D1557539

1–2 TIMOTHY
TITUS

WISDOM COMMENTARY
Volume 53

1–2 Timothy
Titus

Annette Bourland Huizenga

Sarah Tanzer
Volume Editor

Barbara E. Reid, OP
General Editor

A Michael Glazier Book

LITURGICAL PRESS
Collegeville, Minnesota

www.litpress.org

A Michael Glazier Book published by Liturgical Press

1	2	3	4	5	6	7	8	9

Library of Congress Cataloging-in-Publication Data

Names: Huizenga, Annette Bourland, author.
Title: 1–2 Timothy, Titus / Annette Bourland Huizenga ; Sarah Tanzer, volume
    editor ; Barbara E. Reid, OP, general editor.
Other titles: Titus
Description: Collegeville, Minnesota : LITURGICAL PRESS, 2016. | Series:
    Wisdom commentary ; v. 53 | "A Michael Glazier Book." | Includes
    bibliographical references and index.
Identifiers: LCCN 2016009628 (print) | LCCN 2016013474 (ebook) | ISBN
    9780814682036 | ISBN 9780814682289 (ebook)
Subjects: LCSH: Bible. Pastoral epistles—Commentaries.
Classification: LCC BS2735.53 .H85 2016 (print) | LCC BS2735.53 (ebook) | DDC
    227/.8307—dc23
LC record available at http://lccn.loc.gov/2016009628

To my own Timothy,
a true partner

Contents

Abbreviations

AB	Anchor Bible
ANTC	Abingdon New Testament Commentaries
Barn.	*Epistle to Barnabas*
BibInt	*Biblical Interpretation*
BibInt	Biblical Interpretation Series
BZNW	Beihefte zur Zeitschrift für die neutestamentliche Wissenschaft
CBQ	*Catholic Biblical Quarterly*
CBQMS	Catholic Biblical Quarterly Monograph Series
CJ	*Classical Journal*
CurTM	*Currents in Theology and Mission*
Did.	*Didache*
FCB	Feminist Companion to the Bible
Hist. eccl.	Eusebius, *Ecclesiatical History*
IBC	Interpretation: A Bible Commentary for Teaching and Preaching
ICC	International Critical Commentary
IFT	Introductions in Feminist Theology
Ign. *Pol.*	Ignatius, *To Polycarp*

JBL	*Journal of Biblical Literature*
JFSR	*Journal of Feminist Studies in Religion*
JSOTSup	Journal for the Study of the Old Testament Supplement Series
Neot	*Neotestamentica*
NIBCNT	New International Biblical Commentary on the New Testament
NICNT	New International Commentary on the New Testament
NPNF[1]	*Nicene and Post-Nicene Fathers*, Series 1
NTOA	Novum Testamentum et Orbis Antiquus
OBT	Overtures to Biblical Theology
PL	Patrologia Latina
Pol. *Phil.*	Polycarp, *To the Philippians*
SBL	Society of Biblical Literature
SemeiaSt	Semeia Study Series
SUNT	Studien zur Umwelt des Neuen Testaments
SymS	Symposium Series
WBC	Word Biblical Commentary
WUNT	Wissenschaftliche Untersuchungen zum Neuen Testament
Val.	*Against the Valentinians*
Virg.	*On the Veiling of Virgins*

Acknowledgments

While writing this book I have been constantly aware of intellectual and personal support from other scholars, colleagues, friends, and family members. It has been a joy to discover and to interact with the stimulating ideas of the various interpreters of the Pastoral Letters, and a greater delight to include many of their thoughts in the contents of this commentary. I am truly indebted to their insights into these texts and I am humbled by their willingness to contribute to the volume.

My colleagues at the University of Dubuque Theological Seminary are unfailingly encouraging of my work. I am especially thankful for a sabbatical granted by the president and trustees of the university in the fall of 2015, which allowed me ample time to complete the book. Many thanks also to Dr. Judith Kovacs (University of Virginia) and Dr. David Moessner (Texas Christian University) for writing letters in support of my sabbatical application. Three University of Dubuque librarians—Mary Anne Knefel, Susan Reiter, and Jonathan Helmke—gave invaluable assistance in obtaining books and articles and in navigating digital resources.

Friends and family have listened to me talk about this volume for a few years now. Their patient attention and sometimes not-so-subtle nudges provided me the space and energy to keep on writing. I am grateful to Orley, Peg (†), Joan, Nick (†), Benjamin, Seana, Meg, Richie, and our creative and playful grandchildren, Piper, Toby, Sadie, Rocky, and Maggie. Sadly, just a few weeks after finishing the manuscript, my mother, Peg Bourland, passed away. She was a loving and self-effacing parent, who remained surprised and amazed at the good qualities and accomplishments of her children, never fully realizing that she was a deep spring of whatever talents and virtues we have managed to live out. I have dedicated this book to my husband Timothy, who has been a steady source of love, encouragement, and confidence for me in our life together.

Contributors

Jouette M. Bassler is professor emerita of New Testament at Perkins School of Theology, Southern Methodist University. She is the author of numerous articles on a variety of New Testament topics and several books on Paul, including *Divine Impartiality: Paul and a Theological Axiom* (Scholars Press, 1982); *1 Timothy, 2 Timothy, Titus* (Abingdon Press, 1996); and *Navigating Paul: An Introduction to Key Theological Concepts* (Westminster John Knox Press, 2007).

Dr. Colleen M. Conway is professor of religion at Seton Hall University. She is the author of *Behold the Man: Jesus and Greco-Roman Masculinity* (Oxford University Press, 2008) and numerous articles on gender in the New Testament.

Eloy Escamilla holds an MDiv/MA from Catholic Theological Union. He is the director of religious education, youth ministry, and faith formation at Our Lady of Guadalupe parish in Chicago. He leads Bible workshops at the Claretian Bible Schools of the USA–Canada Province.

Dr. Eh Tar Gay serves as academic dean, associate professor of New Testament, and director of the Gender Studies Center at the Myanmar Institute of Theology, Insein Township, Myanmar. She received her PhD from the University of Birmingham (2011), writing her dissertation on "Authority and Submission in Some New Testament Letters: Postcolonial Feminist Reading from Myanmar." Her research and teaching interests include gender, power, and violence; feminist theology; postcolonial readings of the New Testament; and the New Testament and current issues.

Jennifer A. Glancy is professor of religious studies at Le Moyne College in Syracuse, New York. Her publications include *Slavery in Early Christianity* (Oxford University Press, 2010; paperback edition, Fortress Press, 2006); *Corporal Knowledge: Early Christian Bodies* (Oxford University Press, 2010); and *Slavery as Moral Problem: In the Early Church and Today* (Fortress Press, 2011).

Ekram Kachu received her MDiv from the University of Dubuque Theological Seminary and has been ordained as a ruling elder by the Presbytery of Des Moines (PC-USA). She serves as Organizing Pastor of The First Arabic Presbyterian Church of Des Moines.

Marianne Bjelland Kartzow is working as a professor in New Testament studies at the Faculty of Theology at the University of Oslo, Norway. After finishing her PhD on the Pastoral Epistles (2007), she has been interested in questions of method and theory and worked extensively with Luke–Acts. She is the author of two monographs: *Gossip and Gender: Othering of Speech in the Pastoral Epistles* and *Destabilizing the Margins: An Intersectional Approach to Early Christian Memory* (Walter de Gruyter, 2009).

Emerson Powery is professor of biblical studies and coordinator of ethnic and area studies at Messiah College and an adjunct instructor in Bible at Lancaster Theological Seminary. He is one of the editors of *True to Our Native Land: An African American New Testament Commentary* (Fortress Press, 2007) and will soon publish "The Bible and Slavery in American Life" in *The Oxford Handbook of the Bible in America* (Oxford University Press, forthcoming) and co-authored *The Genesis of Liberation: Biblical Interpretation in the Antebellum Narratives of the Enslaved* (Westminster John Knox, 2016). His passion is to grapple with how the Bible functions in underrepresented communities.

Anna Rebecca Solevåg is associate professor at VID Specialized University (Stavanger, Norway). She is the author of *Birthing Salvation: Gender and Class in Early Christian Childbearing Discourse* (Brill, 2013). Her research currently revolves around biblical interpretation and issues of disability, gender, and sexuality.

Wolfgang Stegemann is professor emeritus of New Testament at Augustana College, Neuendettelsau, Germany, and associate editor of *Kirche und Israel* (*Church and Israel*), an international journal on Christian-Jewish dialogue. His research interests include the social history of early Christianity, Luke–Acts, and the history and theology of ancient Judaism.

Elsa Tamez is Mexican-Costarrican. She is emeritus professor of biblical studies of the Latin American Biblical University. She completed her doctoral degree in theology at the University of Lausanne, Switzerland. She has written several books and many articles. Among her books translated in English: *Bible of the Oppressed* (Orbis Books, 1982); *The Scandalous Message of James* (Crossroad, 1990); *Amnesty of Grace: Justification by Faith from a Latin American Perspective* (Abingdon Press, 1993); *Struggles for Power in Early Christianity: A Study of the First Letter of Timothy* (Orbis Books, 2007). She has received several awards for her contribution on contextual biblical hermeneutics.

Dr. Jay Twomey is associate professor and head of the Department of English and Comparative Literature at the University of Cincinnati. He is the author of *The Pastoral Epistles Through the Centuries* (Wiley-Blackwell, 2009) and *2 Corinthians: Crisis and Conflict* (Sheffield Phoenix, 2013), and co-editor with Richard Walsh of *Borges and the Bible* (Sheffield Phoenix, 2015). He is especially interested in the cultural and literary reception of Paul.

Rev. Elijah Zehyoue is an associate pastor and pastoral resident at Calvary Baptist Church in Washington, DC. He is a graduate of Morehouse College and received an MDiv from The University of Chicago Divinity School. Elijah's ministry includes preaching, writing, and advocating for social justice.

Foreword

"Come Eat of My Bread . . . and Walk in the Ways of Wisdom"

Elisabeth Schüssler Fiorenza
Harvard University Divinity School

J ewish feminist writer Asphodel Long has likened the Bible to

> a magnificent garden of brilliant plants, some flowering, some fruiting,
> some in seed, some in bud, shaded by trees of age old, luxurious growth.
> Yet in the very soil which gives it life the poison has been inserted. . . .
> This poison is that of misogyny, the hatred of women, half the human
> race.[1]

To see Scripture as such a beautiful garden containing poisonous ivy
requires that one identify and name this poison and place on all biblical
texts the label "Caution! Could be dangerous to your health and survival!"
As critical feminist interpretation for well-being this Wisdom Commentary seeks to elaborate the beauty and fecundity of this Scripture-garden

---

1. Asphodel Long, *In a Chariot Drawn by Lions: The Search for the Female in the Deity*
(London: Women's Press, 1992), 195.

and at the same time points to the harm it can do when one submits to its world of vision. Thus, feminist biblical interpretation engages two seemingly contradictory insights: The Bible is written in kyriocentric (i.e., lord/master/father/husband-elite male) language, originated in the patri-kyriarchal cultures of antiquity, and has functioned to inculcate misogynist mind-sets and oppressive values. At the same time it also asserts that the Bible as Sacred Scripture has functioned to inspire and authorize wo/men[2] in our struggles against dehumanizing oppression. The hermeneutical lens of wisdom/Wisdom empowers the commentary writers to do so.

In biblical as well as in contemporary religious discourse the word *wisdom* has a double meaning: It can either refer to the quality of life and of people and/or it can refer to a figuration of the Divine. Wisdom in both senses of the word is not a prerogative of the biblical traditions but is found in the imagination and writings of all known religions. Wisdom is transcultural, international, and interreligious. Wisdom is practical knowledge gained through experience and daily living as well as through the study of creation and human nature. Both word meanings, that of capability (wisdom) and that of female personification (Wisdom), are crucial for this Wisdom Commentary series that seeks to enable biblical readers to become critical subjects of interpretation.

Wisdom is a state of the human mind and spirit characterized by deep understanding and profound insight. It is elaborated as a quality possessed by the sages but also treasured as folk wisdom and wit. Wisdom is the power of discernment, deeper understanding, and creativity; it is the ability to move and to dance, to make the connections, to savor life, and to learn from experience. Wisdom is intelligence shaped by experience and sharpened by critical analysis. It is the ability to make sound choices and incisive decisions. Its root meaning comes to the fore in its Latin form *sapientia*, which is derived from the verb *sapere*, to taste and to savor something. Hence, this series of commentaries invites readers to taste, to evaluate, and to imagine.

In the figure of *Chokmah-Sophia-Sapientia-Wisdom*, ancient Jewish scriptures seek to hold together belief in the "one" G*d[3] of Israel with both masculine and feminine language and metaphors of the Divine.

2. I use wo/man, s/he, fe/male and not the grammatical standard "man" as inclusive terms and make this visible by adding /.

3. I use the * asterisk in order to alert readers to a problem to explore and think about.

In distinction to traditional Scripture reading, which is often individualistic and privatized, the practice and space of Wisdom commentary is public. Wisdom's spiraling presence (*Shekhinah*) is global, embracing all creation. Her voice is a public, radical democratic voice rather than a "feminine," privatized one. To become one of Her justice-seeking friends, one needs to imagine the work of this feminist commentary series as the spiraling circle dance of wisdom/Wisdom,[4] as a Spirit/spiritual intellectual movement in the open space of wisdom/Wisdom who calls readers to critically analyze, debate, and reimagine biblical texts and their commentaries as wisdom/Wisdom texts inspired by visions of justice and well-being for everyone and everything. Wisdom-Sophia-imagination engenders a different understanding of Jesus and the movement around him. It understands him as the child and prophet of Divine Wisdom and as Wisdom herself instead of imagining him as ruling King and Lord who has only subalterns but not friends. To approach the N*T[5] and the whole Bible as Wisdom's invitation of cosmic dimensions means to acknowledge its multivalence and its openness to change. As bread—not stone.

In short, this commentary series is inspired by the feminist vision of the open cosmic house of Divine Wisdom-Sophia as it is found in biblical Wisdom literatures, which include the N*T:

> Wisdom has built Her house
> She has set up Her seven pillars . . .
> She has mixed Her wine,
> She also has set Her table.
> She has sent out Her wo/men ministers
> to call from the highest places in the town . . .
> "Come eat of my bread
> and drink of the wine I have mixed.
> Leave immaturity, and live,
> And walk in the way of Wisdom." (Prov 9:1-3, 5-6)

---

4. I have elaborated such a Wisdom dance in terms of biblical hermeneutics in my book *Wisdom Ways: Introducing Feminist Biblical Interpretation* (Maryknoll, NY: Orbis Books, 2001). Its seven steps are a hermeneutics of experience, of domination, of suspicion, of evaluation, of remembering or historical reconstruction, of imagination, and of transformation. However, such Wisdom strategies of meaning making are not restricted to the Bible. Rather, I have used them in workshops in Brazil and Ecuador to explore the workings of power, Condomblé, Christology, imagining a the*logical wo/men's center, or engaging the national icon of Mary.

5. See the discussion about nomenclature of the two testaments in the introduction, page xxxvii.

Editor's Introduction to Wisdom Commentary

"She Is a Breath of the Power of God" (Wis 7:25)

Barbara E. Reid, OP

General Editor

Wisdom Commentary is the first series to offer detailed feminist interpretation of every book of the Bible. The fruit of collaborative work by an ecumenical and interreligious team of scholars, the volumes provide serious, scholarly engagement with the whole biblical text, not only those texts that explicitly mention women. The series is intended for clergy, teachers, ministers, and all serious students of the Bible. Designed to be both accessible and informed by the various approaches of biblical scholarship, it pays particular attention to the world in front of the text, that is, how the text is heard and appropriated. At the same time, this series aims to be faithful to the ancient text and its earliest audiences; thus the volumes also explicate the worlds behind the text and within it. While issues of gender are primary in this project, the volumes also address the intersecting issues of power, authority, ethnicity, race, class, and religious belief and practice. The fifty-eight volumes include the books regarded as canonical by Jews (i.e., the Tanakh); Protestants (the "Hebrew Bible" and the New Testament); and Roman Catholic, Anglican, and Eastern Orthodox Communions (i.e.,

Tobit, Judith, 1 and 2 Maccabees, Wisdom of Solomon, Sirach/Ecclesiasticus, Baruch, including the Letter of Jeremiah, the additions to Esther, and Susanna and Bel and the Dragon in Daniel).

A Symphony of Diverse Voices

Included in the Wisdom Commentary series are voices from scholars of many different religious traditions, of diverse ages, differing sexual identities, and varying cultural, racial, ethnic, and social contexts. Some have been pioneers in feminist biblical interpretation; others are newer contributors from a younger generation. A further distinctive feature of this series is that each volume incorporates voices other than that of the lead author(s). These voices appear alongside the commentary of the lead author(s), in the grayscale inserts. At times, a contributor may offer an alternative interpretation or a critique of the position taken by the lead author(s). At other times, she or he may offer a complementary interpretation from a different cultural context or subject position. Occasionally, portions of previously published material bring in other views. The diverse voices are not intended to be contestants in a debate or a cacophony of discordant notes. The multiple voices reflect that there is no single definitive feminist interpretation of a text. In addition, they show the importance of subject position in the process of interpretation. In this regard, the Wisdom Commentary series takes inspiration from the Talmud and from *The Torah: A Women's Commentary* (ed. Tamara Cohn Eskenazi and Andrea L. Weiss; New York: Women of Reform Judaism, Federation of Temple Sisterhood, 2008), in which many voices, even conflicting ones, are included and not harmonized.

Contributors include biblical scholars, theologians, and readers of Scripture from outside the scholarly and religious guilds. At times, their comments pertain to a particular text. In some instances they address a theme or topic that arises from the text.

Another feature that highlights the collaborative nature of feminist biblical interpretation is that a number of the volumes have two lead authors who have worked in tandem from the inception of the project and whose voices interweave throughout the commentary.

Woman Wisdom

The title, Wisdom Commentary, reflects both the importance to feminists of the figure of Woman Wisdom in the Scriptures and the distinct wisdom that feminist women and men bring to the interpretive process. In the Scriptures, Woman Wisdom appears as "a breath of the power of God, and a pure emanation of the glory of the Almighty" (Wis 7:25), who was present and active in fashioning all that exists (Prov 8:22-31; Wis 8:6). She is a spirit who pervades and penetrates all things (Wis 7:22-23), and she provides guidance and nourishment at her all-inclusive table (Prov 9:1-5). In both postexilic biblical and nonbiblical Jewish sources, Woman Wisdom is often equated with Torah, e.g., Sir 24:23-34; Bar 3:9–4:4; 38:2; 46:4-5; 2 Bar 48:33, 36; 4 Ezra 5:9-10; 13:55; 14:40; 1 Enoch 42.

The New Testament frequently portrays Jesus as Wisdom incarnate. He invites his followers, "take my yoke upon you and learn from me" (Matt 11:29), just as Ben Sira advises, "put your neck under her [Wisdom's] yoke and let your souls receive instruction" (Sir 51:26). Just as Wisdom experiences rejection (Prov 1:23-25; Sir 15:7-8; Wis 10:3; Bar 3:12), so too does Jesus (Mark 8:31; John 1:10-11). Only some accept his invitation to his all-inclusive banquet (Matt 22:1-14; Luke 14:15-24; compare Prov 1:20-21; 9:3-5). Yet, "wisdom is vindicated by her deeds" (Matt 11:19, speaking of Jesus and John the Baptist; in the Lucan parallel at 7:35 they are called "wisdom's children"). There are numerous parallels between what is said of Wisdom and of the *Logos* in the Prologue of the Fourth Gospel (John 1:1-18). These are only a few of many examples. This female embodiment of divine presence and power is an apt image to guide the work of this series.

Feminism

There are many different understandings of the term "feminism." The various meanings, aims, and methods have developed exponentially in recent decades. Feminism is a perspective and a movement that springs from a recognition of inequities toward women, and it advocates for changes in whatever structures prevent full human flourishing. Three waves of feminism in the United States are commonly recognized. The first, arising in the mid-nineteenth century and lasting into the early twentieth, was sparked by women's efforts to be involved in the public sphere and to win the right to vote. In the 1960s and 1970s, the second wave focused on civil rights and equality for women. With the third wave, from the 1980s forward, came global feminism and the emphasis on the contextual nature of interpretation. Now a fourth wave may be emerging, with a stronger emphasis on the intersectionality of women's concerns with those of other marginalized groups and the increased use of the internet as a platform for discussion and activism.[1] As feminism has matured, it has recognized that inequities based on gender are interwoven with power imbalances based on race, class, ethnicity, religion, sexual identity, physical ability, and a host of other social markers.

Feminist Women and Men

Men who choose to identify with and partner with feminist women in the work of deconstructing systems of domination and building structures of equality are rightly regarded as feminists. Some men readily identify with experiences of women who are discriminated against on the basis of sex/gender, having themselves had comparable experiences; others who may not have faced direct discrimination or stereotyping recognize that inequity and problematic characterization still occur, and they seek correction. This series is pleased to include feminist men both as lead authors and as contributing voices.

Feminist Biblical Interpretation

Women interpreting the Bible from the lenses of their own experience is nothing new. Throughout the ages women have recounted the biblical stories, teaching them to their children and others, all the while interpreting them afresh for their time and circumstances.[2] Following is a very brief sketch of select foremothers who laid the groundwork for contemporary feminist biblical interpretation.

One of the earliest known Christian women who challenged patriarchal interpretations of Scripture was a consecrated virgin named Helie, who lived in the second century CE. When she refused to marry, her

1. See Martha Rampton, "Four Waves of Feminism" (October 25, 2015), at http://www.pacificu.edu/about-us/news-events/four-waves-feminism; and Ealasaid Munro, "Feminism: A Fourth Wave?," https://www.psa.ac.uk/insight-plus/feminism-fourth-wave.

2. For fuller treatments of this history, see chap. 7, "One Thousand Years of Feminist Bible Criticism," in Gerda Lerner, *Creation of Feminist Consciousness: From the Middle Ages to Eighteen-Seventy* (New York: Oxford University Press, 1993), 138–66; Susanne Scholz, "From the 'Woman's Bible' to the 'Women's Bible,' The History of Feminist Approaches to the Hebrew Bible," in *Introducing the Women's Hebrew Bible*, IFT 13 (New York: T & T Clark, 2007), 12–32; Marion Ann Taylor and Agnes Choi, eds., *Handbook of Women Biblical Interpreters: A Historical and Biographical Guide* (Grand Rapids, MI: Baker Academic, 2012).

parents brought her before a judge, who quoted to her Paul's admonition, "It is better to marry than to be aflame with passion" (1 Cor 7:9). In response, Helie first acknowledges that this is what Scripture says, but then she retorts, "but not for everyone, that is, not for holy virgins."[3] She is one of the first to question the notion that a text has one meaning that is applicable in all situations.

A Jewish woman who also lived in the second century CE, Beruriah, is said to have had "profound knowledge of biblical exegesis and outstanding intelligence."[4] One story preserved in the Talmud (b. Berakot 10a) tells of how she challenged her husband, Rabbi Meir, when he prayed for the destruction of a sinner. Proffering an alternate interpretation, she argued that Psalm 104:35 advocated praying for the destruction of sin, not the sinner.

In medieval times the first written commentaries on Scripture from a critical feminist point of view emerge. While others may have been produced and passed on orally, they are for the most part lost to us now. Among the earliest preserved feminist writings are those of Hildegard of Bingen (1098–1179), German writer, mystic, and abbess of a Benedictine monastery. She reinterpreted the Genesis narratives in a way that presented women and men as complementary and interdependent. She frequently wrote about feminine aspects of the Divine.[5] Along with other women mystics of the time, such as Julian of Norwich (1342–ca. 1416), she spoke authoritatively from her personal experiences of God's revelation in prayer.

In this era, women were also among the scribes who copied biblical manuscripts. Notable among them is Paula Dei Mansi of Verona, from a distinguished family of Jewish scribes. In 1288, she translated from Hebrew into Italian a collection of Bible commentaries written by her father and added her own explanations.[6]

Another pioneer, Christine de Pizan (1365–ca. 1430), was a French court writer and prolific poet. She used allegory and common sense to

3. Madrid, Escorial MS, a II 9, f. 90 v., as cited in Lerner, *Feminist Consciousness*, 140.

4. See Judith R. Baskin, "Women and Post-Biblical Commentary," in *The Torah: A Women's Commentary*, ed. Tamara Cohn Eskenazi and Andrea L. Weiss (New York: Women of Reform Judaism, Federation of Temple Sisterhood, 2008), xlix–lv, at lii.

5. Hildegard of Bingen, *De Operatione Dei*, 1.4.100; PL 197:885bc, as cited in Lerner, *Feminist Consciousness*, 142–43. See also Barbara Newman, *Sister of Wisdom: St. Hildegard's Theology of the Feminine* (Berkeley: University of California Press, 1987).

6. Emily Taitz, Sondra Henry, Cheryl Tallan, eds., *JPS Guide to Jewish Women 600 B.C.E.–1900 C.E.* (Philadelphia: JPS, 2003), 110–11.

subvert misogynist readings of Scripture and celebrated the accomplishments of female biblical figures to argue for women's active roles in building society.[7]

By the seventeenth century, there were women who asserted that the biblical text needs to be understood and interpreted in its historical context. For example, Rachel Speght (1597–ca. 1630), a Calvinist English poet, elaborates on the historical situation in first-century Corinth that prompted Paul to say, "It is well for a man not to touch a woman" (1 Cor 7:1). Her aim was to show that the biblical texts should not be applied in a literal fashion to all times and circumstances. Similarly, Margaret Fell (1614–1702), one of the founders of the Religious Society of Friends (Quakers) in Britain, addressed the Pauline prohibitions against women speaking in church by insisting that they do not have universal validity. Rather, they need to be understood in their historical context, as addressed to a local church in particular time-bound circumstances.[8]

Along with analyzing the historical context of the biblical writings, women in the eighteenth and nineteenth centuries began to attend to misogynistic interpretations based on faulty translations. One of the first to do so was British feminist Mary Astell (1666–1731).[9] In the United States, the Grimké sisters, Sarah (1792–1873) and Angelina (1805–1879), Quaker women from a slaveholding family in South Carolina, learned biblical Greek and Hebrew so that they could interpret the Bible for themselves. They were prompted to do so after men sought to silence them from speaking out against slavery and for women's rights by claiming that the Bible (e.g., 1 Cor 14:34) prevented women from speaking in public.[10] Another prominent abolitionist, Sojourner Truth (ca. 1797–1883), a former slave, quoted the Bible liberally in her speeches[11] and in so doing challenged cultural assumptions and biblical interpretations that undergird gender inequities.

7. See further Taylor and Choi, *Handbook of Women Biblical Interpreters*, 127–32.

8. Her major work, *Women's Speaking Justified, Proved and Allowed by the Scriptures*, published in London in 1667, gave a systematic feminist reading of all biblical texts pertaining to women.

9. Mary Astell, *Some Reflections upon Marriage* (New York: Source Book Press, 1970, reprint of the 1730 edition; earliest edition of this work is 1700), 103–4.

10. See further Sarah Grimké, *Letters on the Equality of the Sexes and the Condition of Woman* (Boston: Isaac Knapp, 1838).

11. See, for example, her most famous speech, "Ain't I a Woman?," delivered in 1851 at the Ohio Women's Rights Convention in Akron, OH; http://www.fordham.edu/halsall/mod/sojtruth-woman.asp.

Another monumental work that emerged in nineteenth-century England was that of Jewish theologian Grace Aguilar (1816–1847), *The Women of Israel*,[12] published in 1845. Aguilar's approach was to make connections between the biblical women and contemporary Jewish women's concerns. She aimed to counter the widespread notion that women were degraded in Jewish law and that only in Christianity were women's dignity and value upheld. Her intent was to help Jewish women find strength and encouragement by seeing the evidence of God's compassionate love in the history of every woman in the Bible. While not a full commentary on the Bible, Aguilar's work stands out for its comprehensive treatment of every female biblical character, including even the most obscure references.[13]

The first person to produce a full-blown feminist commentary on the Bible was Elizabeth Cady Stanton (1815–1902). A leading proponent in the United States for women's right to vote, she found that whenever women tried to make inroads into politics, education, or the work world, the Bible was quoted against them. Along with a team of like-minded women, she produced her own commentary on every text of the Bible that concerned women. Her pioneering two-volume project, *The Woman's Bible*, published in 1895 and 1898, urges women to recognize that texts that degrade women come from the men who wrote the texts, not from God, and to use their common sense to rethink what has been presented to them as sacred.

Nearly a century later, *The Women's Bible Commentary*, edited by Sharon Ringe and Carol Newsom (Westminster John Knox Press, 1992), appeared. This one-volume commentary features North American feminist scholarship on each book of the Protestant canon. Like Cady Stanton's commentary, it does not contain comments on every section of the biblical text but only on those passages deemed relevant to women. It was revised and expanded in 1998 to include the Apocrypha/Deuterocanonical books, and the contributors to this new volume reflect the global face of contemporary feminist scholarship. The revisions made in the third edition, which appeared in 2012, represent the profound advances in feminist biblical scholarship and include newer voices. In both the second and third editions, *The* has been dropped from the title.

---

12. The full title is *The Women of Israel or Characters and Sketches from the Holy Scriptures and Jewish History Illustrative of the Past History, Present Duty, and Future Destiny of the Hebrew Females, as Based on the Word of God*.

13. See further Eskenazi and Weiss, *The Torah: A Women's Commentary*, xxxviii; Taylor and Choi, *Handbook of Women Biblical Interpreters*, 31–37.

Also appearing at the centennial of Cady Stanton's *The Woman's Bible* were two volumes edited by Elisabeth Schüssler Fiorenza with the assistance of Shelly Matthews. The first, *Searching the Scriptures: A Feminist Introduction* (New York: Crossroad, 1993), charts a comprehensive approach to feminist interpretation from ecumenical, interreligious, and multicultural perspectives. The second volume, published in 1994, provides critical feminist commentary on each book of the New Testament as well as on three books of Jewish Pseudepigrapha and eleven other early Christian writings.

In Europe, similar endeavors have been undertaken, such as the one-volume *Kompendium Feministische Bibelauslegung*, edited by Luise Schottroff and Marie-Theres Wacker (Gütersloh, Gütersloher Verlagshaus, 2007), featuring German feminist biblical interpretation of each book of the Bible, along with apocryphal books, and several extrabiblical writings. This work, now in its third edition, has recently been translated into English.[14] A multivolume project, *The Bible and Women: An Encylopaedia of Exegesis and Cultural History*, edited by Irmtraud Fischer, Adriana Valerio, Mercedes Navarro Puerto, and Christiana de Groot, is currently in production. This project presents a history of the reception of the Bible as embedded in Western cultural history and focuses particularly on gender-relevant biblical themes, biblical female characters, and women recipients of the Bible. The volumes are published in English, Spanish, Italian, and German.[15]

Another groundbreaking work is the collection The Feminist Companion to the Bible Series, edited by Athalya Brenner (Sheffield: Sheffield

14. *Feminist Biblical Interpretation: A Compendium of Critical Commentary on the Books of the Bible and Related Literature*, trans. Lisa E. Dahill, Everett R. Kalin, Nancy Lukens, Linda M. Maloney, Barbara Rumscheidt, Martin Rumscheidt, and Tina Steiner (Grand Rapids, MI: Eerdmans, 2012). Another notable collection is the three volumes edited by Susanne Scholtz, *Feminist Interpretation of the Hebrew Bible in Retrospect*, Recent Research in Biblical Studies 7, 8, 9 (Sheffield: Sheffield Phoenix Press, 2013, 2014, 2016).

15. The first volume, on the Torah, appeared in Spanish in 2009, in German and Italian in 2010, and in English in 2011 (Atlanta, GA: SBL). Four more volumes are now available: *Feminist Biblical Studies in the Twentieth Century*, ed. Elisabeth Schüssler Fiorenza (2014); *The Writings and Later Wisdom Books*, ed. Christl M. Maier and Nuria Calduch-Benages (2014); *Gospels: Narrative and History*, ed. Mercedes Navarro Puerto and Marinella Perroni (2015); and *The High Middle Ages*, ed. Kari Elisabeth Børresen and Adriana Valerio (2015). For further information, see http://www.bibleandwomen.org.

Academic Press, 1993–2015), which comprises twenty volumes of commentaries on the Old Testament. The parallel series, Feminist Companion to the New Testament and Early Christian Writings, edited by Amy-Jill Levine with Marianne Blickenstaff and Maria Mayo Robbins (Sheffield: Sheffield Academic Press, 2001–2009), contains thirteen volumes with one more planned. These two series are not full commentaries on the biblical books but comprise collected essays on discrete biblical texts.

Works by individual feminist biblical scholars in all parts of the world abound, and they are now too numerous to list in this introduction. Feminist biblical interpretation has reached a level of maturity that now makes possible a commentary series on every book of the Bible. In recent decades, women have had greater access to formal theological education, have been able to learn critical analytical tools, have put their own interpretations into writing, and have developed new methods of biblical interpretation. Until recent decades the work of feminist biblical interpreters was largely unknown, both to other women and to their brothers in the synagogue, church, and academy. Feminists now have taken their place in the professional world of biblical scholars, where they build on the work of their foremothers and connect with one another across the globe in ways not previously possible. In a few short decades, feminist biblical criticism has become an integral part of the academy.

Methodologies

Feminist biblical scholars use a variety of methods and often employ a number of them together.[16] In the Wisdom Commentary series, the authors will explain their understanding of feminism and the feminist reading strategies used in their commentary. Each volume treats the biblical text in blocks of material, not an analysis verse by verse. The entire text is considered, not only those passages that feature female characters or that speak specifically about women. When women are not apparent in the narrative, feminist lenses are used to analyze the dynamics in the text between male characters, the models of power, binary ways of thinking, and dynamics of imperialism. Attention is given to how the whole text functions and how it was and is heard, both in its

---

16. See the seventeen essays in Caroline Vander Stichele and Todd Penner, eds., *Her Master's Tools? Feminist and Postcolonial Engagements of Historical-Critical Discourse* (Atlanta, GA: Society of Biblical Literature, 2005), which show the complementarity of various approaches.

original context and today. Issues of particular concern to women—e.g., poverty, food, health, the environment, water—come to the fore.

One of the approaches used by early feminists and still popular today is to lift up the overlooked and forgotten stories of women in the Bible. Studies of women in each of the Testaments have been done, and there are also studies on women in particular biblical books.[17] Feminists recognize that the examples of biblical characters can be both empowering and problematic. The point of the feminist enterprise is not to serve as an apologetic for women; it is rather, in part, to recover women's history and literary roles in all their complexity and to learn from that recovery.

Retrieving the submerged history of biblical women is a crucial step for constructing the story of the past so as to lead to liberative possibilities for the present and future. There are, however, some pitfalls to this approach. Sometimes depictions of biblical women have been naïve and romantic. Some commentators exalt the virtues of both biblical and contemporary women and paint women as superior to men. Such reverse discrimination inhibits movement toward equality for all. In addition, some feminists challenge the idea that one can "pluck positive images out of an admittedly androcentric text, separating literary characterizations from the androcentric interests they were created to serve."[18] Still other feminists find these images to have enormous value.

One other danger with seeking the submerged history of women is the tendency for Christian feminists to paint Jesus and even Paul as liberators of women in a way that demonizes Judaism.[19] Wisdom Commentary aims

17. See, e.g., Alice Bach, ed., *Women in the Hebrew Bible: A Reader* (New York: Routledge, 1998); Tikva Frymer-Kensky, *Reading the Women of the Bible* (New York: Schocken, 2002); Carol Meyers, Toni Craven, and Ross S. Kraemer, *Women in Scripture* (Grand Rapids, MI: Eerdmans, 2000); Irene Nowell, *Women in the Old Testament* (Collegeville, MN: Liturgical Press, 1997); Katharine Doob Sakenfeld, *Just Wives? Stories of Power and Survival in the Old Testament and Today* (Louisville, KY: Westminster John Knox, 2003); Mary Ann Getty-Sullivan, *Women in the New Testament* (Collegeville, MN: Liturgical Press, 2001); Bonnie Thurston, *Women in the New Testament* (New York: Crossroad, 1998).

18. Cheryl Exum, "Second Thoughts about Secondary Characters: Women in Exodus 1.8–2.10," in *A Feminist Companion to Exodus to Deuteronomy*, FCB 6 (Sheffield: Sheffield Academic Press, 1994), 75–97, at 76.

19. See Judith Plaskow, "Anti-Judaism in Feminist Christian Interpretation," in *Searching the Scriptures: A Feminist Introduction* (New York: Crossroad, 1993), 1:117–29; Amy-Jill Levine, "The New Testament and Anti-Judaism," in *The Misunderstood Jew: The Church and the Scandal of the Jewish Jesus* (San Francisco: HarperSanFrancisco, 2006), 87–117.

to enhance understanding of Jesus as well as Paul as Jews of their day and to forge solidarity among Jewish and Christian feminists.

Feminist scholars who use historical-critical methods analyze the world behind the text; they seek to understand the historical context from which the text emerged and the circumstances of the communities to whom it was addressed. In bringing feminist lenses to this approach, the aim is not to impose modern expectations on ancient cultures but to unmask the ways that ideologically problematic mind-sets that produced the ancient texts are still promulgated through the text. Feminist biblical scholars aim not only to deconstruct but also to reclaim and reconstruct biblical history as women's history, in which women were central and active agents in creating religious heritage.[20] A further step is to construct meaning for contemporary women and men in a liberative movement toward transformation of social, political, economic, and religious structures.[21] In recent years, some feminists have embraced new historicism, which accents the creative role of the interpreter in any construction of history and exposes the power struggles to which the text witnesses.[22]

Literary critics analyze the world of the text: its form, language patterns, and rhetorical function.[23] They do not attempt to separate layers of tradition and redaction but focus on the text holistically, as it is in its

---

20. See, for example, Phyllis A. Bird, *Missing Persons and Mistaken Identities: Women and Gender in Ancient Israel* (Minneapolis: Fortress Press, 1997); Elisabeth Schüssler Fiorenza, *In Memory of Her: A Feminist Theological Reconstruction of Christian Origins* (New York: Crossroad, 1984); Ross Shepard Kraemer and Mary Rose D'Angelo, eds., *Women and Christian Origins* (New York: Oxford University Press, 1999).

21. See, e.g., Sandra M. Schneiders, *The Revelatory Text: Interpreting the New Testament as Sacred Scripture*, rev. ed. (Collegeville, MN: Liturgical Press, 1999), whose aim is to engage in biblical interpretation not only for intellectual enlightenment but, even more important, for personal and communal transformation. Elisabeth Schüssler Fiorenza (*Wisdom Ways: Introducing Feminist Biblical Interpretation* [Maryknoll, NY: Orbis Books, 2001]) envisions the work of feminist biblical interpretation as a dance of Wisdom that consists of seven steps that interweave in spiral movements toward liberation, the final one being transformative action for change.

22. See Gina Hens Piazza, *The New Historicism*, Guides to Biblical Scholarship, Old Testament Series (Minneapolis: Fortress Press, 2002).

23. Phyllis Trible was among the first to employ this method with texts from Genesis and Ruth in her groundbreaking book *God and the Rhetoric of Sexuality*, OBT (Philadelphia: Fortress Press, 1978). Another pioneer in feminist literary criticism is Mieke Bal (*Lethal Love: Feminist Literary Readings of Biblical Love Stories* [Bloomington: Indiana University Press, 1987]). For surveys of recent developments in literary methods, see Terry Eagleton, *Literary Theory: An Introduction*, 3rd ed. (Minneapolis: University of

present form. They examine how meaning is created in the interaction between the text and its reader in multiple contexts. Within the arena of literary approaches are reader-oriented approaches, narrative, rhetorical, structuralist, post-structuralist, deconstructive, ideological, autobiographical, and performance criticism.[24] Narrative critics study the interrelation among author, text, and audience through investigation of settings, both spatial and temporal; characters; plot; and narrative techniques (e.g., irony, parody, intertextual allusions). Reader-response critics attend to the impact that the text has on the reader or hearer. They recognize that when a text is detrimental toward women there is the choice either to affirm the text or to read against the grain toward a liberative end. Rhetorical criticism analyzes the style of argumentation and attends to how the author is attempting to shape the thinking or actions of the hearer. Structuralist critics analyze the complex patterns of binary oppositions in the text to derive its meaning.[25] Post-structuralist approaches challenge the notion that there are fixed meanings to any biblical text or that there is one universal truth. They engage in close readings of the text and often engage in intertextual analysis.[26] Within this approach is deconstructionist criticism, which views the text as a site of conflict, with competing narratives. The interpreter aims to expose the fault lines and overturn and reconfigure binaries by elevating the underling of a pair and foregrounding it.[27] Feminists also use other postmodern approaches,

---

Minnesota Press, 2008); Janice Capel Anderson and Stephen D. Moore, eds., *Mark and Method: New Approaches in Biblical Studies*, 2nd ed. (Minneapolis: Fortress Press, 2008).

24. See, e.g., J. Cheryl Exum and David J. A. Clines, eds., *The New Literary Criticism and the Hebrew Bible* (Valley Forge, PA: Trinity Press International, 1993); Edgar V. McKnight and Elizabeth Struthers Malbon, eds., *The New Literary Criticism and the New Testament* (Valley Forge, PA: Trinity Press International, 1994).

25. See, e.g., David Jobling, *The Sense of Biblical Narrative: Three Structural Analyses in the Old Testament*, JSOTSup 7 (Sheffield: Sheffield University, 1978).

26. See, e.g., Stephen D. Moore, *Poststructuralism and the New Testament: Derrida and Foucault at the Foot of the Cross* (Minneapolis: Fortress Press, 1994); *The Bible in Theory: Critical and Postcritical Essays* (Atlanta, GA: SBL, 2010); Yvonne Sherwood, *A Biblical Text and Its Afterlives: The Survival of Jonah in Western Culture* (Cambridge: Cambridge University Press, 2000).

27. David Penchansky, "Deconstruction," in *The Oxford Encyclopedia of Biblical Interpretation*, ed. Steven McKenzie (New York: Oxford University Press, 2013), 196–205. See, for example, Danna Nolan Fewell and David M. Gunn, *Gender, Power, and Promise: The Subject of the Bible's First Story* (Nashville, TN: Abingdon, 1993); David Rutledge, *Reading Marginally: Feminism, Deconstruction and the Bible*, BibInt 21 (Leiden: Brill, 1996).

such as ideological and autobiographical criticism. The former analyzes the system of ideas that underlies the power and values concealed in the text as well as that of the interpreter.[28] The latter involves deliberate self-disclosure while reading the text as a critical exegete.[29] Performance criticism attends to how the text was passed on orally, usually in communal settings, and to the verbal and nonverbal interactions between the performer and the audience.[30]

From the beginning, feminists have understood that interpreting the Bible is an act of power. In recent decades, feminist biblical scholars have developed hermeneutical theories of the ethics and politics of biblical interpretation to challenge the claims to value neutrality of most academic biblical scholarship. Feminist biblical scholars have also turned their attention to how some biblical writings were shaped by the power of empire and how this still shapes readers' self-understandings today. They have developed hermeneutical approaches that reveal, critique, and evaluate the interactions depicted in the text against the context of empire, and they consider implications for contemporary contexts.[31] Feminists also analyze the dynamics of colonization and the mentalities of colonized peoples in the exercise of biblical interpretation. As Kwok Pui-lan explains, "A postcolonial feminist interpretation of the Bible needs to investigate the deployment of gender in the narration of identity, the negotiation of power differentials between the colonizers and the colonized, and the reinforcement of patriarchal control over spheres where these elites could exercise control."[32] Methods and models from

28. See Tina Pippin, ed., *Ideological Criticism of Biblical Texts: Semeia* 59 (1992); Terry Eagleton, *Ideology: An Introduction* (London: Verso, 2007).

29. See, e.g., Ingrid Rose Kitzberger, ed., *Autobiographical Biblical Interpretation: Between Text and Self* (Leiden: Deo, 2002); P. J. W. Schutte, "When *They, We,* and the Passive Become *I*—Introducing Autobiographical Biblical Criticism," *HTS Teologiese Studies / Theological Studies* vol. 61 (2005): 401–16.

30. See, e.g., Holly Hearon and Philip Ruge-Jones, eds., *The Bible in Ancient and Modern Media: Story and Performance* (Eugene, OR: Cascade Books, 2009).

31. E.g., Gale Yee, ed., *Judges and Method: New Approaches in Biblical Studies* (Minneapolis: Fortress Press, 1995); Warren Carter, *The Gospel of Matthew in Its Roman Imperial Context* (London: T & T Clark, 2005); *The Roman Empire and the New Testament: An Essential Guide* (Nashville, TN: Abingdon, 2006); Elisabeth Schüssler Fiorenza, *The Power of the Word: Scripture and the Rhetoric of Empire* (Minneapolis: Fortress Press, 2007); Judith E. McKinlay, *Reframing Her: Biblical Women in Postcolonial Focus* (Sheffield: Sheffield Phoenix Press, 2004).

32. Kwok Pui-lan, *Postcolonial Imagination and Feminist Theology* (Louisville, KY: Westminster John Knox, 2005), 9. See also, Musa W. Dube, ed., *Postcolonial Feminist*

sociology and cultural anthropology are used by feminists to investigate women's everyday lives, their experiences of marriage, childrearing, labor, money, illness, etc.[33]

As feminists have examined the construction of gender from varying cultural perspectives, they have become ever more cognizant that the way gender roles are defined within differing cultures varies radically. As Mary Ann Tolbert observes, "Attempts to isolate some universal role that cross-culturally defines 'woman' have run into contradictory evidence at every turn."[34] Some women have coined new terms to highlight the particularities of their socio-cultural context. Many African American feminists, for example, call themselves *womanists* to draw attention to the double oppression of racism and sexism they experience.[35] Similarly, many US Hispanic feminists speak of themselves as *mujeristas* (*mujer* is Spanish for "woman").[36] Others prefer to be called "Latina feminists."[37] Both groups emphasize that the context for their theologizing is *mestizaje* and *mulatez* (racial and cultural mixture), done *en conjunto* (in community), with *lo cotidiano* (everyday lived experience) of Hispanic women as starting points for theological reflection and the encounter with the

---

Interpretation of the Bible (St. Louis, MO: Chalice Press, 2000); Cristl M. Maier and Carolyn J. Sharp, *Prophecy and Power: Jeremiah in Feminist and Postcolonial Perspective* (London: Bloomsbury, 2013).

33. See, for example, Carol Meyers, *Discovering Eve: Ancient Israelite Women in Context* (New York: Oxford University Press, 1991); Luise Schottroff, *Lydia's Impatient Sisters: A Feminist Social History of Early Christianity*, trans. Barbara and Martin Rumscheidt (Louisville, KY: Westminster John Knox, 1995); Susan Niditch, *"My Brother Esau Is a Hairy Man": Hair and Identity in Ancient Israel* (Oxford: Oxford University Press, 2008).

34. Mary Ann Tolbert, "Social, Sociological, and Anthropological Methods," in *Searching the Scriptures*, 1:255–71, at 265.

35. Alice Walker coined the term (*In Search of Our Mothers' Gardens: Womanist Prose* [New York: Harcourt Brace Jovanovich, 1967, 1983]). See also Katie G. Cannon, "The Emergence of Black Feminist Consciousness," in *Feminist Interpretation of the Bible*, ed. Letty M. Russell (Philadelphia: Westminster, 1985), 30–40; Renita Weems, *Just a Sister Away: A Womanist Vision of Women's Relationships in the Bible* (San Diego: Lura Media, 1988); Nyasha Junior, *An Introduction to Womanist Biblical Interpretation* (Louisville, KY: Westminster John Knox, 2015).

36. Ada María Isasi-Díaz (*Mujerista Theology: A Theology for the Twenty-first Century* [Maryknoll, NY: Orbis Books, 1996]) is credited with coining the term.

37. E.g., María Pilar Aquino, Daisy L. Machado, and Jeanette Rodríguez, eds., *A Reader in Latina Feminist Theology* (Austin: University of Texas Press, 2002).

divine. Intercultural analysis has become an indispensable tool for working toward justice for women at the global level.[38]

Some feminists are among those who have developed lesbian, gay, bisexual, and transgender (LGBT) interpretation. This approach focuses on issues of sexual identity and uses various reading strategies. Some point out the ways in which categories that emerged in recent centuries are applied anachronistically to biblical texts to make modern-day judgments. Others show how the Bible is silent on contemporary issues about sexual identity. Still others examine same-sex relationships in the Bible by figures such as Ruth and Naomi or David and Jonathan. In recent years, queer theory has emerged; it emphasizes the blurriness of boundaries not just of sexual identity but also of gender roles. Queer critics often focus on texts in which figures transgress what is traditionally considered proper gender behavior.[39]

Feminists also recognize that the struggle for women's equality and dignity is intimately connected with the struggle for respect for Earth and for the whole of the cosmos. Ecofeminists interpret Scripture in ways that highlight the link between human domination of nature and male subjugation of women. They show how anthropocentric ways of interpreting the Bible have overlooked or dismissed Earth and Earth community. They invite readers to identify not only with human characters in the biblical narrative but also with other Earth creatures and domains of nature, especially those that are the object of injustice. Some use creative imagination to retrieve the interests of Earth implicit in the narrative and enable Earth to speak.[40]

38. See, e.g., María Pilar Aquino and María José Rosado-Nunes, eds., *Feminist Intercultural Theology: Latina Explorations for a Just World*, Studies in Latino/a Catholicism (Maryknoll, NY: Orbis Books, 2007).

39. See, e.g., Bernadette J. Brooten, *Love between Women: Early Christian Responses to Female Homoeroticism* (Chicago and London: University of Chicago Press, 1996); Mary Rose D'Angelo, "Women Partners in the New Testament," *JFSR* 6 (1990): 65–86; Deirdre J. Good, "Reading Strategies for Biblical Passages on Same-Sex Relations," *Theology and Sexuality* 7 (1997): 70–82; Deryn Guest, *When Deborah Met Jael: Lesbian Feminist Hermeneutics* (London: SCM Press, 2011); Teresa Hornsby and Ken Stone, eds., *Bible Trouble: Queer Readings at the Boundaries of Biblical Scholarship* (Atlanta, GA: SBL, 2011).

40. E.g., Norman C. Habel and Peter Trudinger, *Exploring Ecological Hermeneutics*, SymS 46 (Atlanta, GA: SBL, 2008); Mary Judith Ress, *Ecofeminism in Latin America*, Women from the Margins (Maryknoll, NY: Orbis Books, 2006).

Biblical Authority

By the late nineteenth century, some feminists, such as Elizabeth Cady Stanton, began to question openly whether the Bible could continue to be regarded as authoritative for women. They viewed the Bible itself as the source of women's oppression, and some rejected its sacred origin and saving claims. Some decided that the Bible and the religious traditions that enshrine it are too thoroughly saturated with androcentrism and patriarchy to be redeemable.[41]

In the Wisdom Commentary series, questions such as these may be raised, but the aim of this series is not to lead readers to reject the authority of the biblical text. Rather, the aim is to promote better understanding of the contexts from which the text arose and of the rhetorical effects it has on women and men in contemporary contexts. Such understanding can lead to a deepening of faith, with the Bible serving as an aid to bring flourishing of life.

Language for God

Because of the ways in which the term "God" has been used to symbolize the divine in predominantly male, patriarchal, and monarchical modes, feminists have designed new ways of speaking of the divine. Some have called attention to the inadequacy of the term *God* by trying to visually destabilize our ways of thinking and speaking of the divine. Rosemary Radford Ruether proposed *God/ess*, as an unpronounceable term pointing to the unnameable understanding of the divine that transcends patriarchal limitations.[42] Some have followed traditional Jewish practice, writing *G-d*. Elisabeth Schüssler Fiorenza has adopted *G*d*.[43] Others draw on the biblical tradition to mine female and non-gender-specific metaphors and symbols.[44] In Wisdom Commentary, there is not one standard way of expressing the divine; each author will use her or

41. E.g., Mary Daly, *Beyond God the Father: A Philosophy of Women's Liberation* (Boston: Beacon, 1973).

42. Rosemary Radford Ruether, *Sexism and God-Talk: Toward a Feminist Theology* (Boston: Beacon, 1983).

43. Elisabeth Schüssler Fiorenza, *Jesus: Miriam's Child, Sophia's Prophet; Critical Issues in Feminist Christology* (New York: Continuum, 1994), 191 n. 3.

44. E.g., Sallie McFague, *Models of God: Theology for an Ecological, Nuclear Age* (Philadelphia: Fortress Press, 1987); Catherine LaCugna, *God for Us: The Trinity and Christian Life* (San Francisco: Harper Collins, 1991); Elizabeth A. Johnson, *She Who Is: The*

his preferred ways. The one exception is that when the tetragrammaton, YHWH, the name revealed to Moses in Exodus 3:14, is used, it will be without vowels, respecting the Jewish custom of avoiding pronouncing the divine name out of reverence.

Nomenclature for the Two Testaments

In recent decades, some biblical scholars have begun to call the two Testaments of the Bible by names other than the traditional nomenclature: Old and New Testament. Some regard "Old" as derogatory, implying that it is no longer relevant or that it has been superseded. Consequently, terms like Hebrew Bible, First Testament, and Jewish Scriptures and, correspondingly, Christian Scriptures or Second Testament have come into use. There are a number of difficulties with these designations. The term "Hebrew Bible" does not take into account that parts of the Old Testament are written not in Hebrew but in Aramaic.[45] Moreover, for Roman Catholics, Anglicans, and Eastern Orthodox believers, the Old Testament includes books written in Greek—the Deuterocanonical books, considered Apocrypha by Protestants. The term "Jewish Scriptures" is inadequate because these books are also sacred to Christians. Conversely, "Christian Scriptures" is not an accurate designation for the New Testament, since the Old Testament is also part of the Christian Scriptures. Using "First and Second Testament" also has difficulties, in that it can imply a hierarchy and a value judgment.[46] Jews generally use the term Tanakh, an acronym for Torah (Pentateuch), Nevi'im (Prophets), and Ketuvim (Writings).

In Wisdom Commentary, if authors choose to use a designation other than Tanakh, Old Testament, and New Testament, they will explain how they mean the term.

Translation

Modern feminist scholars recognize the complexities connected with biblical translation, as they have delved into questions about philosophy of language, how meanings are produced, and how they are culturally

---

Mystery of God in Feminist Theological Discourse (New York: Crossroad, 1992). See further Elizabeth A. Johnson, "God," in *Dictionary of Feminist Theologies*, 128–30.

45. Gen 31:47; Jer 10:11; Ezra 4:7–6:18; 7:12-26; Dan 2:4–7:28.

46. See Levine, *The Misunderstood Jew*, 193–99.

situated. Today it is evident that simply translating into gender-neutral formulations cannot address all the challenges presented by androcentric texts. Efforts at feminist translation must also deal with issues around authority and canonicity.[47]

Because of these complexities, the editors of Wisdom Commentary series have chosen to use an existing translation, the New Revised Standard Version (NRSV), which is provided for easy reference at the top of each page of commentary. The NRSV was produced by a team of ecumenical and interreligious scholars, is a fairly literal translation, and uses inclusive language for human beings. Brief discussions about problematic translations appear in the inserts labeled "Translation Matters." When more detailed discussions are available, these will be indicated in footnotes. In the commentary, wherever Hebrew or Greek words are used, English translation is provided. In cases where a wordplay is involved, transliteration is provided to enable understanding.

Art and Poetry

Artistic expression in poetry, music, sculpture, painting, and various other modes is very important to feminist interpretation. Where possible, art and poetry are included in the print volumes of the series. In a number of instances, these are original works created for this project. Regrettably, copyright and production costs prohibit the inclusion of color photographs and other artistic work. It is our hope that the web version will allow a greater collection of such resources.

Glossary

Because there are a number of excellent readily available resources that provide definitions and concise explanations of terms used in feminist theological and biblical studies, this series will not include a glossary. We refer you to works such as *Dictionary of Feminist Theologies*, edited by Letty M. Russell with J. Shannon Clarkson (Louisville, KY: Westminster John Knox, 1996), and volume 1 of *Searching the Scriptures*, edited by Elisabeth Schüssler Fiorenza with the assistance of Shelly Matthews (New York: Crossroad, 1992). Individual authors in the Wisdom Com-

---

47. Elizabeth Castelli, "*Les Belles Infidèles*/Fidelity or Feminism? The Meanings of Feminist Biblical Translation," in *Searching the Scriptures*, 1:189–204, here 190.

mentary series will define the way they are using terms that may be unfamiliar.

Bibliography

Because bibliographies are quickly outdated and because the space is limited, only a list of Works Cited is included in the print volumes. A comprehensive bibliography for each volume is posted on a dedicated website and is updated regularly. The link for this volume can be found at wisdomcommentary.org.

A Concluding Word

In just a few short decades, feminist biblical studies has grown exponentially, both in the methods that have been developed and in the number of scholars who have embraced it. We realize that this series is limited and will soon need to be revised and updated. It is our hope that Wisdom Commentary, by making the best of current feminist biblical scholarship available in an accessible format to ministers, preachers, teachers, scholars, and students, will aid all readers in their advancement toward God's vision of dignity, equality, and justice for all.

Acknowledgments

There are a great many people who have made this series possible: first, Peter Dwyer, director, and Hans Christoffersen, publisher of the academic market at Liturgical Press, who have believed in this project and have shepherded it since it was conceived in 2008. Editorial consultants Athalya Brenner-Idan and Elisabeth Schüssler Fiorenza have not only been an inspiration with their pioneering work but have encouraged us all along the way with their personal involvement. Volume editors Mary Ann Beavis, Carol J. Dempsey, Amy-Jill Levine, Linda M. Maloney, Ahida Pilarski, Sarah Tanzer, Lauress Wilkins Lawrence, and Seung Ai Yang have lent their extraordinary wisdom to the shaping of the series,

xl   *1–2 Timothy, Titus*

have used their extensive networks of relationships to secure authors and contributors, and have worked tirelessly to guide their work to completion. Two others who contributed greatly to the shaping of the project at the outset were Linda M. Day and Mignon Jacobs, as well as Barbara E. Bowe of blessed memory (d. 2010). Editorial and research assistant Susan M. Hickman has provided invaluable support with administrative details and arrangements. I am grateful to Brian Eisenschenk and Christine Henderson who have assisted Susan Hickman with the Wiki. There are countless others at Liturgical Press whose daily work makes the production possible. I am especially thankful to Lauren L. Murphy, Andrea Humphrey, Lauress Wilkins Lawrence, and Justin Howell for their work in copyediting.

Author's Introduction

Gendered Letters

What does it mean that humankind is created male and female?

What behaviors are especially feminine or masculine?

Which domestic and ecclesial functions ought to be assigned based on a person's biological sex?

How should women and men understand their value in relation to each other?

Such questions have troubled Christians since the founding of the first churches when, it is reported, men and women participated together in worship, mission, and leadership. Early Christian texts disclose many profound conflicts about gender roles, about perceptions of femininity and masculinity, and about the relative status of women and men within the communities.

Disagreements about gender ideals existed *within* individual congregations: How ought women to be clothed when they pray? How should unmarried women behave?

Tensions arose *between* groups as believers argued about church administration: Could women function as teachers, as deacons, as prophets? How should widows serve and be cared for within the communities?

Those outside the faith speculated about the relationships between men and women in these households of faith: Were Christian men incapable of controlling their wives? Why were women in charge of some events? Who was kissing whom during their rituals?

Gendered Instruction in the Household of God

More so than other New Testament texts, the letters known as 1 Timothy, 2 Timothy, and Titus, called collectively the Pastoral Letters, express strong opinions about these conflicts around gender. Their author is familiar with Jewish, Christian, and Roman popular and philosophical discussions about the different natures of and distinct roles for women and men. His own beliefs epitomize the "traditional" gender ideology: that because men and women are biologically different, they ought to behave differently in the family and society.

One key feature of the gender-differentiated hierarchy that the Pastorals' author adopts is *patriarchy*: the "rule of fathers." In a patriarchal arrangement, the free male head-of-household is given political, legal, and financial power that is denied to his wife, children, and slaves. Their social status is defined as in subjection to the man in authority over them as husband, father, and master. The author of the Pastorals views God as "Father," the patriarchal head-of-a-very-large-household, so that the idea of "God's household" functions as the ground of a practical theology that decrees every "family member" ought to take up their subordinated position in relation to this father and master God and after that to God's designated male leaders: Paul and his representatives, Timothy and Titus.

Indeed, the Pastorals assert that the organization of the whole cosmos is based on God's οἰκονομία, "household management" (1 Tim 1:4). This foundational concept sets the stage for these three letters in which households and their members, relationships, and purposes consistently appear as teaching topics. Our author believes that both household and house-church—however they may have overlapped in reality—live and move and have their being under God their father and overseer. God's activities on behalf of humanity and the churches are echoed in the domestic roles assigned to free Roman male citizens as husbands, fathers, and masters.

When the author commands, "be subject to rulers and authorities" (Titus 3:1), he is endorsing not only patriarchy but also *kyriarchy*. This term, invented by Elisabeth Schüssler Fiorenza, signifies the overarching authority of "lords."

> In classical antiquity, the rule of the emperor, lord, slave master, husband—the elite, freeborn, propertied gentleman to whom all disenfranchised men and all wo/men were subordinated—is best characterized by the neologism *kyriarchy*. In antiquity, the social system of kyriarchy was institutionalized either as empire or as a democratic political form

of ruling that excluded all freeborn and slave wo/men from full citizenship and decision-making powers. Kyriarchy is best theorized as a complex pyramidal system of intersecting multiplicative social and religious structures of superordination and subordination, of ruling and oppression. Kyriarchal relations of domination are built on elite male property rights and privileges as well as on the exploitation, dependency, inferiority, and obedience of wo/men who signify all those subordinated. Such kyriarchal relations are still at work today in the multiplicative intersectionality of class, race, gender, ethnicity, empire, and other structures of discrimination.[1]

There is no doubt that the gender ideology of the Pastorals is patriarchal and kyriarchal since it values the male, the masculine, and the supposedly strong over the female, the feminine, and the hypothetically weak. Kyriarchy's "intersecting multiplicative social and religious structures" surface conspicuously in our author's treatments of relationships between enslaved persons (female and male) and "free" slaveholders (both male and female), as well as in his "imperial" theological assertions about God and Christ.

The Pastoral Letters Collection

This commentary, like many others, treats 1 Timothy, 2 Timothy, and Titus as a collection of three letters written by the same author. As in modern times, it was a familiar practice for well-known authors in the ancient world to gather their letters for publication. Additionally, letter collections ascribed to famous philosophers and their students were compiled so that they could be studied as a group. Some followers of the apostle Paul undoubtedly did this with the letters he wrote, since these appear together (in varied sequences) in many ancient New Testament manuscripts and in lists of texts read by early Christian churches. While the Pastoral Letters are three single components of this larger Pauline letter collection, they are still consistently positioned as a smaller cluster (including the letter to Philemon) of "letters to individuals" following what are called the "letters to churches" (Romans through 2 Thessalonians, in canonical order).

Another indication that the Pastorals may appropriately be interpreted as an interrelated collection is that they show remarkable similarities to

---

1. Elisabeth Schüssler Fiorenza, *Empowering Memory and Movement: Thinking and Working Across Borders* (Minneapolis: Augsburg Fortress Press, 2014), 525.

each other and, at the same time, some strong dissimilarities to the other Pauline letters. Tertullian (third century CE) and Augustine (fifth century CE) name the topic of church organization as one link between the Pastorals.[2] Other topics common to all three Pastorals are countering opponents, household management (marriage, children, slaves, and wealth), the church's reputation in society, and education (both teaching and learning). Although the rest of Paul's letters also address these issues, the Pastorals use a vocabulary and style of argumentation that are strikingly distinctive, especially when reading the documents in Greek.

What's more, many of the opinions and theological statements in the Pastorals agree with each other but do not match up with those found in the letters known to be written by Paul (Romans, 1 and 2 Corinthians, Galatians, Philippians, 1 Thessalonians, and Philemon). For example, when Paul criticizes his opponents in Romans, 2 Corinthians, Galatians, and Philippians, he gives specifics points of disagreement with them. In the Pastorals, the author attacks his opposition in more general terms as teaching "different doctrine" (ἑτεροδιδασκαλεῖν, 1 Tim 1:3) but only rarely describes the contents of this problematic teaching. Likewise it is difficult to imagine the Paul who wrote the complicated argument on salvation by faith found in Romans and Galatians asserting instead that "she [probably meaning a believing woman] will be saved through childbearing, provided they continue in faith and love and holiness, with modesty" (1 Tim 2:15). Significantly for the aims of this commentary, the views of the Pastorals on the nature and roles of women diverge from the activities of believing women in Paul's apostolic mission as he himself depicts them (e.g., Rom 16; 1 Cor 11:2-16; Phil 4:2-3). On these three subjects—opponents, salvation, and women—among others, the Pastoral Letters present a consistent worldview and one that varies from the outlook of Paul in the seven letters listed above.

In the last quarter century, some scholars have moved away from the approach of reading the Pastorals as an interconnected letter collection and instead have stressed the value of analyzing 1 Timothy, 2 Timothy, and Titus as individual documents. This sort of procedure is undoubtedly beneficial for understanding each letter, and yet in order to gain a more expansive sense of the Pastorals, they still need to be interpreted in light of each other. As I. Howard Marshall definitively states: "Despite some dissent, the three letters are by one author. . . . This means that

---

2. Tertullian, *Adversus Marcionem* 5.21, and Augustine, *De Doctrina Christiana* 4.16.

the letters can be considered together as a group of writings. . . . They represent a common outlook."[3] Recognizing the Pastorals as a small harmonized collection recommends the usefulness of a study method based on rereadings and cross-references among the three letters. Since the Pastorals have a solid position within the larger Pauline letter collection, it is also instructive to read them alongside these other canonical letters.

A Pseudonymous Author

It is one thing to discern that the Pastorals are all written by the same author and still another thing to identify who that author is. From the second century until around 1800 CE, the Pastorals were accepted as letters from Paul himself. However, the notion of non-Pauline authorship gradually took hold among scholars, so that by the mid-twentieth century, a solid majority agreed that they were not written by Paul. The evidence for this view consists of the numerous elements that distinguish the Pastorals from the authentic Pauline letters, which I have already summarized above and will continue to point out in later chapters. There are some commentators who argue that the differences in language and contents do not necessarily mean that the author of the Pastorals is not Paul. Maybe as Paul aged his writing style changed. Or he employed a secretary who was allowed greater leeway in the letters' composition. Or exceptional conflicts arose in a later decade that required Paul to address topics in an atypical fashion. However, none of these possibilities has proved very convincing, in large part because none alone can explain the whole range of recognized disparities in style and content. For most scholars, it is the substantial *accumulation* of all the literary, historical, and theological differences that makes the case for a pseudonymous author a more plausible solution to the question.

Another piece of evidence in favor of a pseudonymous author emerges from the curriculum of Greco-Roman education: for the (mostly male) students, it was a customary assignment to compose a text in the name and *persona* of a well-known figure. Unlike today, this was considered not as an attempt at forgery but rather as both a learning strategy and an honoring of the influence of that person. In such a literary culture, it is possible to envision a late first-century leader in a Pauline church

---

3. I. Howard Marshall, *The Pastoral Epistles*, ICC (Edinburgh: T & T Clark, 1999), 1.

writing letters that would imitate and reinterpret Paul's teachings for his particular location.

This widely held academic opinion of a pseudonymous author is not ordinarily encountered in modern churches, in spite of the fact that many pastors have been taught that Paul did not compose the Pastorals. In traditions where Bible education is emphasized, lay readers are probably well-aware that the letters themselves start right off with Paul's name, and since many study the Scriptures for personal devotional reasons, there seems to be no necessary reason for questioning the claim. Moreover, in liturgical traditions, worshipers do not often hear readings from the Pastorals at the services. Only short and divided passages have been selected, and these appear just eleven times in the Roman Catholic Lectionary, with nine of these also adopted for the Revised Common Lectionary. The chances that a sermon might be preached on one of these texts must be slim, and when it does occur, the wise preacher ought to be reluctant to tackle the subject of how a pseudonymous author came to be included in the New Testament canon.

An additional problem arises on occasion when a lay reader does learn that Paul probably did not write the Pastorals: the suspicion of a pseudonym allows these letters to be diminished in influence since they have lost their apostolic stamp of approval. In fact, some scholars who argue for Pauline authorship are especially concerned that the Pastorals do not become devalued as Christian texts. Luke Timothy Johnson worries "They [the Pastorals] are not technically outside the canon, but they may as well be for all the attention they receive, especially when elements in the Pastorals (such as their statements on women) are repugnant to present-day readers."[4] Of course, deciding that the Pastorals are Paul's own work may not make their teachings about women any less "repugnant," and at any rate, the letters are still present in the New Testament canon. As a result, the effects of their instruction—on women and men, on slavery and wealth, doctrinal conflicts and church offices—have been powerful forces in the history of Western societies that are experienced to this very day.

One further note: you may have wondered why I refer to this pseudonymous author as "he" or "him." Since we know so little about the actual author, how can I be sure that the Pastorals were written by a man

---

4. Luke Timothy Johnson, *First and Second Letters to Timothy*, AB 35A (New York: Doubleday, 2001), 57.

and not by a woman? Certainly a female believer might hold and agree with the opinions found in these letters. The main reason I think it more likely that the author is male is related to his level of education. Roman historians estimate that no more than 10–15 percent of the urban population at that time would have been literate enough to write such texts. The vast majority of those people would have been male, because education for females was very restricted. The author's written composition and style place him among those men of high enough status to have completed what we would think of as secondary schooling. Another reason I use masculine pronouns for the author is due to his own self-presentation. The author wants the reader to believe he is a man, a particular man, the legendary apostle Paul. If the author were known (or found out) to be a woman, the Pastorals' teachings would have become meaningless, duplicitous, and falsified because women were "not allowed to teach, or to have authority over a man" (1 Tim 2:12). As you will read throughout this commentary, in the communities envisioned by the author, only (higher-status) men were allowed to speak and teach, preside and make decisions. Since he poses as one such admirable male leader who serves as an example for other faithful men, I have decided to adopt his masculine presentation.

A Constructed Social Location

Every New Testament letter represents just one side of a communication process: we have the senders' opinions, understandings, and reactions, while those of the recipients can only be imagined or inferred from the ideas and arguments offered in the letter. Later readers, lacking familiarity with the details behind the correspondence, must try to tease out the facts from the sender's characterization of the setting.

In the case of the Pastorals, the pseudonymous author has added even more complexity to their interpretation because he has created a setting that never existed. He is not "really" Paul, and the proposed recipients Timothy and Titus are not actually present in his day. If they were, they could presumably verify the letters as authentically Pauline. This means that the city of Ephesus (for 1 and 2 Timothy) and the island of Crete (for Titus) are not necessarily indications of historical destinations. The exact teachings and activities of the opponents of the real author likewise remain unclear. Of special concern for this commentary is the actual behavior of women in the communities. In several passages, the author paints a picture of undisciplined females who are upsetting the stability of households and house-churches (e.g., 1 Tim 5:13-15; 2 Tim 3:6-7; Titus 2:3-5), but we cannot be sure to what extent this was happening in reality. A similar situation applies when we consider his commands to enslaved persons: were the slaves really disrespectful to their masters (1 Tim 6:2), and were they talking back and pilfering (Titus 2:9-10)?[5] Because we have only his perspective of the situation on the ground, we do not know what prompted the author to compose these letters, only that he felt some need to address issues that he identifies as problems for his own communities. He has placed these teachings back in time, putting them into the very words of Paul. This means that, while he tackles issues of concern to him, it is the revered apostle Paul who is depicted as a pre-scient teacher who predicts and deplores elements of the author's present situation.

As for the recipients, perhaps he hopes that his readers will assume that Timothy and Titus received the Pastorals as private communication, but then they or someone else preserved the letters until they were "re-discovered" at an appropriate time. Even though each of the Pastorals is written under just one name and sent to another individual, it is clear that the author expects their contents to be shared with other members of the church(es). He instructs Timothy: "and what you have heard from me through many witnesses entrust to faithful people [men] who will be able to teach others as well" (2 Tim 2:2; my insertion). Without ques-tion, the Pastorals emphasize the teaching roles of Paul, Timothy, and Titus, and the author offers the letters as the "core curriculum" for the education of Christians. Therefore, these letters are not "private" in the sense of confidential correspondence; rather, they obviously anticipate reception by a much wider audience, who are, in a way, "reading over the shoulders" of Timothy and Titus.

Although the pseudonymous author has submerged the real occasion(s) for the Pastorals, modern readers may still presume that he has painted a realistic picture of the structure and dynamics of at least some Christian communities of his own place and time. As a result, he formulates a representation that would be historically plausible to the earliest readers, offering an assortment of ingredients drawn from stories about and texts from Paul that are chosen for their applicability to the ecclesial situations faced by the apostle. While the dating of the Pastorals

---

5. On these possibilities, see Emerson B. Powery's comments in his "Interpretive Essay: The Pastor's Commands to Enslaved Christians: 1 Timothy 6:2 and Titus 2:9-10," below, pp. 162–65.

is much debated (suggestions range from the last third of the first century CE to much later in the second century CE), a date around 100 CE would account for the author's knowledge of other Pauline letters. This date also allows for changes since Paul's lifetime in the conflicts, activities, and social issues affecting church life.

Within this commentary, then, I interpret the Pastorals as a small collection composed by a later church leader under the name of the apostle Paul. This man adapted Paul's letter-writing strategies to his own constructed social location. The author of the Pastorals seems to know so much about the entire Pauline approach to written teachings that we can safely assume that he possessed detailed knowledge of Paul's correspondence (and other oral and written traditions about Paul) and indeed probably had access to actual copies of some of the letters. He thought of himself as a teacher in the Pauline tradition, an authoritative one who could "correctly" convey Paul's instructions in the proper form and style.

Recurring Topics in the Pastorals

Many of the topics treated in the Pastorals will be familiar to readers of other Pauline letters, but our author addresses them in his own identifiable writing style and argues on the basis of his distinctive worldview. Promoting the paradigm of the "household of God" (οἶκος θεοῦ; 1 Tim 3:15), he writes about ecclesial structures, ritual, and leadership positions. His focus on this religious household has its counterpart in guidance for the actual households of believers—for married partners, parents, widows, children, and slaves, and for the management of family wealth and possessions. He names and critiques internal opponents to his instructions while also advising the house-churches on how to conduct themselves within their broader social surroundings. The author conceives of his writing project as part of an educational process whereby community members will demonstrate a Christian version of the moral excellence advocated by Greco-Roman philosophical traditions.

For each topic, the letters draw on and yet also differ from the perspective and advice given in letters known to be from Paul. In a further step that is especially pertinent for this commentary, the author explicitly deals with each of these recurring topics when he refers to women, their social roles, church activities, and virtuous development. As we shall see in each of the Pastorals, the author focuses on the moral conduct of women. He seems to perceive female believers as most liable to fail in virtue and most likely to exemplify immoral behavior within the house-churches and in their relations with outsiders. The result is that "women's morality" becomes fundamental to all of his teachings, so fundamental in fact that he has given more direct instructions for women than are found in any other Christian writing of the church's first century.

Approaching the Pastoral Letters

In this commentary I offer one feminist's perspective on the Pastorals. That my interpretations are not the only feminist understandings of these texts will be obvious from reading the valuable exegetical comments provided by the other contributors: Jouette M. Bassler; Colleen M. Conway; Neil Elliott; Eloy Escamilla; Eh Tar Gay; Jennifer A. Glancy; Ekram Kachu; Marianne Bjelland Kartzow; Emerson B. Powery; Anna Rebecca Solevåg; Wolfgang Stegemann; Elsa Tamez; Jay Twomey; and Elijah R. Zehyoue. In addition, my thoughts are grounded in and improved by the work of other feminist biblical scholars who have written about the Pastoral Letters: Joanna Dewey; Margaret Y. MacDonald; Linda M. Maloney; Clarice J. Martin; Annette Merz; Carolyn Osiek; Elisabeth Schüssler Fiorenza; Ulrike Wagener; Frances M. Young; and Korinna Zamfir.[6] Research on slavery and slave societies in the ancient world has taken on a heightened importance as Americans deliberate the role of race in our own social history. I have gained much insight into the Pastorals' teachings about slaves from the studies of classicists Keith Bradley, Jennifer A. Glancy, J. Albert Harrill, Sandra R. Joshel, Sheila Murnaghan, and Richard P. Saller.[7] Finally, I deeply appreciate three Chicago-area scholars who supported the writing of this commentary. Barbara Reid, vice president and academic dean of the Catholic Theological Union and general editor of the Wisdom Commentary Series, first asked me to serve as author and continually and warmly encouraged me in the project. Sarah Tanzer, professor of New Testament and Early Judaism at McCormick Theological Seminary and the volume editor for this book, has been a lively, careful, and essential first reader of each draft; her collegial approach has been a source of strength to me. Margaret M. Mitchell, Shailer Mathews Professor of New Testament and Early Christian Literature and then-dean of the Divinity School at the University of Chicago, invited me to teach a course on the Pastoral Letters. That teaching experience not only re-immersed

6. The studies of these scholars are cited in various chapters.
7. The analyses of these authors appear in the commentary on 1 Tim 6 and Titus 2 below.

me in the Pastorals but also provided me with insightful student conversation partners. Every scholar mentioned in this paragraph has helped to challenge and develop my understandings of the letters, and I am grateful to benefit from this expanded interpretive circle.

My working definition of *feminism* derives from the basic idea that women and men deserve equal rights under the law, at the workplace, in the home, at schools and other communal organizations, and, for our purposes, especially in the churches. This essential commitment leads me to question hierarchical social structures, to distrust gender constructs, and to resist injustices based on perceived differences of race, sexuality, class, and religion. Such questioning, distrust, and resistance are just as necessary for feminist biblical interpretation. Viewing the Scriptures through the lens of this "hermeneutic of suspicion" helps to "uncover many levels of patriarchal bias, some in the Bible itself, others developed by later interpreters and recorded and perpetuated in theological works, scholarly biblical commentaries and histories, and in popular devotional literature."[8] Throughout this commentary, I ask questions that bring gender, status, and authority to the fore: How does the composition of letters in the name of Paul impinge on *the women* in the intended audience? Compared with men, how are *women* depicted as teachers and learners? What theological beliefs does the author use to justify his instructions *about women and men* in his communities? What does he presume about the conventional social *hierarchy* of his culture? How does he handle the *status divisions* caused by differences in gender, family origins, and wealth? How have these canonical teachings *shaped the lives* of people throughout history and in various social locations?

My answers to such questions derive primarily from approaches used by historical-critical scholars and in particular from close readings of the Pastorals based on literary analysis and comparisons with other written sources from the Greco-Roman world. I consider the cultural expectations and rhetorical strategies that seem to have influenced our author as well as relevant pieces of archaeological and epigraphical evidence. As a feminist reader trying to situate these texts in their particular social location, I do not intend to justify his opinions or soften the oppressive effects of his teachings. Instead I hope to show that his Roman Imperial position is historically far distant from our postmodern world.

8. Katharine Doob Sakenfeld, "Hermeneutic of Suspicion," in *Dictionary of Feminist Theologies,* ed. Letty M. Russell and J. Shannon Carson (Louisville, KY: Westminster John Knox, 1996), 27.

The overarching problem—for feminists, for present-day Christians, for women and men more generally, and for commentary writers more specifically—is that these letters as a group contain arguably the most sexist, exclusivist, and socially oppressive teachings in the New Testament. Even though a huge historical and social gap exists between us and the world of the Pastorals, it is not at all difficult to locate living people, groups, and societies that continue to be inhibited, insulted, and harmed by these instructions. Because of the church's interpretations of the Pastorals and because the letters themselves claim to be inspired by God, male domination has been reinforced in a wide range of religious and civic institutions so that in many times and places women have been dismissed, abused, and simply not valued as full persons. Furthermore, the Pastorals' teachings for masters and slaves ensured that generations of people suffered under slavery, and their descendants continue to bear the brunt of societal racism. Such oppressions exemplify why the Pastoral Letters are troubling texts.

A straightforward and widespread approach to the Pastorals is to minimize their presence in the New Testament canon. One may simply avoid reading them or just select a few trouble-free verses for devotional or liturgical purposes, as the lectionary committees have done. One could deny the religious authority vested in these letters or set aside the Pastorals' teachings with a statement like "That was then, this is now." The approach of this commentary is different. I intend to demonstrate the unmistakable patriarchal roots of the author's gender ideology, to question his inflexible kyriarchal worldview, and to wrestle openly with the negative consequences that have occurred when his words were taken seriously by the Christian churches. By encouraging a deeper engagement with these letters, I want to contribute to the many challenging conversations that are already happening around issues of gender, race, and power. By studying the Pastorals Letters with our minds sharpened and our hearts turned toward a generous freedom, we can struggle most productively with the influences of their teachings, past and present, and we can create a future church and a future world that are more just, truly inclusive, and indelibly marked by God's grace.

1 Timothy 1

Order and Disorder

Before reading this letter it is important to remember not only that the sender "Paul" and the recipient "Timothy" are pseudonyms for the real persons but also that the situation of the church in Ephesus is artificial as well. That is, there is no independent evidence about the conflicts this church was supposedly experiencing in the actual times when Paul and Timothy were co-workers. Nevertheless, in order for the letter to be received as authoritative and relevant, the author's description must correspond near enough to the historical reality of his congregations. His writing would need to reflect the sorts of persons, tensions, and movements already familiar to his audience and would also need to be understood as a valid response to those situations.

As with all letters attributed to Paul in the New Testament,[1] 1 Timothy opens with the apostle's name as the letter-writer (1:1). However, usually in the other letters, at least one co-sender is named and most often this is Timothy (2 Cor 1:2; Phil 1:1; Col 1:1; 1 Thess 1:1; 2 Thess 1:1; Phlm 1). Only the letters to the Romans and the Ephesians identify Paul as sole author.[2] Of course, since the supposed circumstances of the Pastorals

---

1. In canonical order these are: Romans, 1–2 Corinthians, Galatians, Ephesians, Philippians, Colossians, 1–2 Thessalonians, 1–2 Timothy, Titus, and Philemon.

2. First Corinthians identifies Sosthenes as a co-sender (1:1); Galatians adds "all the members of God's family who are with me" as co-senders (1:1).

1 Tim 1:1-2

¹Paul, an apostle of Christ Jesus by the command of God our Savior and of Christ Jesus our hope,
  ²To Timothy, my loyal child in the faith:

Grace, mercy, and peace from God the Father and Christ Jesus our Lord.

dictate that Timothy is the recipient of two of the letters, he cannot be a co-author. What sets the openings of all three Pastorals apart from those of the rest of the Pauline collection is that they have both a single author (Paul) *and* a single addressee (either Timothy or Titus). Thus, at a first reading, these letters are designed as correspondence between two individual (male) church leaders, rather than as letters written to entire communities. In spite of this, a closer reading of these "letters between individuals" reveals that in reality they are meant to be heard, studied, and acted upon by believers and groups within the author's larger field of vision. That the church ultimately included the Pastorals in the canon shows that they were useful for such a collective audience and not just for Timothy and Titus. It is as if members of the author's house-churches peer over the shoulders of Paul's named co-workers and examine the private correspondence of their historic leaders.

The relationship between the sender and recipient is defined by a familial label: Timothy is called the true, genuine, legitimate, "loyal child in faith" (1 Tim 1:2; see also, Titus 1:4 and 2 Tim 1:2). This then implies that Paul is Timothy's father in faith, although our author does not state this as clearly as Paul does in 1 Cor 4:14-17 (see also 1 Thess 2:11). In this way, the very beginning of this letter primes the reader for a particular social context: the Roman patriarchal household. "Paul" is an older authoritative man who is likened to a father of the younger Timothy who is his legitimate apostolic son, his heir, and his successor. As the letter continues, the idea of Timothy's legitimacy—as if he were a child born within a legal marriage or one who is legally adopted—must be kept in mind because Paul has a piece of paternal property (παραθήκη, "deposit," 1 Tim 6:20; 2 Tim 1:12, 14)[3] to hand down to Timothy: the "instruction" (1 Tim 1:5, 18), also called "the sound teaching" (1:10). For

---

3. See my comments on this word in "Translation Matters: 'What Has Been Entrusted,'" p. 96.

³I urge you, as I did when I was on my way to Macedonia, to remain in Ephesus so that you may instruct certain people not to teach any different doctrine, ⁴and not to occupy themselves with myths and endless genealogies that promote speculations rather than the divine training that is known by faith.⁵But the aim of such instruction is love that comes from a pure heart, a good conscience, and sincere faith. ⁶Some people have deviated from these and turned to meaningless talk, ⁷desiring to be teachers of the law without understanding either what they are saying or the things about which they make assertions.

Pauline communities reading this letter, the apostolic authority—which is embedded in Paul's very name as well as in the claims about his call by God—is similarly passed down in order to validate the leadership and teachings of his successors, including Timothy. Since the typical family hierarchy also resonates in the naming of God as "Father" (although only here in 1 Timothy) and of Christ Jesus as "master" or "Lord" (1:2), the authorization flows from the top down: from fathers to sons, from God and Christ to Paul and then to Timothy. This is the process by which Timothy receives the charge: his work is approved and empowered by a divine and human kyriarchal chain of command.

For the author, the concept of God as supreme head-of-a-very-large-household (1 Tim 1:17; 3:15; 6:15-16) means that everyone else stands in an inferior position to this superior God. However, Paul and Timothy are God's designated human representatives, which means that they are responsible for bringing about the proper subordination of those who are teachers of a "different doctrine" (1:3-4). These people have supposedly "deviated" (1:6) from the "divine training that is known by faith" (1:4).

Who are these deviating persons? The author refers to them as "certain people" (1 Tim 1:3, 6, 19; also Gal 1:7), an uncomplimentary label typically used in polemical writings of that time. We do not know the gender of these teachers because the Greek employs the "generic" masculine for groups that might include both women and men. When specific opponents are named in the Pastorals, these are all men (e.g., 1 Tim 1:20), but since women are prohibited from teaching (2:12) and are given various other corrective instructions (2:9-10; 5:11-15), some of them may be accused here as well. At any rate, these are persons who are or were part of the believing communities and over whom "Timothy" is expected

⁸Now we know that the law is good, if one uses it legitimately. ⁹This means understanding that the law is laid down not for the innocent but for the lawless and disobedient, for the godless and sinful, for the unholy and profane, for those who kill their father or mother, for murderers, ¹⁰fornicators, sodomites, slave traders, liars, perjurers, and whatever else is contrary to the sound teaching ¹¹that conforms to the glorious gospel of the blessed God, which he entrusted to me.

TRANSLATION MATTERS: "TRAINING"

The Greek word translated by the NRSV as "training" (1:4) is οἰκονομία. Other English translations suggested are: "plan," "stewardship," "office," or "economy." Still, this word conspicuously evokes the Greco-Roman household since its prefix is related to the word οἶκος, which means "house" or "household." The term *oikonomia* serves also as a title for ancient philosophical and practical treatises written on household management (reflecting the idea of "home economics"). In such texts, the authors give advice on marriage, childrearing, and slave supervision, as well as agricultural practices and family religious observances. Similarly, in 1 Tim 1:4, the idea of instructions on "God's household management" conveys a powerful image of the kind of teaching and community life that Timothy is supposed to establish, an image that is reinforced later in the letter when the author refers to "how one ought to behave in the household of God" (1 Tim 3:15).

to have some influence. They are internal adversaries, not outside agitators. They have a connection to the household of God.

What are their differing teachings? Again, the evidence is unclear. Our author specifies that they "occupy themselves with myths and endless genealogies" (1 Tim 1:4) and have "turned to meaningless talk" (1:6). Some aspects of Jewish law also seem to be in question (1:7), yet these teachers are accused more generally of teaching the law erroneously rather than specifically requiring circumcision or adherence to ritual regulations. In this first chapter, a brief assertion is made that following the approved "instruction" brings both external and internal results: "love that comes from a pure heart, a good conscience, and sincere faith" (1:5). Like all the other New Testament writers, this author understands that faith in Jesus Christ must be demonstrated by a loving way of life that is wholly consistent with one's mental and emotional attitudes toward God. Therefore, he attacks the teachers of different doctrine on both counts: they neither talk the talk nor walk the walk.

TRANSLATION MATTERS: "DISOBEDIENT"

The Pastoral Letters are sprinkled with terms about order and disorder. The origin of the Greek word group is the precise and organized arrangement of military forces ready for battle. In 1 Tim 1:9, the word translated "disobedient" (ἀνυπότακτος) comes from these roots. It might also be rendered "unruly," "independent," "undisciplined," "insubordinate," or "rebellious."

The Greek verb for being in proper order within a hierarchy is ὑποτάσσω. It may be translated "I submit to" or "I am subordinate to." The Pastorals use these terms especially for dis/orderly relationships between persons in the household (i.e., 1 Tim 1:9; 2:11; 3:4; Titus 1:6, 10; 2:5, 9), but also for the submissive behavior that people owe to governing authorities (Titus 3:1).

Within this hazy depiction, the author seeks to de-legitimate the other teachers by means of an *ad hominem* attack. First Timothy 1:8-10 accuses them of not using the law in the right way and further associates them with serious illegal and immoral behavior. Four pairs of terms state that the law is laid down for "the lawless and disobedient, for the godless and sinful, for the unholy and profane, for those who kill their father or mother" (1:9). These are followed by six single words for a total of fourteen pejorative labels, all of which are unlawful under Roman and/or Jewish law. They are summarized by the catch-all phrase "and whatever else is contrary to the sound teaching that conforms to the glorious gospel of the blessed God" (1:10-11). Although each of these socially abhorrent slurs disparages the behavior and not the doctrinal stances of the teachers, the author views their intellectual exercises as causes of such immoral behavior.

For modern readers, such polemical writing based on a thorough condemnation of opponents may be disconcerting if not entirely off-putting. This is not because we are unused to such attacks in many of our own societal and political settings where disagreements often lead to anger, threats, irrational conclusions, and deep interpersonal and social divides. Rather, we tend toward a naïve view that Christian community life ought to be different from life in the real world. At the least, we think, the dynamics in the earliest churches must have been more caring and free of caustic debate and discord. The Pastorals, among other early Christian texts, give evidence that there was no Golden Age of church life; conflicts have existed from the very beginning.

The rhetoric of the author of the Pastorals is controlled by his social location; he handles the opposition in ways that are culturally acceptable

TRANSLATION MATTERS: ANCIENT VICES

Two of the fourteen insults deserve separate comment because their presence in Christian Scripture has fostered oppression for two groups of persons. In my comments on these verses, I critique the author's polemical strategies more broadly.

1. ἀρσενοκοίταις ("sodomites") has received much attention in the last few decades since it is in one of the "clobber texts" used by some Christians in order to exclude LGBTQ persons from church offices. The word is a combination of "male" and "bed" as a euphemism for sexual intercourse, and it appears for the first time in all Greek literature in 1 Cor 6:9 and then here in 1 Timothy. In both verses, the term is included for rhetorical purposes as part of a list of vices considered to be repugnant in that social location. However, the NRSV choice of "sodomites" is anachronistic and problematic because we do not know exactly what the term meant to the authors or audience.[4]

2. ἀνδραποδισταῖς ("slave traders") appears only here in the New Testament and is a compound word for "man-stealers" or "kidnappers." While American abolitionists and modern readers might rejoice to interpret this as an "early Christian condemnation of slavery or the slave trade, [instead] the language of 1 Timothy articulates attitudes commonplace among masters in the Roman Empire. . . . The ancient world believed in the moral goodness of slavery yet condemned the immorality of slave traders."[5] This evidence means that, rather than making a socially revolutionary statement, the term "slave traders" undoubtedly intensifies our author's attacks on the other teachers.[6]

for himself and his audience. His approach to the other teachers is that they must be brought into line by intimidation and pressure. In order to maintain orderly behavior among the rest of his audience, he lifts up the opponents as negative examples while offering the rewards of God's mercy and salvation to those who abide instead by his own teachings. His worldview differs from a postmodern position that promotes personal freedom and dignity, values universal human rights, and operates within a sweeping global interconnectedness. Therefore, rather than

4. For a short discussion of translation and interpretation, see David J. Lull, "Jesus, Paul, and Homosexuals," *CurTM* 34 (June 2007): 203–4. For a longer essay, see Dale B. Martin, "*Arsenokoitês* and *Malakos*: Meanings and Consequences," in *Biblical Ethics & Homosexuality: Listening to Scripture*, ed. Robert L. Brawley (Louisville, KY: Westminster John Knox, 1996), 124–29.

5. J. Albert Harrill, *Slaves in the New Testament: Literary, Social, and Moral Dimensions* (Minneapolis: Fortress Press, 2006), 141.

6. In the chapter on Titus 2, the "Interpretive Essay" by Emerson Powery asserts that the author of the Pastorals *is* opposed to the slave trade. See pp. 161–62 below.

¹²I am grateful to Christ Jesus our Lord, who has strengthened me, because he judged me faithful and appointed me to his service, ¹³even though I was formerly a blasphemer, a persecutor, and a man of violence. But I received mercy because I had acted ignorantly in unbelief, ¹⁴and the grace of our Lord overflowed for me with the faith and love that are in Christ Jesus. ¹⁵The saying is sure and worthy of full acceptance, that Christ Jesus came into the world to save sinners—of whom I am the foremost. ¹⁶But for that very reason I received mercy, so that in me, as the foremost, Jesus Christ might display the utmost patience, making me an example to those who would come to believe in him for eternal life. ¹⁷To the King of the ages, immortal, invisible, the only God, be honor and glory forever and ever. Amen.

adopting the author's perspectives on conflict and disagreement that have been inscribed in the canonical texts, the interpreter ought to consider instead various strategies for conflict transformation that have emerged from other entities such as the historical Peace Churches (Society of Friends, Mennonites, and Church of the Brethren), nonviolent resistance movements, and the fields of group dynamics, family systems theory, and legal mediation. The Pastorals' use of abusive language and their advocacy of ostracism and shunning of opposition ought to have no place in contemporary religious or civic groups.

The author asserts as a summary that both the teachers and their instruction are the very opposite of the "sound teaching" of 1 Tim 1:10,[7] while his own teaching is consistent with the "the glorious gospel of the blessed God" (1:11). Verse 11 ends with "which he entrusted to me," a phrase that bridges to the next section of the letter, which is a description of Paul's experience of coming to be an apostle.

This biographically based passage that appears late in Year C of the New Revised Common Lectionary conveys an image of a merciful God reaching out to Paul, who then functions as a model for the rest of humankind. On God's and Christ's side, the author mentions positive attributes: strengthening and appointing (1 Tim 1:12); mercy (1:13, 16); grace, faith, and love (1:14); and patience and eternal life (1:16). On Paul's side, we find gratitude (1:12, 17) and acceptance of the gifts of God (1:16), as well as the admission of the faults of his previous life (1:13) as the

---

7. On this favorite Pastorals phrase, see in this volume "Translation Matters: 'Sound Doctrine,'" p. 146.

1 Tim 1:18-20

[18]I am giving you these instructions, Timothy, my child, in accordance with the prophecies made earlier about you, so that by following them you may fight the good fight, [19]having faith and a good conscience. By rejecting conscience, certain persons have suffered shipwreck in the faith; [20]among them are Hymenaeus and Alexander, whom I have turned over to Satan, so that they may learn not to blaspheme.

TRANSLATION MATTERS: "FIGHT THE GOOD FIGHT"

In 1 Tim 1:18, this command means to engage in military combat. In 1 Tim 6:12 and 2 Tim 4:7, the same English translation is given, but there the Greek indicates that the "fight" is more like an athletic competition. The author draws on the military language again in 2 Tim 2:3-4. Both the military and athletic images presume male opponents, advancing the notion that "Timothy" is in a win-lose confrontation with the so-called false teachers.

"foremost" of sinners (1:15). "Paul" lists three sins, calling himself "a blasphemer, a persecutor, and a man of violence" (1:13), whereas in the undisputed letters of Paul, the apostle admits only to "persecuting" the assemblies (1 Cor 15:9; Gal 1:13; and Phil 3:6).[8] In spite of Paul's sins, God regards Paul as "faithful" (1 Tim 1:12), perhaps because he "acted ignorantly in unbelief," although that excuse is not used in Phil 3:6. Our author sounds a Pauline note when he mentions "the grace of our Lord" (1 Tim 1:14). Since God extends grace to such a sinner as this, it necessarily must be extended also to all other sinners (1:15). In fact, Paul has become a prototype for everyone who subsequently comes to believe in Jesus Christ (1:16). Any reader of this letter can consider the transformation of Paul's life to be a reliable example of how God deals with sinners: by saving them through Christ Jesus (1:15). Such an act of God can only result in a human response of praise and blessing (1:17).

These last few verses return to themes raised earlier in the chapter. Our author re-emphasizes the father-child relationship between Paul and Timothy, in particular that Paul designates Timothy as the recipient of his "instructions" (1 Tim 1:18). In addition, Timothy supposedly received authorization by means of "prophecies made earlier" about him, although

---

8. Paul's harassment of believers is also mentioned in Acts 8:1 and 9:1-2.

this event is not documented elsewhere in the New Testament. By following the instructions and the prophecies, it is said that Timothy will be able to "fight the good fight" because he will then possess "faith and a good conscience," an echo of "the aim of such instruction" (1:5).

Finally, another censure of the opponents indicts the anonymous "certain persons" (as in 1 Tim 1:3) by supplying two names—Hymenaeus and Alexander—and describing the punishment meted out by "Paul," which appears to be exclusion from the community of faith (1:19b-20). While the reason given for this action is that it is "corrective discipline" (so that "they may learn not to blaspheme"), the ostracism seems inconsistent, at the least, with the story of God's mercy shown to Paul, the "foremost of sinners" (1:15).

1 Timothy 2

Praying Men and Silenced Women

As indicated by the opening phrase—"first of all"—1 Timothy 2 shifts the focus. Instead of giving instructions to Timothy in particular, as expressed in the direct address to him (1:18) and in the use of second-person pronouns (1:3, 18), now the author looks beyond Timothy to all the believers in the listening/reading audience. By the word "audience," I mean "auditors" or "hearers" because most people in the Roman Empire could not have read these letters for themselves. It is estimated that only 10 to 15 percent of men were literate and even fewer women. In the cities, where the majority of Pauline churches were founded, literacy rates would be at the higher end of the range. Still, in the small house-churches, only two or three people would have high-level reading skills, and these were most likely men from the wealthier households that could afford tutoring and educational fees. For their meetings, we should probably picture the male head-of-household handling and reading aloud any Jewish Scriptures as well as whatever early Christian texts the group possessed. The rest of the assembly gathered to hear the word of God and the apostolic teachings in his voice, a dynamic that served to increase the male leader's authority and to encourage the subordination of the non-readers.

¹First of all, then, I urge that supplications, prayers, intercessions, and thanksgivings should be made for everyone, ²for kings and all who are in high positions, so that we may lead a quiet and peaceable life in all godliness and dignity. ³This is right and is acceptable in the sight of God our Savior, ⁴who desires everyone to be saved and to come to the knowledge of the truth. ⁵For there is one God;

there is also one mediator
between God and
humankind,
Christ Jesus, himself human,
⁶who gave himself a ransom
for all
—this was attested at the right time. ⁷For this I was appointed a herald and an apostle (I am telling the truth, I am not lying), a teacher of the Gentiles in faith and truth.

What the author of 1 Timothy considers to be top priority is a certain way of praying. While several kinds of prayers are listed, he first states that prayers are to be offered for "everyone" (2:1) and then narrows his focus to praying specifically for rulers (2:2). These verses recall Rom 13:1-7 where Paul himself discusses the relationships between God, the believers, and the political rulers. In that earlier letter, Paul begins with "let every person be subject to the governing authorities for there is no authority except from God, and those authorities that exist have been instituted by God" (Rom 13:1a). Writing from a later time, the author of the Pastorals gives specific instructions on how to pray for rulers, saying that this is part of God's plan for salvation (2:1-4). Significantly, the believers are not to pray *to* "the kings and all those in high authority," but *for* them, or more literally "on their behalf" (2:2). This distinction became a key point for Christians in the next few centuries, as they sought to explain their approach to civic duty.

Roman Imperial Religion

Like many other societies before and since, the Romans excelled at mixing politics and religion. The emperor took on supreme earthly authority so that he functioned as both a political and religious figure. Who would not give honor and adoration to such mighty conquerors and sovereigns of the known world? Their armies built roads and aqueducts and secured the peace. Their rule of law stabilized the economy. To many, it appeared that the god(s) ordained these rulers and this style of governance for the Empire. In fact, when they died, many emperors were elevated to divine status, so that offering sacrifices and prayers at temples built for them and their family members became a popular practice for currying imperial favor. This was especially true in the cities of Asia Minor, a conquered province, where Ephesus and Sardis competed to show their devotion to the emperor and to attract the benefits of his patronage to their cities. For example, in Ephesus, the named location of Timothy and his churches (1 Tim 1:3), wealthy citizens built temples for the imperial cult in the first and second centuries CE, set up monumental statues of Augustus and his wife Livia in the *stoa* and later of Claudius in the marketplace and adorned other gates and buildings with signs of loyalty to the emperor and his governors. We can assume that the author of the Pastorals knew very well how this pattern of recognition and reverence for the emperor might influence the house-churches in Ephesus.

Such veneration of the divine imperial power caused persistent theological problems for monotheists like the Jews and Christ-believers in the Imperial Age. From their Jewish roots, the Christians adopted certain titles and labels for God and Jesus that were also being applied to and by the emperors. The emperor was known as "lord" (κύριος, 1 Tim 1:2; 6:14-15), "savior" (σωτήρ, 1 Tim 1:1, 15; 2:3), "father" ("of the

fatherland"; *pater* in Latin; πατήρ in Greek; 1 Tim 1:2), and "king" (βασιλεύς, 1 Tim 1:17; 6:15). (The emperor was also called "son of god," which in Latin is *divi filius*, but the title "son of God" does not appear for Jesus in the Pastorals.) Such imperial labels appeared on coins, inscriptions, documents, and buildings throughout the Empire.

How could Jewish-based monotheists pledge loyalty and submission to the emperor when their theology allowed for only one supreme ruler, the almighty God, who alone is "savior" (1 Tim 2:3-4)? By appropriating such imperial designations, early Christian writers essentially placed their God above any of the emperors. A Roman official might be justifiably concerned about sedition if he had heard the author declare: "For there is one God; there is also one mediator between God and humankind, Christ Jesus, himself human" (1 Tim 2:5).

By the late first to early second century CE when the Pastorals were written, Christians were just coming to the attention of governors and other provincial rulers, and not in a positive way. A letter exchange (ca. 111–113 CE) between the Roman emperor Trajan and Pliny, the governor of Pontus-Bithynia in north Asia Minor (a few hundred miles from Ephesus), describes some events concerning Christians. Governor Pliny explains how he interrogated some persons who had been turned into the authorities on the suspicion that they were Christ-believers.

An anonymous document was published containing the names of many persons. Those who denied that they were or had been Christians, when they invoked the gods in words dictated by me, offered prayer with incense and wine to your [i.e., Trajan's] image, which I had ordered to be brought for this purpose together with statues of the gods, and moreover cursed Christ—none of which those who are really Christians, it is said, can be forced to do—these I thought should be discharged. Others named by the informer declared that they were Christians, but then denied it, asserting that they had been but had ceased to be, some three years before, others many years, some as much as twenty-five years. They all worshipped your image and the statues of the gods, and cursed Christ.[1]

What is significant here is that Pliny knew that Christian faith stood in opposition to worship of the emperor's "image" (along with statues of the "gods"). So if an accused person prayed to the imperial image and offered incense and wine to the same, she or he was obviously not a Christian believer. True Christians prayed for the governing authorities rather than to them or to their images.

Annette Huizenga

These verses of 1 Timothy indicate some of the looming potential for disagreement and hostility between assembly and empire and suggest some ways for conciliating with the Roman authorities. When the author advocates for this style of prayer, he promises that "we may lead a quiet and peaceable life in all godliness and dignity" (1 Tim 2:2; echoing 1 Thess 4:11-12). The Christian assemblies were developing a noteworthy interest in living quietly out of the public eye, especially that of the governor.

The political implications of these verses surface yet again when the author claims that Christ Jesus is the "one mediator between God and humankind" (1 Tim 2:5). This was another function that the emperors claimed for themselves, in their role of "chief priest" (*Pontifex Maximus*)

---

1. Pliny, *Letters* 10.96–97.

of the empire, a role "given" to them by virtue of their military victories, amassed wealth, and unchallenged political authority. Yet 1 Timothy has a distinctive and different understanding of the mediator: his mediation occurs as a result of his humanness and his self-giving (2:5-6). This act differentiates him from the acts of imperial oppression.

Similarly, the human Christ Jesus is likewise set up as superior to the angels, prophets, priests, and even Moses of the Jewish tradition (as in Gal 3:19-20 and Heb 8:6; 9:15; 12:14). The influence of Christ Jesus as mediator extends far and wide because he "gave himself a ransom for all" (1 Tim 2:6). The phrase "for all" explains why prayers ought to be offered "for everyone" in 1 Tim 2:1. The universality of God's intentions also links to the statement that God "desires *everyone* to be saved and to come to the knowledge of the truth" (2:4).

TRANSLATION MATTERS: "A HERALD AND AN APOSTLE"

The titles "herald" (κῆρυξ) and "apostle" (ἀπόστολος) eventually developed special meanings within Christian circles, but in the wider Greco-Roman world they also connote diplomatic roles of the government. Although sometimes used interchangeably, "herald" could signify "a messenger between warring parties" (LSJ), while "apostle" meant "ambassador" or "envoy" more generally. Thus Paul is presented in 1 Tim 2:7 and elsewhere in the NT as an "appointed" official of God's own imperial administration. Such terms seem to establish God, Christ, and Paul as rivals to the Roman emperors and their governance.

Unlike most other deities in the Mediterranean world, the God of the Jews and Christians is depicted as having no geographical or functional limitations: this God was responsible for the operation and salvation of the entire cosmos. While this might bring comfort to the ancient audience, it is crucial for the modern reader to recognize that 1 Timothy, like other early Christian writings, does not replace a kyriarchal[2] political system with a democratic or socialist or populist one but rather positions the God of Jesus at the pinnacle of this lordship hierarchy. Therefore, even though the conflict between God's empire and the Roman one seems to be successfully resolved, yet with this one and only God as true king, savior, father, and master, a pyramidal patriarchal social structure is re-established and reinforced as the product of the divine will.

---

2. For the definition of "kyriarchy," see in this volume "Introduction," p. xlii.

1 Tim 2:8-10

⁸I desire, then, that in every place the men should pray, lifting up holy hands without anger or argument; ⁹also that the women should dress themselves modestly and decently in suitable clothing, not with their hair braided, or with gold, pearls, or expensive clothes, ¹⁰but with good works, as is proper for women who profess reverence for God.

A possible improvement to the kyriarchal imagery of the one God at the top of the pyramid—the one whose mighty power will overcome even Caesar and rain destruction on all enemies—is found in the act of "Christ Jesus, himself human, who gave himself a ransom for all" (1 Tim 2:5-6). This tangible manifestation of a generous and philanthropic divinity stands in tension with the image of the conquering warrior-God.

The next section opens with a strong declaration in the first-person singular: "I [meaning, Paul] desire that in every place the *men should . . .*" (1 Tim 2:8).[3] This single instruction to men is followed by some seven verses of instructions for women that go far beyond their conduct during prayer (2:9-3:1a). The author begins with how women ought to dress and adorn their physical bodies, rejecting the material "consumer items" and replacing them with a more metaphorical kind of adornment: "good works" (2:10). The feminine "good works" are not specified in this passage, but we find some of them mentioned later in the letter's teachings about widows (5:10). While I contest the notion that good faithful women ought to be inconspicuous, modest, and even "silent" (2:11-12), there is a valuable teaching here for readers from industrialized Western economies. The prominent display of one's affluence does not provide a sense of ultimate meaning for the individual, nor does it bring about a just and peaceful world. Amassing wealth—as an individual or a nation—contributes to the oppression of the poor and creates social conflict. The author has more to say about the topic of money in 1 Tim 6.

This high proportion of teachings for and about women suggests that their activities were somehow problematic for the author and his communities; he perceives that at least some female believers were not acting according to the social conventions, so he wants to monitor and guide their behavior. We do not know exactly what these women were doing that attracted his attention. Elsa Tamez views them as wealthy women

3. See the discussion of this NRSV translation in "Translation Matters: 'I Desire,'" p. 178.

TRANSLATION MATTERS: VIRTUES FOR WOMEN

First Timothy 2:8-10 uses ideals common to women's moral education in the ancient world. Philosophers, playwrights, satirists, and even the average person (male and female) repeated the cultural convention that modesty in a woman's outer appearance signifies that her internal character is likewise virtuous. The key virtue is σωφροσύνη, which has a range of meanings: "moderation," "chastity," "temperance," or "self-control." When applied to females (as opposed to males) "moderation" means that a woman is sexually faithful to her own husband. This sexual fidelity is extended to all the activities that a good woman ought to demonstrate as a wife, mother, and household manager. A woman who possesses this virtue is most highly regarded by others. It is the premier standard by which she is judged.

In the NRSV version of 1 Tim 2:9, the noun σωφροσύνη has been translated as the adverb "decently." That translation greatly underplays the importance of this word to the role and status of women in that world. I would prefer that this whole phrase be translated "the women should dress themselves with modesty and sexual faithfulness" in order to emphasize how a woman's outer appearance and actions function as her virtuous adornment.

The remaining specific elements that 1 Timothy includes—expensive clothing, braided hair, pearls, and gold—also are linked to feminine "moderation" by other writers (Jewish, Greek, Roman, and Christian) throughout the empire. All agree with our author that adornment for a woman means to cover her body modestly so that she does not draw attention to herself. As just one example, around the turn of the Common Era, the female philosopher Periktione wrote

> One must presume that the harmonious woman is full of prudence and moderation. . . . She must train her body to a natural measure of provision in regard to clothing and bathing and anointing and hairstyles and such things for adornment as gold and precious stones. For the women who eat and drink and cover themselves in every expensive thing, and wear the things that women wear, are prepared for error of every dishonor related to marriage beds and for other unjust acts. . . . Therefore she will not wear gold or precious stone from India or from another country, nor will she braid her hair very artfully, or anoint herself with oil laden with Arabian scent, nor will she color her face, making it white or red or her eyebrows and eyes black, or work on her gray hair with dyes, or bathe frequently. For the woman seeking these things, seeks admirers of womanly lack of self-control.[4]

Like the author of the Pastorals, Periktione expects women to renounce "expensive" adornments because such things indicate female sexual impropriety. A woman who wants to be recognized as possessing "moderation" will follow their advice.

---

4. Periktione, *On the Harmony of a Woman*, Stob., Anth. 4.27–28.19 (my translation).

who were using their prestige to exert authority in the house-churches.[5] We know of many high-status Roman women in Asia Minor. One such woman is described in this inscription from the city of Perga (ca. 120 CE).

> *Plancia Magna*
>
> Daughter of Marcus Plancius Varus
> and daughter of the city.
> Priestess of Artemis
> and both first and sole public priestess
> of the mother of the gods
> for the duration of her life
> pious and patriotic.

Certainly no one as elevated as Plancia Magna was a member of the Christian assembly in Ephesus, but lower-status women still emulated, in lesser ways, the clothing, jewelry, and hairstyles of the women in the imperial family and among their provincial elite. Participants in the small house-churches might take notice of a new set of gold hoop earrings or comment on a new way of arranging their hair. If a woman could afford it, perhaps a robe would be designed, woven, and dyed for special religious events. Tamez points out how the display of ostentation would emphasize the social distinctions in the assembly. Would less wealthy women in the group then feel jealousy or self-pity? Would the men sense an enticement and/or feel competitive about the wealth of other households?

When reading Elsa Tamez's analysis below alongside my own comments in "Virtues for Women," we see how difficult it is to decipher which elements are the author's opinions about the situation on the ground and which represent the social location of the community of the Pastorals. The author has used stereotypical language and topics, yet he has directed these teachings toward some real situation that he perceives as historically plausible for his audience. Korinna Zamfir reminds us that the effect of such a complicated text is that it "*obscures* social reality."[6]

---

5. See pp. 18–19.
6. Korinna Zamfir, *Men and Women in the Household of God: A Contextual Approach to Roles and Ministries in the Pastoral Epistles*, NTOA 103 (Göttingen: Vandenhoeck & Ruprecht, 2013), 27.

From Struggles for Power in Early Christianity:

A Study of the First Letter to Timothy

The exhortation [in 1 Timothy] to dress in a modest and simple manner, where good works are more important than luxurious attire, cannot be seen simply as a straightforward motif frequent within the moral values of antiquity. Many commentators mention in passing that the advice to dress without ostentation was a common philosophical topic among thinkers and satirists of that time. . . .

Nevertheless, we believe that the author does not come up with this topic out of the air, in passing, to counsel all the women of the Christian community on how they should dress. The reference to sophisticated hairstyles, gold, pearls, and expensive clothing, in a community in which the majority of the members are poor, alerts all readers to pay attention to this point because it gives a crucial clue for the reconstruction of the situation. It raises the possibility that the principal problem that the author brings up is not simply about women in general, leaders of the community, but about rich women, . . . women who were probably very dominant. . . . At this time, the end of the first century and the beginning of the second century, the tensions caused by the presence of wealthy men and women intensified within the Christian communities. This growing tension between the different social classes in the community was aggravated when some members appeared in luxurious clothing alongside those who dressed poorly. For this reason, we insist that the principal critique is ostentation, not indecency.

But the fundamental problem is not the manner of dress but the behavior of those wearing the ostentatious clothing. The most profound tensions probably were produced between church leaders and the wealthy believers of the community rather than between the wealthy and those of scarce resources. The clothing simply serves to point out the social differences and, in passing, to observe the rejection of all ostentation.

How is it possible that the rich women have achieved power within the community? For us in Latin America today, the answer is easy: it is an everyday occurrence in our Christian communities. Wealth and power easily open doors in all circles, not just in the secular world. . . .

To tell women how they should dress, even though here it is to avoid the contrast of the clothing worn by the rich and the poor of the assembly, is part of patriarchal ideology. The terms "decently," "modestly," "restraint," and "discretion," for example, in spite of the fact that the author contrasts them with ostentatious hairdos, jewels, and costly clothing, still reflect the values that patriarchal society assigns to the feminine gender. By applying to women the terms *aidous* ("discretion, modesty") and *sōphrosunēs* ("self-control, restraint"), the author causes the reader to think of "chastity," sexual purity. It is because patriarchal ideology has associated women, throughout history, with sex and temptation. Shame is for women who dress with insolence and liberty. That is why, as we have seen, the men of the household—fathers, brothers, uncles, grandfathers— had the task of controlling the women so they would not be sexually provocative and damage the family's honor.

So the author of the letter gives instructions that the rich women not use jewels and expensive clothing in order to reduce the social inequality within the Christian community, but at the same time the patriarchal ideology tells women how they should dress, using terms with connotations associated with chastity. For our reading of the Bible, what is important is to contrast the ostentatious with what is modest and simple, not with chastity. The problem is not the women's sexual provocation, but the ostentation of the wealthy women of the community.[7]

Elsa Tamez

During the 1990s I served as a pastor at a nondenominational church near downtown Chicago. Located up the street from a Bible college, we often had strict evangelical and even fundamentalist students come to our Sunday services. Many of them had never encountered a female pastor, so that invariably, whether I preached, directed worship, or celebrated the Lord's Supper, the church staff would receive written and oral rebukes stating (usually in the King James Version): "But I suffer not a woman to teach nor to usurp authority over the man but to be in silence" (1 Tim 2:12). The meaning of this verse and its proper application to my worship leadership appeared obvious to the students, thus they suspected both the church and me of anti-biblical practices. Most of them never returned to our congregation.

As the author of the Pastorals wrote these verses, he surely could not have imagined how effectively they would be used over the centuries to repress female believers—to silence their voices, control their activities,

7. Elsa Tamez, *Struggles for Power in Early Christianity: A Study of the First Letter to Timothy* (Maryknoll, NY: Orbis Books, 2007), 5–6, 9, 36–37.

1 Tim 2:11–3:1a

[11]Let a woman learn in silence with full submission. [12]I permit no woman to teach or to have authority over a man; she is to keep silent. [13]For Adam was formed first, then Eve; [14]and Adam was not deceived, but the woman was deceived and became a transgressor. [15]Yet she will be saved through childbearing, provided they continue in faith and love and holiness, with modesty. [3:1a] The saying is sure.

and eviscerate their leadership in churches. He could not have known that pious church authorities would exhort women instead to take up their supposedly God-ordained roles of wife and mother. Although he wrote for his own time and place, I believe he would be quite satisfied to learn that his instructions have influenced gender perceptions not only in the church but in the long history of Western societies. Like the author of the Pastorals, the two largest Christian denominations in the United States—Roman Catholic and Southern Baptist—continue to prohibit women from holding the highest church leadership positions, and an ideal "femininity" like that of the Pastorals may be found in many modern church's teachings about marriage and childrearing. As described by Dr. Eh Tar Gay, a similar ecclesial and social situation exists in Myanmar (also known as Burma), where, as in many colonized countries, Western missionaries exerted a strong influence on the adoption of Christianity.

Reinterpreting 1 Tim 2:9-15

Is there any culture that cannot be changed? Is there any tradition that is static? Is there any one theological perspective that has no contradiction? Some believe that there are two cultures: a culture that may be changed because it is made by humans and a culture that should not be changed because it is God-given and foundational for a good life. Some people apply this understanding to interpreting the Bible, especially interpreting texts like 1 Tim 2:9-15. For them, some teachings in the text represent the cultures that may be changed, but the central theological doctrines stand outside of human culture and ought not be changed. In my opinion, there is neither static truth nor only one theology. This can be seen vividly in that there are many Christian denominations that read and interpret the Bible differently. Some observe the restrictions on women in the Pastoral Letters as absolute truth while some reform those restrictions. In this essay, I examine the interpretation of the teachings in

1 Tim 2:9-15 from the perspective of Myanmar Christians and describe how the differing cultures of the Bible and today intersect with each other.

In Myanmar, Christians are a small minority, about 4 percent of the total population of fifty-four million. Christianity is regarded as a foreign religion by many people in Myanmar because our missionaries (mostly Roman Catholic and Baptist) came from the West. Myanmar Buddhists, who make up about 90 percent of the population, assume that we Christians have a different culture, which is identified with the Western culture. Our government officials also regard Christianity as a colonial religion. Myanmar culture, which has a long association with Buddhism, can be regarded as Myanmar-Buddhist culture in which respect, hospitality, gentleness, and modesty are practiced. Women, especially mothers, are considered as important persons who preserve and hand the culture down to the younger generations. The man is recognized as the head of the family and a provider of the livelihood for the family. Boys are strongly encouraged to pursue higher education while girls are encouraged to raise children and fulfill domestic duties in the family. This is the typical communal pattern of the culture of a Myanmar family, and because of this pattern,

Myanmar women are considered to be second-class citizens in the family and the society.

In 1 Tim 2:9-15, we find three restrictions on women's activities that have already been changed or that are no longer wholly practiced among Myanmar Christians. These restrictions negatively affect the whole being of a woman.

First, Women have often been exploited and discriminated against based on what they wear. For example, in 1 Cor 11:3-16, Paul encourages women to wear the veil. Although the author of the Pastorals does not require wearing a veil, he does command women to dress modestly, and virtuous women did veil themselves at various events. In some cultures today, this practice continues to be encouraged because wearing the veil is considered a sign of modesty and provides security for a woman. Without a veil, women are looked down upon or even threatened.

Wearing a veil is not mandated for Myanmar Christian women because it was not part of traditional Myanmar culture or dress for women. However, since women in Myanmar are believed to be the preservers of our heritage, they are strongly encouraged to wear the traditional dress. This costume is authentic and conservative, a sari-type of skirt called the *longyi*, which extends down to the feet. It is thought that unless women wear the traditional costumes the culture will be lost.

Second, the author's restrictions on women's intellectual life can be seen vividly in 1 Tim 2:11-12 and in the similar statement found in 1 Cor 14:34-35. Many churches nowadays allude to these verses as a reason to disallow women's ordination to church leadership roles. Since in Myanmar-Buddhist culture the religious leaders must be male, Myanmar Christian communities share the same sort of mentality. However, many churches in Myanmar do permit women to teach both in public schools and religious schools. Many women are also becoming theological educators; thus, my own institution, the Myanmar Institute of Theology, has an equal number of male and female faculty. Because women are supposed to be family caretakers, raising children at home and then teaching children and other students in public, women's roles in the educational sphere are seen by society and the church as more acceptable than making decisions and serving as a pastor. The cultural perception of women in education has changed so that the prohibitions from 1 Tim 2 are no longer valid regarding women's learning and teaching in the Myanmar churches or religious sphere.

Third, the phrase "saved through childbearing" (1 Tim 2:15) was very important for women in the first century because it assumes that only mothers would be saved.[8] The author seems to indicate that salvation through belief in Jesus was meant only for the male believers. Because of this restriction, barren women would be discriminated against, and women's roles and their faith expression were limited. Actually this verse also has political, social, and economical implications in addition to theological and spiritual ones. The text reflects the life of women under the Roman emperors who encouraged women to give birth to the sons who could be good citizens of the empire. The children could be useful for the economic stability of the household and would inherit the family wealth, stand up for the family honor, carry on the family names, and preserve the traditions of the clan and tribe. Women would be forced to depend on a man's support or domination in marriage and childbearing. However, Christian women these days in Myanmar do not accept this statement from the Pastorals that they will be saved through childbearing but instead believe that they will be saved through faith in Jesus.

8. Joanna Dewey, "1 Timothy," in *Women's Bible Commentary*, ed. Carol A. Newsom and Sharon H. Ringe (Louisville, KY: Westminster John Knox Press, 1998), 446–47.

In 1 Tim 2:14, there is one main theological point that needs to be re-examined and changed in order to support the personhood and work of women. This teaching states that, because Eve was the first and only one to be deceived and to become a transgressor, all later women have a share in her experience and inherit her female sinful nature. This traditional understanding is fully embedded in Myanmar Christian society: since they believe that the original sin comes from women, it follows that religious leadership roles should not be undertaken by women. In this way Christian women in Myanmar suffer from the consequences of the text's core theology about the origin of sin.

However, even in the Bible there are several inconsistent interpretations about the meaning of the events in Genesis 3. For example, 1 Tim 2:14 contradicts Rom 5:12, which says, "Therefore, just as sin came into the world through one man, and death came through sin, and so death spread to all because all have sinned." Here Paul says that sin came through one man instead of through a woman. The Pastorals' theology about the origin of sin does not need to be accepted because there are at least two opinions within the New Testament. If Christian

denominations recognized the contradiction between 1 Timothy and Romans about Adam's and Eve's roles in transmitting sin, they might begin to change their position about ordaining women to pastoral leadership roles.

We find in the passage several ethical virtues that not only women but also men should practice: good deeds in religion, faith, love, holiness, and modesty. In the Pastorals these virtues are commanded not only for women but also for men.[9] In fact, such "good works" are valuable for human relationships in every time and every culture. These kinds of virtues can be found not only in New Testament books but also in the teachings of other religions, including Buddhism in Myanmar, where they are also to be followed by both men and women. Such good qualities are important to the healthy functioning of every culture.

The biblical cultures and beliefs are not static. Through the centuries, there have already been many changes in how Christians interpret and act out the teachings of the Bible. My readings of 1 Tim 2:9-15 call attention to the fact that there are restrictions on women that have already been changed or are no longer valid in the culture of Myanmar and its churches. I have pointed out that the belief that women are responsible for

9. 1 Tim 4:12; 5:10; 6:6-8, 11, 18; 2 Tim 2:22, 24; 3:10; Titus 1:7-8; 2:1-8; 3:1-2.

the origin of sin should be changed in order to give confidence to Christian women in many denominations who seek to follow God's call to pastoral leadership. Finally, I believe that all Christians, whether male or female, ought to practice the kind of "good works" prescribed by the Pastoral Letters. Good works are not an exceptional culture of any particular religion. They are the virtues demanded by all religions.

Eh Tar Gay

Since these few verses have been so authoritatively influential regarding women's position within church and society, feminist biblical scholars have written numerous books, essays, and critiques of their teachings.[10] I cannot possibly duplicate their arguments and insights in this commentary, but my thoughts draw on the solid foundation they have provided.

10. I list just a few of the books here, in order of publication: Elisabeth Schüssler Fiorenza, *In Memory of Her: A Feminist Theological Reconstruction of Christian Origins* (New York: Crossroad, 1983; 2nd ed., 1993); Dennis R. MacDonald, *The Legend and the Apostle: The Battle for Paul in Story and Canon* (Philadelphia: Westminster, 1983); Joanna Dewey, "1 Timothy," "2 Timothy," "Titus," in *The Women's Bible Commentary*, ed. Carol A. Newsom and Sharon H. Ringe (Louisville, KY: Westminster/John Knox, 1992), 353–61; Ulrike Wagener, *Die Ordnung des "Hauses Gottes": Der Ort von Frauen in der Ekklesiologie und Ethik der Pastoralbriefe* WUNT 2, vol. 65 (Tübingen: J.C.B. Mohr [Paul Siebeck], 1994); Margaret Y. MacDonald, *Early Christian Women and Pagan Opinion: The Power of the Hysterical Woman* (New York: Cambridge University Press, 1996); Carolyn Osiek and David L. Balch, *Families in the New Testament World: House-hold and House Churches* (Louisville, KY: Westminster/John Knox, 1997); Annette Merz, *Die fiktive Selbstauslegung des Paulus: Intertextuelle Studien zur Intention und Rezeption der Pastoralbriefe*, NTOA/SUNT 52 (Göttingen: Vandenhoeck & Ruprecht; Fribourg: Academic Press, 2004); Carolyn Osiek and Margaret Y. MacDonald, *A Woman's Place: House Churches in Earliest Christianity*, with Janet H. Tulloch (Minneapolis: Fortress Press, 2006); Elsa Tamez, *Struggles for Power in Early Christianity* (Maryknoll, NY: Orbis Books, 2007); Anna Rebecca Solevag, *Birthing Salvation: Gender and Class in Early Christian Childbearing Discourse*, BibInt 121 (Leiden: Brill, 2013); and Korinna Zamfir, *Men and Women in the Household of God: A Contextual Approach to Roles and Ministries in the Pastoral Epistles* (Göttingen: Vandenhoeck & Ruprecht, 2013).

TRANSLATION MATTERS: SILENT LEARNING

The Greek word translated as "silence" in 1 Tim 2:11 and as "to keep silent" in 2:12 is the same word: ἡσυχία. Another Greek word, σιωπή, is also sometimes translated as "silence." A third related word is the verb σιγάω, meaning "to be still/silent." All three words have two meanings: (1) "silence" as in no sound, and (2) "stillness," "rest," or "calm" as in no movement. All are applied to anyone, male or female, who is identified as a student. In the New Testament, this concept also arises in 1 Cor 14:34-35: "As in all the churches of the saints, women should be silent [the verb σιγάτωσαν] in the churches. For they are not permitted to speak, but should be subordinate, as the law also says. If there is anything they desire to know [literally, "they wish to learn"], let them ask their husbands at home." This is one of those echoes of an undisputed Pauline letter that suggests that the author of the Pastorals was quite familiar with Paul's own teachings. But our author might have read similar ideals in one of the Pythagorean letters, *Melissa to Kleareta*, which connects the concept of silence to proper adornment. It states that the first requirement for the good wife is the metaphorical "being adorned with silence" (line 6). Or he might have known of Plutarch's essay called *On Listening to Lectures*: "In every case, silence is a safe adornment for a young man" (*Mor.* 39B). The author of the Pastorals writes from a social location where silence from subordinated persons shows respect toward those of higher status.

In 1 Tim 2:11-12, the emphasis is on the proper behavior of faithful women within the context of the church's teaching and learning process. The author insists that the most appropriate role for women is as learners, and for him their learning ought to be done "in silence with full submission [ὑποταγή]."[11] Such learning in silence signifies respect for the teacher and reinforces the subordinate position of the learner. Since women are already subordinated to men in the household and the house-church, the author wants to place them securely in the role of subordinate learners.

While modern pedagogical theories stress that the best students are engaged with the material and the teacher through active and integrative strategies, many ancient teachers perceive learners to be more like "empty vessels" waiting to be filled up with the knowledge of the teacher. The question and response strategy of Socrates—known to us as the "Socratic method"—may be an exception to this perception of students. As described in several dialogues written by Plato, Socrates appears to treat his students as capable of critical thinking that leads to logical and

---

11. This Greek noun is related to the verb ὑποτάσσω ("to be subordinate to"), already discussed above, "Translation Matters: 'Disobedient,'" p. 5.

solid conclusions. Nonetheless, a teacher-student hierarchy is still maintained since Socrates the teacher is the more prominent, knowledgeable figure who seeks to train the uninformed, illogical students to be more rational and consistent in their beliefs.

To underscore that women are learners only and always, the author forcefully states: "I permit no woman to teach or to have authority over a man; she is to keep silent" (1 Tim 2:12). The word translated "have authority over" (αὐθεντεῖν) appears in the New Testament just this one time, and it is not entirely clear what kind of activity it refers to. However, given the literary structure of the verses, it seems to reflect the same idea as the verb "to teach" (διδάσκειν), in part because both words are in the infinitive form. The full logic can be outlined like this:

   A   Let a woman learn in *silence* with full submission

     B   I permit no woman **to teach**

     B¹   or **to have authority over** a man

   A¹   she is to *keep silent*.

The author has tried to establish a definitive and enduring rule that will remind women of their subordinate ranking in the church hierarchy and that will pressure them to remain in it. To that he adds two pieces of evidence from Jewish Scripture that bolster his command. First, he states: "For Adam was formed first, then Eve" (1 Tim 2:13), which for him seems to mean that the first is better. In our age of technological expansion, we often think of the first production as a "prototype," with later models bringing improvements on the original. But for our author, there is something superior about Adam, and all subsequent male humans, simply because he was the first to be created in Gen 2:7.

Second, referring to Gen 3:6 and 13, the author claims "Adam was not deceived, but the woman was deceived and became a transgressor." He believes that somehow "the woman" had a different experience of decep-

TRANSLATION MATTERS: "DECEIVED"

When the NRSV uses the translation "deceived" in 1 Tim 2:14 for both human creatures, it neglects an important nuance of the verb. The Greek says that Adam was not at all "deceived" (ἀπατᾶσθαι) while the woman was "thoroughly/completely deceived" (ἐξαπατᾶσθαι). The verb difference intensifies the idea that the primary male and the secondary female responded to temptation in completely different ways.

tion that Adam avoided. This verse has been influenced by other Jewish interpretations of Gen 3 that speculated that there was some sexual element in the serpent's temptation of Eve. Paul himself made this link: "I feel a divine jealousy for you, for I promised you in marriage to one husband, to present you as a chaste virgin to Christ. But I am afraid that as the serpent deceived [or, "thoroughly deceived," as in 1 Tim 2:14] Eve by its cunning, your thoughts will be led astray from a sincere and pure devotion to Christ" (2 Cor 11:2-3).

The fact that the author of the Pastorals does not call Eve by name means that she represents all women: she is the principal pattern of female nature. Mother Eve serves as a negative example, showing how she and her female offspring might behave due to their untrustworthy nature as women. The author believes that women are not only *likely* to act immorally in certain situations (specifically, teaching and having authority over men) but *destined* to act like this due to their "inherited" biology. Since the first woman was more vulnerable to the wiles of the serpent, the author argues that subsequent women may not teach but should learn in silence.

In 1 Tim 2:14, the eroticized temptation of the woman by the serpent is sharply contrasted with the astonishing claim that "Adam was not deceived." This explains why the author denies teaching positions to all women as "daughters of Eve" while allowing the possibility that any man as a "son of Adam" might aspire to that function. The example of Eve is expected to restrict the activities of female members in the audience. Of course, this text influences male audience members as well: they could and did use this instruction as justification for prohibiting women from community leadership.

TRANSLATION MATTERS: WHO WILL BE SAVED?

The NRSV translation reveals a problem with understanding the Greek text of 1 Tim 2:15. The verse starts out referring to the subject as "she," but then it switches to "they" as the subject. The most likely interpretation is one that maintains the connection between Eve and all other female human beings. The singular "she" would refer to "Eve" (2:13) or "the woman" (2:14), while the plural "they" goes back to the women addressed in 2:9-10 and 2:11-12. Another word links back to these earlier verses. The last word in 2:15 is again σωφροσύνη (here translated "modesty," while in 2:9 it was translated as "decently"). Another possible reading is that it is a mother's children who must "continue in faith and love and holiness, with modesty." This would stress a woman's function of "childbearing" and extend it into the long period of childrearing.

An alternative occupation for faithful women is put forward in 1 Tim 2:15: "Yet she will be saved through childbearing, provided they continue in faith and love and holiness, with modesty." Such a gender-specific claim about salvation distinguishes the theology of the Pastorals from that of the historical Paul, whose views on how one is saved do not differentiate between the sexes. For example, in Rom 5:10 the "we" who will be saved encompasses all believers: "For if while *we* were enemies, *we* were reconciled to God through the death of his Son, much more surely, having been reconciled, will *we be saved* by his life" (italics added). Similarly, in a discussion about believers married to unbelievers, Paul makes two exactly parallel exhortations: "Wife, for all you know, you might *save* your husband. Husband, for all you know, you might *save* your wife" (1 Cor 7:16; italics added). While it is unclear how Paul expects the unbelieving spouse might be saved by the believer, it is obvious that for him one's gender is not a factor in that endeavor.

The assertion that motherhood brings about a woman's salvation is difficult to interpret, and many explanations have been devised to clarify it. John Chrysostom, archbishop of Constantinople around the year 400 CE, ponders the meaning of the phrase, asking: "Then what about the virgins? And what about the barren? What about the widows whose husbands died before they bore children? Are they lost? Do they have no hope? . . . What in the world, then, does he [Paul] mean to say here?"[12] After raising such pointed questions, John decides that the statement ought to be understood as urging both mothers *and* fathers to raise their children properly. Fortunately, the assertion that women's salvation depends on childbearing was never generally accepted or promoted by mainstream churches and theologians. However, modern feminist readers can still trace the influence of this instruction throughout the Pastorals, wherever our author advocates childbearing and childrearing within the context of a faithful marriage as religious obligations for Christian women (1 Tim 5:10, 14; 2 Tim 1:5; and Titus 2:4).

A short list of virtues closes 1 Tim 2:15: "faith and love and holiness." This threefold phrase reminds us of another triad that appears in 1 Cor 13:13: "faith, hope, and love," which is echoed also in 1 Thess 1:3; 5:8. The author of the Pastorals has replaced "hope" with "holiness" (ἁγιασμός), a word that acquires a special feminine implication. For him,

---

12. *Homily on 1 Timothy* 9.1, translated and discussed by Margaret M. Mitchell, in "Corrective Composition, Corrective Exegesis: The Teaching on Prayer in 1 Tim 2:1-15," in *1 Timothy Reconsidered,* ed. Karl P. Donfried (Louvain: Peeters, 2008), 61.

TRANSLATION MATTERS: "THE SAYING IS SURE"

The expression πιστὸς ὁ λόγος ("the saying is sure"), which appears for the first time in Greek literature here in the Pastorals, is short and pithy and composed of two meaningful terms. The first word, πιστός, is an adjective and could also be translated as "faithful," "trustworthy," or "dependable." Among many other references in the New Testament, 2 Tim 2:13 also describes the Lord as πιστός. The second term (preceded by the definite article in the Greek) is λόγος. This can refer to a "saying" in either written or oral form but has other connotations as well, depending on the context: "assertion," "declaration," "subject matter," "word," "prophecy," "message," and "instruction." Although there is a wide range of meaning for each Greek word, the phrase has the overall effect of formally endorsing his teachings.

a believing woman obtains both "holiness" and salvation through participating in marital sex with its hoped-for outcome of children. His concept is entirely contrary to what Paul himself states: "And the unmarried woman and the virgin are anxious about the affairs of the Lord, so that they may be *holy* [ἁγίας] in body and spirit; but the married woman is anxious about the affairs of the world, how to please her husband" (1 Cor 7:34; italics added). In brief, Paul asserts that unmarried women are able to be more faithful to the Lord than married women. Our author contradicts this idea, perhaps because some women in his house-church audience were taking Paul's teachings to heart by avoiding or leaving marriage. There are hints of such goings-on in 1 Tim 4:3, where the author wants to counter some false teachers who "forbid marriage."

The author puts a strong stamp of approval on this shocking theological statement by adding: "The saying is sure" (1 Tim 3:1a). This slogan appears twice more in 1 Timothy and is also repeated in 2 Timothy and Titus. Even though the chapter break seems to link this saying to the instructions about the office of bishop that follow, every other time the phrase occurs in the Pastorals it is attached to a theological statement about salvation or eternal life:

- 1 Tim 1:15: *"The saying is sure and worthy of full acceptance*, that Christ Jesus came into the world to *save* sinners—of whom I am the foremost."

- 1 Tim 2:15–3:1a: "Yet she will be *saved* through childbearing, provided they continue in faith and love and holiness, with modesty. *The saying is sure."*

- 1 Tim 4:8-9: "while physical training is of some value, godliness is valuable in every way, holding promise for both the present life and *the life to come. The saying is sure and worthy of full acceptance.*"

- 2 Tim 2:10-11: "Therefore I endure everything for the sake of the elect, so that they may also obtain the *salvation* that is in Christ Jesus, with eternal glory. *The saying is sure.*"

- Titus 3:6-8: "This Spirit he poured out on us richly through Jesus Christ our Savior, so that, having been justified by his grace, we might become heirs according to the hope of *eternal life. The saying is sure.*"

Our author uses this added formula in order to emphasize the truth of what he has already stated and to validate the particular teaching to which it is attached. The contexts for these five occurrences of the phrase indicate that here too the author seeks to put even more forceful authority behind the assertion that "she will be saved through childbearing." Fortunately for the sake of most believing women through the centuries, his authorization has been ignored or at least not interpreted literally by theologians and church bodies. Still, the author's repeated instructions that women should bear and rear children (1 Tim 5:10, 14; Titus 2:4; also, 2 Tim 1:5) have served to perpetuate a long-lasting Christian culture where (successful) mothering is perceived as a gender-appropriate and honorable role for women.

1 Timothy 3

Leaders for the Household of God

In 1 Timothy 3, our author gives instructions about leaders of the community: the overseer (often translated "bishop") and servers ("deacons"). He strings together lists of virtues and vices that serve as qualifications for the leadership roles but never explains exactly how the leaders are chosen or what they are expected to do within the church. This lack of specificity has allowed for various interpretations about the roles of "bishops" and "deacons," resulting in complicated processes and layers of theology around clergy ordination in both the Eastern and Western branches of the church. Until recently, even among many denominations with a "lower" view of ordination and a more congregational polity, the main element of the Pastorals' teaching that was preserved is that official church leaders ought to be men. The author believes that male leadership is a key component of "how to behave in the household of God" (1 Tim 3:15).

The author, in Paul's name, has charged Timothy not to allow women to teach or to act in leadership roles but to require them to remain silent and subordinate. He then moves on to describe who (besides Timothy and himself) is eligible to teach and to lead within the house-church. Not surprisingly, the potential leaders are men who are recognized as competent heads of their own households. The actual "job description" is

1 Tim 3:1b-7

3:1b Whoever aspires to the office of bishop desires a noble task. ²Now a bishop must be above reproach, married only once, temperate, sensible, respectable, hospitable, an apt teacher, ³not a drunkard, not violent but gentle, not quarrelsome, and not a lover of money. ⁴He must manage his own household well, keeping his children submissive and respectful in every way— ⁵for if someone does not know how to manage his own household, how can he take care of God's church? ⁶He must not be a recent convert, or he may be puffed up with conceit and fall into the condemnation of the devil. ⁷Moreover, he must be well thought of by outsiders, so that he may not fall into disgrace and the snare of the devil.

TRANSLATION MATTERS: "OFFICE OF BISHOP"

The NRSV translates the Greek word ἐπισκοπή as "office of bishop," which gives the wrong impression of the author's intent. First of all, the church structure represented in the Pastorals does not seem to have evolved to the point of having ritually appointed "offices," which begins later in church history. Second, at this time, the term "bishop" does not denote a regional head of numerous churches as also developed over the decades of the second century CE. Here the word means more literally "overseer" (or "supervisor") and suggests the functions and activities of this male leader rather than his religious title or office. The differences in translation are apparent by simply substituting the word "overseer" wherever "bishop" appears in the NRSV.

not spelled out. We do not learn how he might lead a worship gathering or organize the group's finances. Instead, we read about the personal characteristics that a man must have to qualify for this assignment. These qualifications are similar to the virtues expected of any man in good standing either in the house-church or in society at large. An overseer who demonstrated such qualities would be a well-respected member of society, and that respect would carry over to the Christian community (1 Tim 3:7).

Many of the virtues required of one aspiring to be an overseer also appear in the Pastorals' lists of qualities for women. Both male and female believers ought to be "sensible" (σώφρων, 1 Tim 2:9, 15; 3:2; 2 Tim 1:7; Titus 1:8), "respectable" (κόσμιος, 1 Tim 2:9; 3:2), and not drunkards (1 Tim 3:3, 8; Titus 1:7; 2:3). Yet, even though some of the virtuous activities for women are the same as or similar to those required for men—

praying (1 Tim 2:8; 5:5), hospitality (1 Tim 3:2; 5:10), providing for one's household (1 Tim 3:4; 5:4, 8, 16)—in many of these cases there is an explicit gender-based difference in how these virtues are to be displayed. Every Christian in the letters' audience is "to be zealous for good works" (ζηλωτὴν καλῶν ἔργων, Titus 2:14), but whether one is male or female determines the range of "good works" one ought to seek after and possibly attain. As a prime example, the word διδακτικός, "skilled at teaching," is found only in the list for an overseer (1 Tim 3:2) and for Timothy himself (2 Tim 2:24-25). This is additional evidence that the activity of teaching is a masculine attribute and, even then, one that is restricted to the foremost male leaders in the communities: overseers, Timothy, and, of course, Paul (1 Tim 2:7; 2 Tim 1:11). Therefore, it should come as no surprise to the reader of the Pastorals that women are specifically prohibited from teaching.

TRANSLATION MATTERS: "MARRIED ONLY ONCE"

The NRSV translation of this phrase is quite different from the Greek μιᾶς γυναικὸς ἄνδρες, which means literally "husbands of one wife." It is sometimes translated more colloquially, "one-woman men." The exact phrase recurs in 1 Tim 3:12 for deacons and in Titus 1:6 for elders, while the reverse idea—"wife of one husband" or "one-man woman"—appears in 1 Tim 5:9. A few possible meanings have been suggested over the centuries: (1) a man married only once to a woman who is still alive and who practices complete marital fidelity; (2) a widowed man who remains faithful to the memory of his first and only wife by not remarrying; (3) a man who practices a kind of serial monogamy after being widowed or divorced; and (4) as disallowing bigamists. The most likely interpretation seems to be a combination of (1) and (2), since it was a popular Roman marital ideal that one remained faithful to one's spouse by not remarrying even after his or her death.

As the tradition of clerical celibacy developed in the Western church, this requirement proved difficult to interpret. In the fourth century, the church historian Eusebius argued that, while 1 Timothy teaches that male church leaders ought to be married, they ought "to abstain thereafter from conjugal intercourse with their wives" (*Demonstration of the Gospel* 1.9). In the decades following, Ambrose, Ambrosiaster, and John Chrysostom all rejected the idea that bishops had an obligation to be married. This line of interpretation endorses and extends the theological position that there is "something wrong" with women, especially their female bodies, so that men appointed to church offices ought to restrict their (sexual) contact with them.[1]

1. Ancient sources cited in Raymond F. Collins, *Accompanied by a Believing Wife: Ministry and Celibacy in the Earliest Church Communities* (Collegeville, MN: Liturgical Press, 2013), 164–66.

While all male believers who exemplify all these standards for leadership are potentially eligible to seek the role of overseer, in reality lower-status men could not attain such a position. Some higher level of literacy, enough for one to be "skilled at teaching," was required, which ruled out some men. For male Christian slaves, one basic obstacle was that they could not legally marry, which meant that their children were not legitimate and that they could not even form their own household. Similarly, any citizen or freed man whose partner was a female slave would also be disqualified.

TRANSLATION MATTERS: "THE DEVIL"

First Timothy 3:6 warns about "the condemnation of the devil," which seems to be connected to the reference to "the snare of the devil" in 3:7 (see also 2 Tim 2:26). The word διάβολος ("devil") is used as a title for the figure of Satan, and it is capitalized in some translations. The word more literally means "slanderer" and may also be applied to human persons. The author of the Pastorals uses that meaning when he lists qualities for women to avoid (1 Tim 3:11; Titus 2:3). In those instances, he seems to view women as particularly prone to this kind of negative (and gossipy?) speech.[2]

The modern reader also ponders how many fathers did not (or could not!) keep their "children submissive and respectful in every way" (1 Tim 3:4) and whether that standard would be strictly applied. Since our author is very concerned about the insubordination of some community members who are teaching "different doctrine" (see 1:3) and about women who are stepping outside their conventional roles (2:11-12), he looks toward capable male heads-of-households who have dealt with disobedient children and perhaps also with noncompliant slaves and even wives. A rhetorical question (3:5) spells out the kyriarchal assumption: those believers who are competent husbands/fathers/slaveholders will be able to handle theological and ethical deviations involving the believers. Nevertheless, a newly converted man, even if he is already experienced at household management, is not prepared to lead a church (3:6). Further training in the truth and in the ethics of the faith is still required because an appropriately virtuous and experienced male overseer represents the entire community to those outside it. Any disgrace that he causes or suffers reflects poorly on the *ekklēsia*. Such dishonor would bring both him and his people near to "the snare of the devil" (3:7).

---

2. For more comments on women as gossips, see Marianne Bjelland Kartzow's in chapter 5 below, pp. 62–63.

[8] Deacons likewise must be serious, not double-tongued, not indulging in much wine, not greedy for money; [9] they must hold fast to the mystery of the faith with a clear conscience. [10] And let them first be tested; then, if they prove themselves blameless, let them serve as deacons. [11] Women likewise must be serious, not slanderers, but temperate, faithful in all things. [12] Let deacons be married only once, and let them manage their children and their households well; [13] for those who serve well as deacons gain a good standing for themselves and great boldness in the faith that is in Christ Jesus.

TRANSLATION MATTERS: "DEACONS"

The Greek word translated as "deacon" is διάκονος, a word used generally for "server" or "helper." As with the NRSV translation "bishop" (3:1b), "deacon" implies a church office that has developed over time into a variety of meanings and responsibilities. While 1 Tim 3:8, 12, and 13 clearly imply some special role, we do not know the exact duties of these helpers, nor what their relationship was to the overseers. Many denominations today have specific processes and functions for persons appointed as deacons, but we should not assume that these were true for the communities of the Pastorals. My own preferred translation would be a more neutral "server" or "assistant."

The author next begins listing the traits required for a different group of church leadership, that of deacons. Some similar qualities have already been stated for the overseer: "not indulging in wine, not greedy for money" (1 Tim 3:8); "married only once" (3:12); and "manage their children and their households well" (3:12). Other traits are new to the list: be "serious, not double-tongued" (3:8); "hold fast to the mystery of the faith with a clear conscience" (3:9); and be "blameless" (3:10). Such additions do not substantially change the import of the qualifications for this community role: these men must be well-respected in their homes and in society. Unlike his instructions for overseers, here the author suggests a process for selecting these helpers, wherein they are first "tested" (3:9) and found worthy.

What is more noteworthy in this section emerges in 1 Tim 3:11 where we read these words: "Women likewise must be serious, not slanderers, but temperate, faithful in all things." For the purpose of tracing leadership roles for women in the earliest churches, the crucial interpretive question is "who are the women being addressed?" Two answers are probable: they are either the wives of the deacons or else they themselves are deacons. The Greek word may be translated either as "wives" or "women," so that does not help determine the answer. Supporting the first option is the fact that this brief verse has been sandwiched between the qualifications for male deacons, which seems to downplay the position of these women. In addition, the translation "wives" provides a good transition after the teaching for "helpers" to be married, while the strong prohibition of women in teaching and authoritative roles in 2:11-15 leaves the reader wondering how any woman would be allowed to act as an approved leader in the house-church. If they are deacons' wives, then as prominent women, they would be visible to serve as moral examples for other women in the assemblies. Or, if a wife's behavior is not exemplary, then her husband would not be considered leadership material.

Model Household

One consequence of the [Pastorals'] use of the *oikos* model as a structuring concept is that it blurs the boundaries between family and community. The two entities of *oikos* and *ekklēsia* are so similar in these letters and so interdependent that it becomes difficult to distinguish them. For example, it has been discussed whether 1 Tim 2:9-15 and 3:11 are concerned with the relationship between a husband and his wife or with the relationship between men and women in the community. In these passages the term for "married woman" (γυνή) is used and explicitly compared to "men" (ἄνδρας, 1 Tim 2:8; 3:12). However, the *oikos* ideology's two-tiered notion of household blurs the distinctions between community and family and makes it impossible to decide which setting is intended. Similarly, it may be asked whether the term "widow" (χήρα) refers to a household members or to a particular church office. The passage concerning widows (1 Tim 5:2-16) is also shaped by the double household model. If a woman's husband cannot take care of her because he is dead, her (male) children or grandchildren should. If she has no "household members" (οἰκείων, 1 Tim 5:8) to care for her, the Household of God should take on this kyriarchal responsibility (5:3-5). Kyriarchal structures govern in both spheres, and the ideal woman— the wife (or widow) with children—is subordinated to men in both spheres. At the time these letters were written and first circulated, Christian communities still gathered in private homes, hence there is also a spatial overlap of the two tiers of the Household of God. Thus, these passages should not be read as only referring to a wife's relation to her husband, but as simultaneously working on two levels.[3]

Anna Rebecca Solevåg

On the other hand, this one-verse instruction is introduced by the word "likewise," which is used in both 1 Tim 2:9 and 3:8 to indicate that a new group is being addressed. Also, since there is no feminine form of the Greek word "deacon," the reference to "women" could be used in order to acknowledge the presence of female helpers. In Rom 16:1, Paul uses the masculine noun to commend "our sister Phoebe, a *deacon* [διάκονον] of the church in Cenchreae." Another point in favor of the second option is that there is no teaching that mentions the wives of overseers, women who surely would have been even more prominent because of their marriage to the higher-level leaders.

I tend to believe that 1 Tim 3:11 denotes the wives of deacons because this author is so consistently suspicious of women in any kind of leadership role. Yet even if our author meant to establish standards for female deacons, the word γυναῖκας would still allude to their being *married* women. Also, if both men and women could serve as "helpers," they may well have had gender-specific duties and/or the female deacons could have worked only with women and the male deacons with men. In any case, everyone identified as a deacon is expected to adhere to the customary forms of the virtues, while strictly avoiding the usually identified vices.

If this verse in 1 Timothy does acknowledge female deacons, then it stands alongside Rom 16:1-2, which names Phoebe as a deacon. Other early Christian references also give evidence that some women were appointed to this office. The church fathers Origen (early third century CE), John Chrysostom (late fourth century CE), Theodoret of Mopsuestia (late fourth century CE), Theodoret of Cyrrhus (early fifth century CE), and Pelagius (early fifth century CE) all assume that the women of 1 Tim

3. Anna Rebecca Solevåg, *Birthing Salvation: Gender and Class in Early Christian Childbearing Discourse* (Leiden: Brill, 2013), 99.

1 Tim 3:14-16

¹⁴I hope to come to you soon, but I am writing these instructions to you so that, ¹⁵if I am delayed, you may know how one ought to behave in the household of God, which is the church of the living God, the pillar and bulwark of the truth. ¹⁶Without any doubt, the mystery of our religion is great:

He was revealed in flesh,
    vindicated in spirit,
    seen by angels,
proclaimed among Gentiles,
    believed in throughout the
        world,
    taken up in glory.

3:11 were deacons.[4] However, these female deacons were often viewed as fulfilling either a gender-specific ministry of working with children and other women or a "service" of providing meals and other material comforts to church leaders and members, as can be seen in the accompanying quote from the *Didascalia of the Apostles*. Much later, in nineteenth-century Europe, a women's vocation called "deaconess" became popular in many Protestant churches. (The feminizing ending of this noun reminds us that the Greek word διάκονος is masculine in gender.) Most of these women trained as nurses and served in hospitals.

Women Deacons

The *Didascalia (Teaching) of the Apostles* 16 (third to fourth century CE) states:

"The man who is elected is for many oversights that are required, but a woman for the service of the women; for there are houses where one canst not send a Deacon to the women on account of the heathen. Send a Deaconess for many things. . . . [W]e affirm that the service of a woman, a Deaconess is necessary and obligatory, because even our Lord and Saviour was served by the hand of women deaconesses, who were Mary the Magdalene and Mary of James, the mother of Joses, and the mother of Zebedee's children, with other women."[5]

4. The ancient sources on this topic are very helpfully pulled together in *Ordained Women in the Early Church: A Documentary History*, ed. Kevin Madigan and Carolyn Osiek (Baltimore, MD: Johns Hopkins University Press, 2005).

5. Margaret Dunlop Gibson, trans. and ed., *Didascalia (Teaching) of the Apostles in Syriac: Edited from a Mesopotamian Manuscript, with Various Readings and Collations of Other Mss* (London: C. J. Clay and Sons, 1903).

Somewhat unexpectedly, the person of Paul surfaces again in a direct address to Timothy (1 Tim 3:14-15), so that the reader recalls the written presence of the supposed letter-writer and the recipient. Since the audience recognizes both men as authoritative teachers in the faith, their reappearance serves to strengthen the influence of the instructions. The phrase translated "these instructions" (3:14) is more simply "these things" and probably refers to the contents of the entire letter, not just what immediately precedes it.[6] Even though Timothy himself is the stated recipient of the instructions—"so that . . . *you* [singular] may know . . ." (3:14-15)—the letter is clearly meant to be read by a wider audience. The author consistently moves from one social group to another, dealing with issues specific to the status of each group. He is not telling Timothy alone "how one ought to behave in the household of God" (3:15) but rather seeks to teach everyone who participates in the community.

The apostolic authority is reinforced by the expressed wish that "Paul" hopes to come soon (reiterated in 1 Tim 4:13), implying that he will check on Timothy's progress in implementing the instructions. "Paul" says he might be delayed for a visit (3:15) that, within the pseudonymous context of the letter, is a possibility that will not be fulfilled: Paul cannot visit because Paul is dead. Likewise, Timothy has also died, or else he might be available to testify to the falseness of the letter. The authority of the teachings of 1 Timothy rests on the names and reputations of the two respected leaders, especially on memories of them as travelling evangelists and missionaries and as founders and teachers of churches. As is apparent from other early Christian texts, Paul's journeys were fraught with difficulties, and he was not infrequently prevented from following his desired itinerary.[7]

The author sets up three equivalent images of the community: "the household of God"; "the church of the living God"; and "the pillar and bulwark of the truth" (1 Tim 3:15). The architectural terms are used symbolically to describe the communal relationships of the believers. Based on Jewish traditions, Jens Herzer suggests that we should think of the Pastorals' community as "a new kind of spiritual *temple*" rather than simply assuming that the Roman household conventions lie behind

---

6. See below, "Translation Matters: 'These Instructions,'" p. 47.

7. See, for example, Rom 15:22-25; 1 Cor 4:17-21; 2 Cor 11:25-27; Phil 4:14-15; 1 Thess 2:17–3:5; Acts 16:6-10; 21:1-6; 27:1-44; Acts of Paul 15–21.

TRANSLATION MATTERS:
"HOUSEHOLD," "CHURCH," AND "PILLAR AND BULWARK"

Each Greek word could be translated somewhat differently than in the NRSV.

(1) "Household" is the choice for οἶκος, a flexible word that can mean the physical structure or "house" as well as the persons who are associated with it. In the Septuagint, the Greek version of the Old Testament, οἶκος θεοῦ, "house of God/of the Lord," refers to a place where God lives, especially a temple (e.g., Exod 23:19; Deut 23:19; 1 Sam 1:7; throughout Ezra and Nehemiah; Ps 84:11; Joel 1:13-16). Other New Testament texts use the phrase "house of God" for the Jerusalem Temple (e.g., Mark 2:26//Matt 12:4//Luke 6:1-5; Heb 10:21; 1 Pet 4:17). Physical houses are often mentioned as parts of narrative settings (e.g., Matt 8:14; 9:23, 28; Mark 9:33; Luke 10:38; Acts 10:6; 21:8). Family members are also identified as "[of the] house of" (e.g., John 4:53; Acts 16:31, 34; 18:8; 1 Cor 1:11; 1 Tim 3:4-5; 2 Tim 1:16; 2 John 10).

(2) "Church" is the widely used English word for ἐκκλησία. The author follows Paul in using this label for the group of believers. The main problem with this translation is that, for Western readers, a church building frequently comes to mind, rather than the idea of a political body or a social gathering more generally. In this commentary, I have tried to avoid the translation "church" for ἐκκλησία, preferring to use "community" or "assembly" instead.

(3) "Pillar and bulwark of the truth" (στῦλος καὶ ἑδραίωμα τῆς ἀληθείας, v. 15), could also be translated as "column and foundation of the truth." The description establishes the community as the group that provides "vertical and horizontal supports" for the true faith.

---

the phrase.[8] Since the "household of God" does often reference an actual "temple of God," it may be that, in addition to alluding to family dynamics, the author wants to bring to mind the ritual physical spaces where God is present with worshipers.

First Timothy 3 closes with a flourish in 3:16, as our author starts with a pronouncement: "Without any doubt, the mystery of our religion is great." The word "mystery" has just appeared in 3:9, where the author requires the deacons to hold fast to "the mystery of the faith." Earlier letters attributed to Paul also speak of "the mystery," but in those instances the term refers to "the secret plans of God" now revealed (e.g., 1 Cor 4:1; 14:2; Col 2:2) or to the Christ as the content of that mystery

---

8. Jens Herzer, "Rearranging the Household of God: A New Perspective on the Pastoral Epistles," in *Empsychoi Logoi Religious Innovations in Antiquity: Studies in Honour of Pieter Willem van der Horst*, Ancient Judaism and Early Christianity 73, ed. Alberdina Houtman et al. (Leiden: Brill, 2008), 561.

(e.g., Col 1:26; Eph 1:9; 3:4).[9] There is a nuanced difference when the Pastorals speak about "mystery of the faith" and "mystery of our religion." The Pastorals' statements emphasize the content ("faith") and the practice ("religion") of human believers rather than the activities of God and Christ.

TRANSLATION MATTERS: LINES OF POETRY

The six indented lines in the NRSV translation of 1 Tim 3:16 indicate that this is a piece of poetry. The layout of two "stanzas" of three lines each suggests that the lines have some kind of literary and/or theological construction. The relationship between the six lines is, however, quite difficult to determine, and no one solution has been generally agreed on. Each phrase is quite short and has a parallel construction in the Greek: a passive verb ending with the same sound, followed by an indirect object.

The Pastorals' emphasis on content and practice is not to say that the earlier Pauline thought regarding the "mystery of Christ" has been set aside. The rest of the verse illustrates that the varied features of "the mystery" are still meaningful to our author, for here he incorporates a few lines from an early poem or hymn that is wholly christological in content, with some hints of a chronological and/or spatial arrangement. The first line endorses the humanity of Christ, as in 1 Tim 2:5, while the second seems to interpret the resurrection as a sign of God's action on Christ's behalf. Christ's appearance to angels might then connote exaltation of him in the heavenly realms. After these things happened, the reader knows that Christ was "proclaimed among the Gentiles," most powerfully by the apostle Paul (1 Tim 2:7), so that the Messiah was "believed in throughout the world." The last clause is more difficult to fit into the timeline if "taken up in glory" is understood as the ascension. Perhaps the ascension must be viewed as the promise of the future glorious enthronement of Christ. In any case, the author positions these lyrical lines in order to maintain the focus of the instructive content and down-to-earth practice of "the mystery" on the actions of God through and within the person of the Christ.

---

9. I. Howard Marshall, *The Pastoral Epistles*, ICC (London: Bloomsbury T&T Clark, 2004), 490.

1 Timothy 4

Marriage Embodies Godliness

F ollowing the poetic closing verses of 1 Timothy 3, our author
refocuses on what he sees as the immediate conflictual situation
of his recipients. This chapter first describes and contradicts the teachings
of the opponents and then instructs "Timothy" how to act as a leader in
that challenging context.

The first two verses evoke aspects of the person and writings of the
apostle Paul: his spiritual authority, his activities as a prophet, his hope
for the near-future return of the Lord, and his hostility toward his opponents. Our author seeks to bolster the influence of his letter by drawing
on the memory of the historical Paul who claimed to have the Spirit as
an authoritative presence within himself and as a convincing source for
his opinion about an issue.[1] By naming the "Spirit," the pseudonymous
author then suggests that "Paul" knows a particular inspired prophecy
on this topic. Both Jewish and Christian Scriptures view the Spirit as the
source of prophetic statements. To name just two examples: (1) the Lord
takes a portion of the Spirit given to Moses and puts it on the seventy
chosen elders who then begin to prophesy (Num 11:24-25); and (2)
throughout 1 Cor 14, Paul links the Spirit to the gift of prophetic speech,
including his own (1 Cor 14:37-38). When referring to the "later times,"

---

1. For example, Rom 9:1; 1 Cor 2:10-13; 7:40; 14:37-38; 2 Cor 1:21-22; 3:18.

¹Now the Spirit expressly says that in later times some will renounce the faith by paying attention to deceitful spirits and teachings of demons, ²through the hypocrisy of liars whose consciences are seared with a hot iron. ³They forbid marriage and demand abstinence from foods, which God created to be received with thanksgiving by those who believe and know the truth. ⁴For everything created by God is good, and nothing is to be rejected, provided it is received with thanksgiving; ⁵for it is sanctified by God's word and by prayer.

the author of the Pastorals reminds the audience of Paul's enthusiastic expectation that the Lord Jesus would return and that this Parousia would mark the end of time (1 Cor 7:29-31; 1 Thess 4:14–5:6). Finally, the author denounces in unabashedly belligerent terms the "some" who oppose his teachings, just as Paul condemned the "superlative apostles," for example, in 2 Cor 11:12-15. The invective employed here and elsewhere in the Pastorals (e.g., 1 Tim 1:19-20; 2 Tim 2:16-18; Titus 1:10-16) disparages the opponents as both spiritually *and* ethically immoral, a favorite tactic of this author.[2]

TRANSLATION MATTERS:
"TO MARRY AND TO ABSTAIN FROM FOODS"

The Greek text in the first part of 1 Tim 4:3 is a bit complicated because it says literally: "forbidding to marry, to abstain from foods" (κωλυόντων γαμεῖν, ἀπέχεσθαι βρωμάτων). Clearly, the opponents do not forbid but rather support abstaining from foods or else the author would not argue in this manner. To clear up this confusion, the NRSV translation reads *"and demand* abstinence from foods" (italics added).

The Greek in the second part of the verse implies that it is only the "foods" that are "created by God." Yet by alluding to the Genesis accounts where male and female human beings are created (1:27-31; 2:18-25), the author also conveys the impression that marriage is likewise a divine creation.

Next we read of two examples of the wrong teaching, both of which point to an ascetic approach to life: forbidding marriage and rejecting the eating of certain foods (1 Tim 4:3). Since the author not only explicitly promotes marriage for community leaders and especially for women

2. See my comments on 1 Tim 1:8-11 in this volume, pp. 5–7.

(3:2, 12; 5:14; Titus 1:6; 2:4) but also holds a family-friendly attitude in general (1 Tim 5:1-2, 3-4, 8-10; also 2 Tim 3:6; Titus 2:11), we can predict that he would strongly disapprove of celibacy or other practices that would lead to changes in the conventional household model. It remains puzzling to me, therefore, that he does not instruct Timothy or Titus to get married or on how to conduct their own marital relationships. It seems probable that in the letters and other traditions handed down to our author, neither Paul nor his two co-workers were married. For example, Paul says that he is unmarried (1 Cor 7:7) and that he does not have a "sister-as-wife" traveling with him (1 Cor 9:5), and he advocates that single people remain unmarried (1 Cor 7:8, 25-26, 32, 35, 38-40). References to Timothy and Titus in early Christian literature never mention they were married, but we know very little about their biographies. Had they heeded Paul's instructions not to marry? Was their missionary work so involving or their belief in the coming of the Lord Jesus so enthusiastic that "normal" family life was either impractical or unnecessary? For our author, such unmarried males must have posed an ethical and theological problem. This might explain in part why he emphasizes the youthfulness of Timothy and Titus (1 Tim 4:12; 5:1-2; 2 Tim 2:22; Titus 2:6-8). Maybe the reader is supposed to think of them as just a bit too young to be married.

In any case, it is incredibly ironic that "Paul" is pictured here as a dedicated champion of the married state in sharp contrast to those who "forbid" marriage since in 1 Cor 7 the apostle himself offers powerful opinions about the distinctive value of remaining unmarried. His discussion of marriage, divorce, the widows, and the unmarried culminates in these declarations:

> I think that, in view of the impending crisis, it is well for you to remain as you are. Are you bound to a wife? Do not seek to be free. Are you free from a wife? Do not seek a wife. But if you marry, you do not sin, and if a virgin marries, she does not sin. Yet those who marry will experience distress in this life, and I would spare you that. I mean, brothers and sisters, the appointed time has grown short; from now on, let even those who have wives be as though they had none.
>
> I want you to be free from anxieties. The unmarried man is anxious about the affairs of the Lord, how to please the Lord; but the married man is anxious about the affairs of the world, how to please his wife, and his interests are divided. And the unmarried woman and the virgin are anxious about the affairs of the Lord, so that they may be holy in body and spirit; but the married woman is anxious about the affairs of

the world, how to please her husband. I say this for your own benefit, not to put any restraint upon you, but to promote good order and unhindered devotion to the Lord. (1 Cor 7:26-29, 32-35)

Two issues seem to motivate Paul's teachings. First, he assumes that the time of the coming of the Lord Jesus (what he calls "the impending crisis") is near enough to his present time that a believer ought not to make much effort to change their particular social status. Presumably he thinks there will be little opportunity in this life to experience or enjoy any differences in status. Second, Paul focuses on what he perceives as the divided loyalties that pull at people who are married: will they be devoted to their spouse or to the Lord? His own primary commitment is to the Lord, and he is free to carry out God's commission in part because he is unmarried (1 Cor 7:7-8). The Pastorals author's encouragement of marriage and explicit rejection of singleness in 1 Tim 4:1-4 stand in tension with the authentically Pauline approval of living the unmarried life as a means of faithful expression toward the Lord.

An advocate of various forms of asceticism, Tatian (a Syrian Christian of the second century) directly opposes the opinions of the author of 1 Timothy. Peter Brown summarizes Tatian's theological reasoning on the topic: "Tatian . . . stressed the 'vertical' dimension of the human person. The joining of the existent, insufficient human being to the Holy Spirit formed the center of gravity of his thought. His insistence on sexual abstinence flowed from this overriding preoccupation."[3] Tatian's thinking was influential, spawning a movement of its own:

> Contemporaries assigned to the views of Tatian and of the many groups loosely associated with him the general term "Encratite"—from *enkrateia*, "continence." The Encratites declared that the Christian Church had to consist of men and women who were continent in the strict sense: they had "contained" the urge to have sexual intercourse with each another. To this basic continence, the Encratites added dietary constraints, abstention from meat and the drinking of wine. These abstentions were intimately linked to the constitutive act of sexual renunciation: for the eating of meat was held to link human beings to the wild, carnivorous nature of animals, as intercourse linked them to the sexual nature of brute beasts. Furthermore, wine was a known source of sexual energy—"for wine imparts warmth to the nerves, soothes the soul,

---

3. Peter Brown, *The Body and Society: Men, Women, and Sexual Renunciation in Early Christianity* (New York: Columbia University Press, 1988), 90.

⁶If you put these instructions before the brothers and sisters, you will be a good servant of Christ Jesus, nourished on the words of the faith and of the sound teaching that you have followed. ⁷Have nothing to do with profane myths and old wives' tales. Train yourself in godliness, ⁸for, while physical training is of some value, godliness is valuable in every way, holding promise for both the present life and the life to come. ⁹The saying is sure and worthy of full acceptance. ¹⁰For to this end we toil and struggle, because we have our hope set on the living God, who is the Savior of all people, especially of those who believe.

¹¹These are the things you must insist on and teach. ¹²Let no one despise your youth, but set the believers an example in speech and conduct, in love, in faith, in purity. ¹³Until I arrive, give attention to the public reading of scripture, to exhorting, to teaching. ¹⁴Do not neglect the gift that is in you, which was given to you through prophecy with the laying on of hands by the council of elders. ¹⁵Put these things into practice, devote yourself to them, so that all may see your progress.¹⁶Pay close attention to yourself and to your teaching; continue in these things, for in doing this you will save both yourself and your hearers.

recalls pleasure, engenders semen, and provokes to venery [sexual indulgence]."[4]

Although the author of the Pastorals also is quite concerned about believers drinking too much wine, his prescription is meant to position human beings within God's *good* creation. That is why he affirms sexual activity (within marriage) as well unrestricted diets. In fact, since the Greek word for "food" (βρῶμα) in 1 Tim 4:3 has the connotation of "solid food" or even "meat," the disagreement between our author and Tatian is even more obvious.

Although our author gives no specific information about the dietary restrictions, he commences a theological counter-argument drawn from the Genesis creation stories (Gen 1:29; 2:9, 16; 3:2; also 9:3). First, he asserts the role of God in the creation of foods (1 Tim 4:3), an act that is characterized as providing for "those who believe and know the truth." That is, true believers understand how to receive what God has created with thanksgiving, which implies that those who will not eat these foods have false beliefs. Then he deepens his exegesis of Genesis 1 by recapping God's own assessments of creation: "everything created by God is good" (4:4; see Gen 1:4, 9, 12, 18, 21, 25, 31). The conclusion of this argument is that no created thing should be rejected when it is accepted in a thankful fash-

4. Ibid., 92–93.

TRANSLATION MATTERS: "THESE INSTRUCTIONS"

The Greek for "these instructions" (1 Tim 4:6) is actually one word: ταῦτα, "these things." Our author is fond of this word (see also 1 Tim 3:14; 4:11; 6:2, 11; 2 Tim 1:12; 2:2, 14; Titus 2:15; 3:8), most often using it to refer to something he has just written. In 1 Tim 4:6, it seems to mean his interpretation of marriage based on Gen 1:27-31 and 2:18-25, which contradicts the opponents' ascetic teachings. However, in 1 Tim 3:14—"I am writing these instructions"—the word connotes everything that comes before and possibly all that follows. The NRSV translation "these instructions" in 3:14 and 4:6 indicates the general "teaching" intentions of the letter.

ion. In fact, two actions "sanctify" creation: (1) God's word in Genesis 1, where God calls creation "good," and (2) prayer, by which the author seems to refer to a mealtime prayer including a "thanksgiving" (4:3, 4). His explanation effectively paints the opponents both as deficient Bible interpreters and also as ungrateful recipients of God's gifts.

The rest of this chapter contains instructions directed toward Timothy, who is presented as a teacher of the whole community. He is subordinated to Paul yet elevated over the other believers because of his exceptional relationship to Paul. After all, Timothy has been called Paul's "loyal child in the faith" (1 Tim 1:2), and we are to think of him as the privileged original and sole recipient of this letter. Since "Paul" is a pseudonym, we may presume that "Timothy" too is pseudonymous and that neither man is still alive to dispute the contents of the letter. However, one can imagine a "private" letter such as this one (plus 2 Timothy and Titus) surfacing in one of the early second-century communities, perhaps as a surprising "discovery" in a household library. Bearing the names of two revered leaders and covering many of the same topics as the other Pauline letters, its authority would be difficult to refute and its contents would be highly valued. Its textual power supports a patriarchal order of teachers: Paul teaches Timothy who teaches other male leaders who teach the rest. Women, of course, have already been banned from teaching (2:12), except for older women who may teach younger women (Titus 2:3-5), and those males who are not heads-of-households are effectively also disempowered. To emphasize Timothy's leadership, his appointment was confirmed through a ritual involving prophecy, the laying on of hands, and a council of elders (4:14). The ritual is not described in detail, but elements of it developed into rites of ordination (signifying apostolic succession) in various churches. The restrictive influence of this teaching hierarchy has endured for centuries in the structures and policies of most Christian churches.

TRANSLATION MATTERS: "GODLINESS"

The Greek word for "godliness" is εὐσέβεια, a word formed from two roots: εὐ- meaning "good" or "well" and σεβ-, which "frequently suggests religious devotion and respect, even if directed toward a human person."[5] Put together, we get the idea of "good/proper reverence." This noun is sometimes translated "religion," "devotion," or "piety." (The Latin equivalent is *pietas*.) This noun and its related forms appear twenty-three times in the Pastorals (1 Tim 1:9; 2:2 [2x], 10; 3:4, 8, 11, 16; 4:7, 8; 5:4; 6:3, 5, 6, 11; 2 Tim 2:16; 3:5, 12; Titus 1:1; 2:2, 7, 12 [2x]). The noun is especially common in the Pastorals but never occurs in the rest of the Pauline letter collection.

These two paragraphs (1 Tim 4:6-16) are marked by language about the educational process. Timothy ought to "put these *instructions* before the brothers and sisters," having already himself been "nourished" as a follower of the "teaching" (4:6, italics added). He is reminded to avoid false teachings, which are described vaguely as "profane myths" (see 1:4) and as "old wives' tales" (βεβήλους καί γραώδεις μύθους, 4:7). The latter term, γραώδεις, derives its negative force from the ancient (and often modern) stereotype of older women as gossips. Instead, Timothy should focus on training himself in godliness (4:7). In twenty-first-century American culture, the idea of "religion" or "piety" carries negative connotations. However, within the Greco-Roman world, this word group is rich in positive meanings, pointing above all to demonstrating a proper respect for the gods. Such respect is shown in both appropriate rituals (prayer, sacrifices, and other observances) and in correct social behaviors, especially toward one's family (e.g., 5:4). Our author also defines godliness as expressing true beliefs (3:16). For Timothy to train himself in "godliness" involves exercising the virtues and holding to the good teaching in his own life (4:6) while also structuring the "household of God" into good order (3:15). The author views one's interactions in everyday society as interconnected with spiritual/eternal realities, for he claims "godliness is valuable in every way, holding promise for both the present life and the life to come" (4:8). This appreciation of the "present life" echoes his opinions about the goodness of creation, created by the one "living God, who is savior of all people" (4:10).

The pervasive educational tone continues with a series of commands about teaching, beginning with "these are the things you must insist on

5. Jerome D. Quinn, *The Letter to Titus*, AB 35 (New York: Doubleday, 1990), 284.

and teach" (1 Tim 4:11). As was common in the ancient world, and is still echoed in classrooms today, the process of teaching happens in two ways: via the example of the teacher (4:12) and in oral communication of content (4:13). One distinctive Christian element appears in our author's promotion of "the public reading of scripture" (4:13), which in the late first century CE meant reading aloud the Jewish Scripture rather than Paul's letters or any other early Christian literature. Even though such contents of the teaching are crucial to the author, he concentrates here on Timothy's personal conduct as a role model to other believers: he is an "example" (τύπος) in living virtuously. That is why he must continue his own education, putting "these things" into practice and devoting himself to them, "so that all may see your progress" (4:15). The author feels an intense concern about the example of the teachers, so he restates it in 1 Tim 4:16: "*Pay close attention to yourself* and to your teaching; *continue* in these things," followed by the powerful claim that "in doing this you will save both yourself and your hearers" (italics added). What greater pledge could the author give both to those who teach correctly and to those who follow such faithful teachers?

1 Timothy 5

Older Women/Older Men

While 1 Timothy 4 dealt explicitly with "sound teaching" (4:1-10) and commands for Timothy's own behavior (4:11-16), the next chapter returns to topics related to specific social groups within the "household of God." The author prescribes appropriate communal relationships based on his theological and ethical opinions about youth and old age, gender roles, marriage, and sexual propriety.

First Timothy 5:1-2 provides a transition into the instructions for the community of believers that is depicted as a family group, the "household of God" (3:15). They are addressed to Timothy alone, positioning him as a "son" in relationship to a "father" and "mothers" and then as if he were a "brother" to other young people, male and female. In this

---

TRANSLATION MATTERS: "OLDER MAN"

The author of the Pastorals uses two slightly different Greek words to refer to an older man: πρεσβύτερος, which is the masculine comparative form of the adjective "old"; and the related noun πρεσβύτης for "old man" in Titus 2:2. The comparative form in 1 Tim 5:1 indicates a basic age distinction between the older and the younger men, but this adjective is also applied to specific older men who hold an office in the community (5:17-19).

The author also uses two different feminine forms for an "older woman": πρεσβυτέρας, a comparative adjective (1 Tim 5:2), and the noun πρεσβῦτις (Titus 2:3). Neither of these words is used for female church leaders but simply refers to women who are grouped according to their age.

---

¹Do not speak harshly to an older man, but speak to him as to a father, to younger men as brothers, ²to older women as mothers, to younger women as sisters—with absolute purity.

way, our author continues to portray Timothy as a younger man (4:12) who has been placed in charge of the assembly. As an example for others, Timothy ought to demonstrate the typical cultural respect for older persons as well as the kind of sibling-love that believers ought to share in Pauline-founded communities.

The parallel construction of these verses ("to a [person] as to a [person]") is broken at the end when the author of the Pastorals adds an additional phrase: "with absolute purity" (5:2b; or "in all holiness"). In other letters of Paul, the word translated as "purity" or "holiness" (ἁγνεία) carries the connotation of sexual purity (1 Thess 4:4; 1 Cor 7:34-35). In this letter, the add-on seems to highlight the situation imagined by the author, where Timothy is a young, presumably heterosexual man who might not have full control of his passions, so that he would be tempted by the younger women. The author foresees more problems arising from the improper behavior of younger women, which he addresses later in the chapter (5:11-15). The addition also conveys the notion that other people, both inside and outside the community, would be observing Timothy's behavior so that he needs to act in an exemplary way and also avoid arousing their suspicions.

The next fourteen verses discuss a particular subset of women in the community: those who are widowed. One of the more difficult aspects of this passage is that the author divides this group into even smaller sets: "real" widows (1 Tim 5:3, 5); widows who have children or grandchildren (5:4); a (hypothetical?) widow who "lives for pleasure" (5:6); widows over sixty years old (5:9-10); younger widows (5:11-15); and widows who are provided for by a female believer (5:16). Interpreters have struggled to make sense of his stated "policies" because his descriptions of the various widows seem disconnected and ambiguous. One thing is clear: the author's overarching concern with all types of widows is how and from whom they ought to receive financial assistance.

It is hard to imagine exactly how many women he might be placing in these categories in any one church because we do not have solid demographic statistics for the ancient Mediterranean world. The population of the city of Ephesus, the supposed location of Timothy in this letter, is

1 Tim 5:3-16

³Honor widows who are really widows. ⁴If a widow has children or grandchildren, they should first learn their religious duty to their own family and make some repayment to their parents; for this is pleasing in God's sight. ⁵The real widow, left alone, has set her hope on God and continues in supplications and prayers night and day; ⁶but the widow who lives for pleasure is dead even while she lives. ⁷Give these commands as well, so that they may be above reproach. ⁸And whoever does not provide for relatives, and especially for family members, has denied the faith and is worse than an unbeliever.

⁹Let a widow be put on the list if she is not less than sixty years old and has been married only once; ¹⁰she must be well attested for her good works, as one who has brought up children, shown hospitality, washed the saints' feet, helped the afflicted, and devoted herself to doing good in every way. ¹¹But refuse to put younger widows on the list; for when their sensual desires alienate them from Christ, they want to marry, ¹²and so they incur condemnation for having violated their first pledge. ¹³Besides that, they learn to be idle, gadding about from house to house; and they are not merely idle, but also gossips and busybodies, saying what they should not say. ¹⁴So I would have younger widows marry, bear children, and manage their households, so as to give the adversary no occasion to revile us. ¹⁵For some have already turned away to follow Satan. ¹⁶If any believing woman has relatives who are really widows, let her assist them; let the church not be burdened, so that it can assist those who are real widows.

TRANSLATION MATTERS: "REAL WIDOWS"

While the Greek word translated as "widow" (χήρα) usually refers to a woman whose husband has died, it can also be used more generally of any woman who is unmarried, including one who is divorced. For example, in the letter *Theano to Nikostrate* (second century CE), the author describes a young woman in an unhappy marriage: "For although you might go and get divorced, then you will try your fortune with another man after being divorced from the first man, and if that man transgresses in similar ways, again [you will try] yet another man (for widowhood [χηρεία] is not bearable for young women), or you will remain alone without a man—that is to say, very unmarried" (lines 52–55). The obvious implication here is that a divorced woman will not want to be alone and even that an unmarried woman is considered to be a somewhat tragic person.

Our author is defining the term more narrowly when he exhorts Timothy to "honor widows who are *really* widows" (5:3). This particular use of the adverb "really" (ὄντως) to modify a noun occurs four times in the New Testament, all of them in 1 Timothy (5:3, 5, 16; 6:19). In this letter, a "real" widow is not simply a woman whose husband has died but seems to be a woman who is somewhat impoverished, has been married only once, and exhibits certain behaviors.

estimated at around 300,000, but the number of Christ-believers there around the year 100 CE would have been very small. For the sake of constructing a scenario, let us assume there were three hundred Christians scattered in different house-churches there and that one hundred and fifty were female. Could we expect that there were thirty to fifty Christian widows? And, given the low life expectancy, how many would be over sixty? Perhaps ten to fifteen? Would not the majority of these be supported by younger family members? What was the economic situation of widows under the age of sixty? Which parts of our author's instructions are based on cultural stereotypes about women, widows, and younger widows, in particular? Which pieces are founded on the real lives of widows within Christian communities of that time?

These are the sorts of important questions raised by the author's instructions, and I find it difficult to draw solid conclusions about what was actually happening within the Christian households and assemblies with which he was acquainted. Certainly, there were widows among the believers, and some (many?) must have lived in insecurity, both social and economic. But throughout these verses, the author expresses *his own emotional insecurity* about women when he commends domestic femininity as the ideal and censures all women who step outside this standard.

Perhaps drawing on the traditional Jewish ethical concern of protecting "widows and orphans," the author focuses here on the issue of caring for the "real widows" with which the passage opens (1 Tim 5:3) and closes (5:16). The first verb in 5:3 is the command "honor" (τίμα), which carries connotations of offering physical and financial support to a person as well as personal reverence and esteem. This verb also appears in the Greek version of the fifth (or fourth) commandment found in Exod 20:12 and Deut 5:16: "honor your father and your mother." In 1 Tim 5, the author instructs Timothy, on behalf of the church, to determine which widows are deserving of such "honor."

The grammar of 1 Tim 5:4—"if a widow has children or grandchildren, *they* should first learn their religious duty"—is a bit confusing. "They" could refer either to the biological descendants of the believing widow who ought to take care of her or to the widow who ought to care for her own family. Most commentators decide that it is the family who should provide for the widow. Whoever is commanded to give such support is said to be "performing a religious duty" (5:3),[1] an activity that our author

---

1. This is the infinitive εὐσεβεῖν, on which, see above "Translation Matters: 'Godliness,'" p. 48.

seeks to encourage by stating that "this is pleasing in God's sight" (5:4). Once more, the author links the reciprocal relationships among the real-life household of spouses, parents, and children to the implicit obligations of members of the metaphorical "household of God."

It seems that any widow who has children and grandchildren is not a "real widow," because the depiction of a "real widow" is a woman who has been left alone (1 Tim 5:5). This woman is so alone that her only hope is set on God rather than on human beings like children and grandchildren. Elsa Tamez succinctly describes this kind of widow as "poor but obedient."[2] The "real widow" is "poor" because she has no family (5:4) and no wealth (5:6). She is "obedient" in the sense that she demonstrates her faith through dependence on God and persistent praying (5:5).

The author expresses a conventional belief about a widow's life: she must experience personal loneliness as well as economic hardship. Certainly, many widows in the patriarchal Roman world found themselves in just this situation. Demographic models based on Latin and Greek memorial inscriptions suggest that women were often likely to outlive their older husbands and that infant mortality resulted in fewer children living to maturity. During the reign of Augustus, imperial decrees had been issued that rewarded women for bearing multiple children and for remarrying soon after being widowed. In order that widows will be provided for, our author promotes remarriage for some of them but not for others, as we will see.

As in many times and places, unmarried women (including the widowed and divorced), noncitizens of both sexes, and the poor were especially vulnerable to the neglect and manipulations of a system devised to benefit those of elite social status. For high-born women, family inheritance could ease their financial difficulties, but most people, male *and* female, had little capital or property resources on which to depend. In addition, except for the *alimenta*, the subsidized distribution of grain to those living in the city of Rome itself, no government-funded assistance programs existed to meet the chronic or emergency needs of the poor in the empire. It is noteworthy that the early communities of believers, including those addressed in 1 Timothy, created measures for caring for the poor, demonstrating the kind of active righteousness that resonates throughout the law and the prophets.[3]

2. Elsa Tamez, *Struggles for Power in Early Christianity: A Study of the First Letter to Timothy* (Maryknoll, NY: Orbis Books, 2007), 47.

3. Examples of other New Testament texts that mention such activity are Acts 2:44-45; 4:34-35; 6:1; Rom 15:25-27; 1 Cor 16:1-2; 2 Cor 8:1-15; 9:6-13; Gal 2:10.

What recourse does this "real" widow have, except to "set her hope on God" and to continue "in supplications and prayers night and day" (1 Tim 5:5)? The author approves of such persistent devotion, which echoes the actions of the widowed prophet Anna (Luke 2:36-37). Later in church history an office of "widow" developed, whereby widows had certain responsibilities to care for orphans and others in need, but that office is not fully formed here in 1 Tim 5. Instead, the perpetual praying of the "real widow" is a sign of her faithful dependence on God rather than a task she executes on behalf of the church.

A short description of another kind of widow appears in 1 Tim 5:6: "the widow who lives for pleasure." Like the widow with children and grandchildren, such a widow is not a "real" widow either; she has the economic means to live "for pleasure" (σπαταλῶσα) or, to give an alternate translation, to live "luxuriously." In the Roman world, as today, wealthy widows, like other wealthy women, had authority over larger households and, therefore, more supervisory responsibilities. Because of their financial resources, they could act more independently in legal and business matters, and they received more civic and religious honors, such as being named as the honorary overseers of athletic contests or as annual priestesses for a certain temple. The author's brief sketch of a rich widow in 1 Tim 5:6 reminds the reader of his earlier condemnation of the women who wear "gold, pearls, and expensive clothes" (2:9). Here, he portrays the wealthy widow in stark terms: she might think she is "really living," but she is actually spiritually dead. Although he is extremely skeptical about the virtue of such widows in particular, the author also speaks more generally to the moral and spiritual troubles of *all* well-off believers in 1 Tim 6.

Widows in Code

The true widows are poor and totally abandoned. They put all their confidence and hope in God. According to the author, those who are not real widows are those who lead a comfortable life, living for pleasure (*spatalōsa*). According to the author of 1 Timothy, wealth and a libertine life go together, although in practice this is not always so. What is happening here is that the author wants to remove those rich leaders who occupy posts simply because of their power and influence without being officially named. The author tries to remove them by appealing to moral questions. For us in Latin America, this is not difficult to understand because in many churches when those in authority wish to remove some woman or even a man, they generally appeal to moral conduct. In antiquity, the rhetorical discourse also used this argument.

Reading between the lines of the text, we see that it is probable that the author wants to take away economic support and erase from the list of the widows' order all widows, poor or not, who according to him do not fulfill the traditional tasks of the patriarchal household and prefer to be working in the church and for the Christian community. The author is worried that the community might be despised by the patriarchal Roman Empire, but this text also reflects the conflict between these women and some male leaders about their functions in the community as men who have households and patriarchal privileges. This can be clearly seen in the case of the young widows and the emphasis that the author puts on the qualities that the widows must have to be on the list of the widows' order (1 Tim 5:9-15). The option for the poor widows in 1 Timothy depends on their obedience to the domestic codes.[4]

Elsa Tamez

In a short command similar to that of 1 Tim 4:11,[5] the author addresses Timothy directly and with the obvious implication that Timothy must pass on these teachings to members of the community (5:7). It is unclear who "they" are who will receive the commands and thus be "above reproach"; it could be the widows or some subset of that group, or it could refer to the heads-of-household who ought to provide for them (5:8). The verb προνοεῖ, translated as "provide for," is associated with rulers and other persons in superior social positions. In any case, the author once again binds this care for vulnerable family members to "the faith," so that one lives out this "faith" in large part through fulfilling moral duties. As we have seen before, his rhetorical strategy is not at all conciliatory or diplomatic in that he vilifies those who do not comply with his teachings. In this verse, he calls them "worse than" unbelievers, a negative label that is used in order to dissuade his audience from neglecting their households.

4. Tamez, *Struggles for Power*, 52–53.
5. See above, "Translation Matters: 'These Instructions,'" p. 47.

The topic shifts suddenly from encouraging familial support for "their own" widows to what seems to be the qualifications for certain widows to receive church support (1 Tim 5:9-10). The simplest interpretation of these widows who will be "put on the list" is that *they* are the "real widows," already differentiated from those widows who are still part of a family as well as from the widows who are living "for pleasure." These are the "poor but obedient widows," in Tamez's phrase. However, there are restrictions even for this select group: they must be at least sixty years old, married only once, and well-known for performing good works.

Although few people, female or male, would have lived as long as sixty years, this age was often stated to be the onset of true elderliness, when one's body could no longer be expected to be in healthy working condition. At sixty years, a woman's reproductive function was over, so that the Augustan legislation on remarriage no longer applied. Since there were no birth certificates, age was often only an estimate, and there was sometimes a proud sort of tendency to round up one's age to a number ending in five or zero. As I speculated above, one wonders how many widows might fit into this category, given that the believing communities of the late first and early second centuries are thought to be quite small.

As noted before, the phrase ἑνὸς ἀνδρὸς γυνή, "married only once," is open to some interpretation.[6] In 1 Tim 5:9, the Greek says literally "woman/wife of one man/husband." Certainly this "widow" is living alone now, but we don't know how often she might have been married in the past. If her husband died when she was young and she felt pressured by economic incentives to remarry quickly, would a second marriage disqualify her from being "put on the list"? Given the option for divorce in the Roman system, as well as Paul's allowing divorce when one is married to an unbeliever (1 Cor 7:12-16), there is even a chance that such a "widow" who was what we would think of as divorced might also qualify for church assistance if she had not remarried. Or perhaps the phrase "wife of one husband" refers more metaphorically to her fidelity within the marriage, meaning that she was recognized as a faithful wife.

---

6. In "Translation Matters: 'Married Only Once,'" p. 33.

TRANSLATION MATTERS: "GOOD WORKS"

The expression ἔργα καλά, "good works," appears frequently in the Pastorals, eight times in a plural form (1 Tim 2:10; 5:10, 25; 6:18; Titus 2:7, 14: 3:8a, 14) and five times in the singular "every good work" (1 Tim 5:10; 2 Tim 2:21; 3:17; Titus 1:16; 3:1). (The Greek adjective translated "good" varies between either καλός or ἀγαθός, but this is an insignificant difference.) The NRSV translation at the end of 1 Tim 5:10 "doing good in every way" obscures these repeated and parallel references to good works.

The third primary criterion is that the widow ought to be "well attested for her good works." Believers of different social groups—women, widows, the rich, younger men, as well as "everyone"—are instructed to exhibit these "good works" as living proof of their faith. In the letters scholars attribute to Paul, "works" in general are not viewed with such positive theological connotations, especially when they are identified as "works of the law" (see, e.g., Rom 3:27-28; Gal 2:16). For a clearer understanding, we need to consider Jerome Quinn's comparison of the use of this distinctive phrase in the Pastorals with the teachings about works in the other Pauline letters (Rom, 1–2 Cor, Gal, Eph, Col, Phil, 1–2 Thess, and Phlm). Quinn has found that "the characteristic emphasis of the PE appears when the plural *erga* are qualified as *agatha* or *kala*. The rest of the Paulines and the Lukan corpus never use *kalon* with *ergon*; . . . half a dozen times the other Paulines qualify *ergon* with *agathon*, but only Eph 2:10 refers to *erga agatha*."[7] This key difference in vocabulary provides more evidence that the Pastorals are not written by Paul himself. Yet even the apostle himself still expected believers to behave in a virtuous manner as a way of "working out" their salvation in Christ (e.g., Gal 5:6, 19-23; 6:4; Phil 2:12-13). The author of the Pastorals picks up on this Pauline idea that salvation leads to "good works." In Titus 2:14, he makes an explicit declaration that Christ's redemption results in a people "who are zealous for good works."

For a widow to qualify for community support she needs to be known as a woman who has done "feminine" good works such as raising children (either her own or maybe orphans), showing hospitality, washing the feet of the saints (probably not in a ritual performance but as representative of a basic service to others), and helping the afflicted (a general

7. Jerome Quinn, *The Letter to Titus*, AB 35 (New Haven, CT: Yale University Press, 2005), 104.

assistance to anyone in need). These "good works" are the prerequisites for her to receive support, rather than a job description that she must now carry out. Note that none of these approved works depicts women in leadership positions within the household or the house-church; rather, the services provided by women correspond to the gender ideology that places them in subordinate positions in both contexts.

In 1 Tim 5:11-15, our author turns his attention to a group he finds quite troublesome within the community. He calls them the "younger widows" (5:11, 14), and it is certainly possible that these women were widowed in their twenties or thirties, given life expectancies at the time. Legislation passed under Emperor Augustus penalized a widow who did not remarry within one year of her husband's death, but it is not known how consistently this law was enforced. Many Romans still held to the cultural ideal of widows and widowers remaining unmarried after the death of a spouse in order to prove how faithful one still was to that marriage.[8]

But we cannot know for certain if these younger women were *ever* married because the author mentions that they have "violated their first pledge" by wanting to marry (1 Tim 5:11-12). This statement hints at the possibility that some young women made a choice to remain unmarried but then reneged on that pledge when, as he says, "their sensual desires alienate them from Christ" (5:11). The social environment would allow for those women to be called or to call themselves "widows," since the word "widow" can more generally mean any "unmarried woman."[9]

We can only speculate about why young female believers might take a pledge of sexual celibacy instead of marriage. It is not necessary to assume that these women hated men as a group or thought of marriage as an oppressive institution. Perhaps out of deep Christian devotion they wanted to follow Paul's advice: "to the unmarried and the widows I say that it is well for them to remain unmarried as I am" (1 Cor 7:8).[10] Paul had originally justified remaining single because he felt a strong eschatological urgency. In 1 Cor 7 he declares: "Yet those who marry will experience distress in this life, and I would spare you that. I mean, brothers and sisters, the appointed time has grown short; from now on, let even those who have wives be as though they had none" (7:28b-29),

8. See "Translation Matters: 'Married Only Once,'" p. 33.

9. See above, "Translation Matters: 'Real Widows,'" p. 52.

10. I have also discussed Paul's ideas in 1 Cor 7 on singleness and marriage in relation to 1 Tim 4:1-4 in this volume, pp. 44–45.

and "the present form of this world is passing away" (7:31b). Even forty-some years after Paul wrote those words, the early Christian movement was still infused with apocalyptic expectations, as evidenced by the composition of the book of Revelation around the year 100 CE (like the Pastorals, Revelation has a setting in Asia Minor). In part because the author of the Pastorals does not seem to feel the same urgency about the Lord's "manifestation" (ἐπιφάνεια) that Paul expresses about the Lord's "coming" (using a different Greek word, παρουσία), the Pastorals' audience is exhorted to fulfill their culturally expected domestic roles as the way to live faithfully while awaiting the end of time.

It seems likely that the younger widows were attracted to the anti-marriage teachings of the author's opponents, the people the author castigated in 1 Tim 4:4 because they "forbid marriage." Certainly the opposition's viewpoint persisted within Christianity because we know that in the second century other Christian writers and movements such as the New Prophecy (called "Montanism" by the fourth century)[11] promoted sexual abstinence for women *and* men, sometimes even within a marriage, as a constructive devotional practice supported by the apostle Paul.[12] Over time, some traditions adopted clergy and religious celibacy as the norm while still attempting to harmonize the inconsistencies in New Testament opinions on singleness, marriage, divorce, widowhood, and remarriage.

Challenges for Widows

The author launches his fury against wealthy women using his patriarchal arsenal against all women. He is not only against rich women but against all women, rich and poor, because they do not comply with the domestic roles. The young widows were not necessarily wealthy. They could be widows who were cared for by the church and therefore did not need to work in their parents' household in domestic tasks such as spinning and weaving. In the church, these widows had time to visit the households and teach

---

11. Information about these prophetic sects that arose in Asia Minor during the second century comes from Eusebius, *Hist. eccl.* 5.18, and Tertullian, *Val.* 5. Tertullian (160?–240? CE) himself later joined a Montanist group.

12. A few examples of early Christian texts that give evidence for sexual celibacy are Rev 14:4; Ign. *Pol.* 5.2; Pol. *Phil.* 5.3; *Acts of Paul* 3.5-12; *Virg.* See also my comments above, "Tatian and the Encratites," pp. 45–46.

and console the families. The author exhorts them to marry and form a traditional patriarchal household and to keep busy in the tasks of the household and taking care of the children.

The language that is used to refer to the young widows reflects a rhetorical discourse that does not have a real foundation but is part of the patriarchal ideology with its gratuitous affirmations in the definition of women. Today, in our patriarchal society, it is also still believed that a young widow "is crazy to get married again, has all the time in the world to gad about outside her home visiting neighbors, men and women, her head filled with nonsense, sticking her nose in everyone's business and talking all the time about nothing." A widow who does not stay in her house is called a "merry widow." But we know that her reality is other. The great majority of women-led households, widows or not, never have time for themselves because they must work day and night to support their children. There are women in a more comfortable position who therefore have time for other things outside the household. That does not mean that they are idle or gossips. In all societies there are huge challenges that women have to take on in order to become human beings. That there are women who gossip and are busybodies is evident; but the same is true of men.[13]

Elsa Tamez

As Elsa Tamez states, the author of the Pastorals uses a powerful rhetorical tactic to deter any proliferation of unmarried women; in a much longer critique than that applied to the wealthy widow (1 Tim 5:6), he attacks the morality of the younger widows. He portrays them as "idle, gadding about from house to house; and they are not merely idle, but also gossips and busybodies, saying what they should not say" (5:13). Each of these negative terms flies in the face of the cultural ideal for feminine virtue, which upholds appropriate household work, staying at home, silence, and/or proper speech for women (see 1 Tim 2:11-12). In words that echo his critique of false teachers in 1 Tim 1:3-7, the author issues a strong warning for these women: any immoral behavior signifies adherence to false doctrines. Symbolically, one has then turned away from Christ (5:11) in order to "follow Satan" (5:15). Marianne Bjelland Kartzow articulates in more modern scholarly terms something of what the author is trying to accomplish by maligning the younger widows.

13. Tamez, *Struggles for Power*, 53–54.

Gossiping Others

[The author] uses a stereotype from his cultural encyclopedia known by his contemporaries, that women have a strong tendency to gossip. Whatever these women did, among all the suggestions given by scholars, whether they had leading positions, opposed the *oikos*-codes, visited the sick, or represented an alternative theological understanding, their activities could easily be labeled as gossip within the ancient gender system. . . . Women who did not follow the accepted standards for behavior and appearance were in danger of getting a bad reputation, a fear that probably was felt by the early Christian women as it was used by those who wanted to re-establish male order.

In the process of constructing early Christian identity the author of the Pastorals defines several groups and persons as outsiders through "othering" them. Confronted with the group of widows and (according to his view) their unfitting behavior, he uses the twofold gendered quality of gossip in order to construct them as "others." The author downloads a misogynic *topos* from his contemporary cultural encyclopedia connecting women to gossip. The widows' interpretation of the Pauline tradition did not fit with his, and this difference formed the core in the "othering process" as we find it in the rhetoric of 1 Tim 5. This insider-outsider dichotomy places the young widows at the wrong side of the scale, making them targets of stereotyping, simplification and male control. They have to keep silent, as the old women and deaconesses were told not to be slanderous. The widows' speech is vilified as merely gossip, and their movements are limited by domestic responsibilities, in fear of what the neighbors might say.

The standards and morals of the Pastoral Epistles generate negative energy, where those who are different have to be eliminated. The insider-outsider contrast we find in the letters is used to divide people into opposing groups, and it forms the core of an othering-process leading to stereotyping, vilification, and even violence. The use of gossip as both an accusation and a threat is gendered power language, and can hardly be useful as a source with anything important to say about the widows in the early church. What this text demonstrates fully, however, is that the process of constructing identity always is in danger of using stereotypes of the other, and history has shown us how dangerous this tendency is.[14]

14. Marianne Bjelland Kartzow, "Female Gossipers and Their Reputation in the Pastoral Epistles," *Neot* 39 (2005): 285–86.

> Gossip is not one of the topics upon which the hegemonic political and theoretical order rests, and it can be said to represent a counter-discourse, providing a place for laughter, alternative knowledge, and creative thinking. Some theologians have imagined the first Christian community to be a place for diversity in religious visions and social organization. Through his involvement in the gossip discourse, the Pastoral Paul invokes gossip's destabilizing potential and gives an unintended hint that there might have been such a place within early Christianity in which various kinds of women and other marginalized groups could let their voices be heard—for him this place represented false teaching or gossip. Unfortunately, though characteristic of how gossip works, outsiders like you and me (and the Pastoral Paul) cannot hear what these voices are saying.[15]
>
> *Marianne Bjelland Kartzow*

In her book, Kartzow shows that in other ancient texts women can be accused of gossiping even when what they say deals with religious affairs or politics, and even when they represent the truth within the texts' universe. Female gossipers are useful for information management or news bearing, although they are blamed, ridiculed, and stereotyped. By using an intersectional lens it seems like gossip belongs to women, children, and slaves and works as a shaming device for men.

Having painted this disturbing possibility for the younger widows who reject marriage, the author unambiguously declares a solution for avoiding that outcome. He instructs "Timothy" that the younger widows ought to marry, bear children, and manage their households (1 Tim 5:14).[16] In other words, these women need to go back to the basics of the three main feminine responsibilities within a household. Not only will this preserve their own moral rectitude but their proper behavior will reduce the amount of some kind of verbal abuse directed at the believers (5:14b). Most interpreters think that the "adversary" mentioned here stands for a human opponent, either someone who has conflicts with

15. Marianne Bjelland Kartzow, *Gossip and Gender: Othering of Speech in the Pastoral Epistles*, BZNW 164 (Berlin: Walter de Gruyter, 2009), 209–10.

16. For more information on the phrase "I would have" (1 Tim 5:14), see below, "Translation Matters: 'I Desire,'" p. 178.

Dangerous Widows

The Pastor . . . , once again, contributes to a long tradition which takes women to be unreliable and dangerous. Chrysostom vaguely generalizes the gender dynamics of this passage, but women are still cause of special concern because, in his commentary, "when the care for the husband is withdrawn," that is, when they no longer have a man watching over them, women "naturally become idlers, tattlers, and busybodies. For he who does not attend to his own concerns will be meddling with those of others, even as he who minds his own business will take no account of and have no care about the affairs of another. And nothing is so unbecoming to a woman, as to busy herself in the concerns of others, and it is no less unbecoming to a man" (Hom. 1 Tim., *NPNF*[1] 13.459). Calvin . . . asserts that what is truly necessary is that men take women in hand to provide them with the kind of Christian life "so as to give the adversary no occasion to revile us." The problem, in his view, is that it is unfortunately all too rare to "find a man who willingly bears the burden of governing a wife! The reason is that it is attended by innumerable vexations," not the least of which, of course, is getting the woman to "submit to the yoke" (Commentary 1964: 260).[17]

Jay Twomey

TRANSLATION MATTERS: "BELIEVING WOMAN"

The word translated as "believing woman" (πιστή) in 1 Tim 5:16 is simply an adjective in the feminine singular form. A few manuscripts have these words inserted before πιστή: "if any *believing man or* . . . ." These manuscripts tend to be after the fifth century CE, later than those that say "believing woman," which is why the NRSV puts the information in a footnote to the verse.

the author or someone outside the community who would be critical of the younger widows' transgressions against the social norms.

Wrapping up his teachings for and about the widows, the author returns to the question of who ought to provide assistance to them (1 Tim 5:16). He envisions "a believing woman who has widows," an oddly worded phrase that suggests to many readers a community of widows supported by a wealthy female believer, perhaps even living in her home. This idea might relate to the short story of Tabitha/Dorcas who was

17. Jay Twomey, *The Pastoral Epistles Through the Centuries*, (Malden, MA: Wiley Blackwell, 2008), 82.

"devoted to good works and other acts of charity" (Acts 9:36) and was known for making clothing for faithful widows (Acts 9:39). Interestingly, the apocryphal *Acts of Peter* mentions one Marcellus, a male believer who cares for widows in his home. On the other hand, when the author singles out "any believing woman," he may just mean that a daughter or granddaughter ought to provide for the widowed women in her family, a sentiment he has already expressed (1 Tim 5:4, 8). Such a female believer needs to take care of those widows so that the "budget" of the assembly would not be overloaded.

This attitude is not unfamiliar to modern Western readers within certain cultural contexts who assume that financial support from one's family should serve as the foundation for caring for an elderly person. One difference now is that we expect the rest of their requirements to be met by government-funded programs rather than by substantial church assistance. With the exception of the practices of some smaller sects, the existing church programs that I know of offer only specialized forms of support, such as organizing social gatherings and providing transportation to appointments. This contrasts with the earliest Christian assemblies, which, like other private associations in the Roman Empire, such as burial societies, developed their own patterns for assisting members of their groups.

Another important difference is that modern countries do not restrict their attentions only to older widows but rather extend them to all older women *and* men and to persons of any age who have special needs. However, as I write this commentary, the economic status of older women in the United States continues to be less secure than that of older men.[18] Older women of color experience particular disadvantages compared with older white women: "In retirement, women of color are particularly vulnerable to economic insecurity. . . . Black and Hispanic women have lower income from Social Security, assets, and pensions than do White women, and they rely on Social Security for a larger portion of their income."[19] Clearly, this more vulnerable economic standing of older women—widowed or not—has been exacerbated by the propagation of gender stereotypes that continue to afflict our present society. In this way, we are still affected by similar patriarchal ideals that were widespread in the Roman Empire.

18. As described in "Older Women Workers and Economic Security," *Women's Bureau of the U.S. Department of Labor: Issue Brief*, US Department of Labor, February 2015, http://www.dol.gov/wb/factsheets/OlderWomen_IssueBrief-F-508.pdf.
19. Ibid.

[17]Let the elders who rule well be considered worthy of double honor, especially those who labor in preaching and teaching; [18]for the scripture says, 'You shall not muzzle an ox while it is treading out the grain', and, 'The laborer deserves to be paid.' [19]Never accept any accusation against an elder except on the evidence of two or three witnesses. [20]As for those who persist in sin, rebuke them in the presence of all, so that the rest also may stand in fear. [21]In the presence of God and of Christ Jesus and of the elect angels, I warn you to keep these instructions without prejudice, doing nothing on the basis of partiality. [22]Do not ordain anyone hastily, and do not participate in the sins of others; keep yourself pure.

[23]No longer drink only water, but take a little wine for the sake of your stomach and your frequent ailments.

[24]The sins of some people are conspicuous and precede them to judgment, while the sins of others follow them there. [25]So also good works are conspicuous; and even when they are not, they cannot remain hidden.

TRANSLATION MATTERS: "ESPECIALLY"

Verse 17 is a bit puzzling because of the Greek word μάλιστα, translated by the NRSV as "especially." This choice indicates that there are elders who "rule" and among them a subset of elders who are "preaching and teaching." But if μάλιστα is translated as "namely," then there is only one group of (male-only) elders in view, and they function in all three roles as rulers, preachers, and teachers. It seems to me that "namely" makes more sense of the author's instructions. In 5:8, the same Greek word is translated as "especially," and again, the choice of "namely" is more understandable in that context as well.

In the next verse, the letter's attention shifts to a set of men called "elders," but the entire section is difficult to interpret under that subject heading because the people and situations referred to are described somewhat ambiguously. First of all, does the word "elders" mean (male) church officials, or simply all the "older men," as in 1 Tim 5:1? Some of the elders "rule well" (5:17), from which we can suppose a group of elders who do not rule well. Our author probably points to a role within the community, since these elders ought to receive some kind of remuneration. As confirmation of his instructions, he cites two sayings from "scripture," the first from Deut 25:4 and the second ascribed to Jesus in Luke 10:7 and Matt 10:10, and used by Paul in 1 Cor 9:9.

Second, ancient and modern readers have speculated about what exactly this "double honor" entails. Is it twice the "salary," and if so, whose salary would be doubled? For an author who is loath to burden the assembly with providing for widows (1 Tim 5:16), this seems an unlikely prospect. A more probable interpretation is that the "double honor" is both the personal respect along with some kind of stipend. Some think that the stipend might not be monetary but rather goods or even additional portions of food and drink at the communal meals. Or the term could be used in a more figurative sense of the extra admiration that is due to those in authority. In light of the several restrictions on community support for widows (5:3-16), these older men fare much better than the women: their only qualification is that they "rule well." These two verses (5:17-18) have been used to justify many diverse "honors" given to male church leaders throughout church history, whether their titles are deacon, elder, pastor, priest, rector, or bishops. Timothy is charged with ensuring that an elder not be subjected to unfounded accusations from others (5:19; whether insiders or outsiders is unclear), another mark of the high regard owed to ecclesial authorities.

Third, who are "those who persist in sin" (1 Tim 5:20)? They could be negligent elders, but later church fathers thought that the teaching of public rebuke applied to anyone in a congregation. The point of this practice, says the author, is not only to correct the sinner but also to inspire "fear" in other believers, presumably so that they themselves will steer away from sin. Such discipline is rarely practiced in Western churches today, and even Augustine had his doubts about its usefulness:

> I know not whether a greater number have been improved or made worse when alarmed under threats of such punishment at the hands of men as is an object of fear. What, then, is the path of duty seeing that it often happens that if you inflict punishment on one he goes to destruction; whereas, if you leave him unpunished, another is destroyed? I confess that I make mistakes daily in regard to this, and that I know not when and how to observe the rule of Scripture: "Them that sin rebuke before all, that others may fear." (*Epistle* 95.3)

The author continues to make firm demands of Timothy, who might here be thought of in the role of the overseer as in Titus 1:9.[20] Echoing the legal process of Deut 19:15-20, Timothy is "warned" to enact the instructions about the male elders "without prejudice" and "partiality" (1 Tim 5:21). The somber tone of the author's language in 5:21 reflects

---

20. For a similar command to Titus himself, see Titus 1:13.

the great importance he places on arranging for good and suitable leaders for the communities. A series of four other warnings follows (5:22-23), which appear to be only loosely linked to what has gone before. Interpreters are uncertain why Timothy is commanded to drink a little wine instead of only water (5:23), but most suggest that this is an anti-ascetic opinion meant to separate Timothy from the false teachings and practices of the opponents.

TRANSLATION MATTERS: "ORDAIN"

In 1 Tim 5:22, the NRSV has chosen the word "ordain" to translate χεῖρας . . . ἐπιτίθει, which more literally means "lay hands upon." This phrase appears in both Testaments for commissioning someone for God's purposes (Num 8:10; 27:23; 1 Tim 4:14; 2 Tim 1:6; Acts 6:6; 13:3). Other uses include the laying on of hands as a part of healing (Matt 9:18; Mark 8:25; Luke 4:40) or as a sign of receiving the Holy Spirit more generally (Acts 8:17; 9:17; 19:6).

In my opinion, the word "ordain" carries the weight of church institutional practices unknown to the author of the Pastorals. Notice that the translators have kept the more literal translation, "laying on of hands," in 1 Tim 4:14 and have added a footnote to 5:22 to indicate the alternate reading.

By revisiting the topics of sin and judgment in the last two verses, the author again evokes the context of a legal trial. In two very similar statements that sound like proverbial sayings, he imagines two kinds of people: those with sins (1 Tim 5:24) and those with good works (5:25). But even within these two groups, the sins of some are quite "conspicuous," while the sins of others not so much; they "follow them." A similar idea is true for good works: there are "conspicuous" ones, contrasted with ones that "cannot remain hidden." All of these deeds—good and bad—will be illuminated at the "judgment" (5:24), which most probably means *the* final judgment given by God. Read together, the two sayings serve to warn the immoral that they face retribution and to encourage the moral that they will be rewarded in the end. Such persistent warnings and rewards endorse the teachings in the letter's next and last chapter.

1 Timothy 6

Home Economics: Enslavement and Wealth

The last chapter in this letter alternates teachings about groups within the assembly with direct commands to Timothy himself. Two specific categories of people are addressed: "slaves" (6:1-2) and the "rich" (6:9-10, 17-19). Along the way, the author once again censures his opponents (6:3, 21). Because he quickly transitions from the proverbial sayings at the end of 1 Tim 5 to the next topic of the behavior of enslaved believers in 1 Tim 6, the division between the chapters is awkward and clouds our understanding of the author's intentions. Did he mean to teach about "slaves" in the same ways that he did about "widows" and "elders"? The NRSV and many other translations seem to agree with this notion, and so a large space is placed near the end of 6:2, which separates the initial verses from those that follow. However, I have decided to treat the chapter as a whole because the main topics—"slaves" and wealth/possessions—were two of the four primary components of classical household management. Also, the topics are tightly connected, since the wealthy persons were those more likely to legally "own" enslaved persons as part of their household possessions, while at the same time slaves were denied any personal property rights.[1]

---

1. Emerson B. Powery argues that slaveholders were indeed present in the Pastorals communities and that the author speaks for the position of masters/mistresses rather than that of enslaved persons. See in this volume "Interpretive Essay: The Pastor's Commands to Enslaved Christians," p. 156.

1 Tim 6:1-2

¹Let all who are under the yoke of slavery regard their masters as worthy of all honor, so that the name of God and the teaching may not be blasphemed. ²Those who have believing masters must not be disrespectful to them on the ground that they are members of the church; rather they must serve them all the more, since those who benefit by their service are believers and beloved. Teach and urge these duties.

TRANSLATION MATTERS: "SLAVE"

In the ancient world, the word δοῦλος literally meant "slave," referring to persons considered to be the "property" of their masters and mistresses. In 1 Tim 6:1, the NRSV chooses "all who are under the yoke of slavery," a smoother translation than the more literal "as many as are slaves under the yoke." Many other translations, including the New International Version, the Common English Version, and *The Message* also use some form of "slave/slavery." But the King James and New American Standard versions use "servants." The New King James Version has unhelpfully changed this to "bondservants," an unfamiliar term for modern readers.

Throughout the New Testament, translators are not entirely consistent in translating δοῦλος as "slave." In Rom 1:1 and Titus 1:1, Paul calls himself a δοῦλος "of God," and both the NRSV and the NIV translate the phrase as "*servant* of God." Why this translation? Does it emerge from a reverence for the apostle, so that it is hard to imagine him as a slave? Does it reflect discomfort about the history of slavery in the Unites States and especially in the churches?

While at least three Greek words may be translated as "servant" in English, it is easy to see that cultural and theological biases influence the choices of the translators. A simple search for the words "servant/s" and "slave/s" in the New Testament shows that the NIV prefers "servant/s" to "slave/s," using the former about twice as often as does the NRSV.

Bible Version	"slave(s)"	"servant(s)"	Total usage
NIV	52	158	210
NRSV	123	75	198

My own choice is to translate the words δοῦλος/δοῦλοι as "slave/s" wherever they occur. This emphasizes the social location of the text, reminding us of the harsh realities that many of the enslaved believers experienced. It also raises the complicated theological idea that church leaders are also somehow "slaves" themselves.

More important, it is crucial for American Christians to recognize and remember how these New Testament texts were used to justify the practice of enslaving

Africans in the American colonies (and, later, the American states). Today, we still need to struggle with what it means to possess and use sacred scriptures that support slavery. How do we relate to such "authoritative" teachings? And how do we make amends for the damages done to enslaved persons in the name of Christian teachings?

Like many domestic households of the Roman Empire, the "household of God" envisioned in 1 Tim 3:15 included persons who were labeled and known as slaves. Someone might "fall" into slavery, having been captured during a military conquest and subsequently sold at an auction. Or she or he might have been born to parents already slaves, or abandoned as an infant by a poor family only to be picked up "for free" and raised by someone else. A few were in debt so deep that they sold themselves into slavery. In each case, slaves (male and female) served at the command of their master or mistress; their bodies were considered property to be utilized in the maintenance and prosperity of a household that was not their own. The evidence from earlier Pauline letters (Gal 3:27-29; 1 Cor 7:21-24; Phlm) confirms that such persons were also members of the Christian assemblies, present in the audience when Paul's words were read aloud and explained to all. Similarly, the author of the Pastorals feels obligated to address the slaves in his audience, and this he does by reinforcing his kyriarchic conceptualization of the relationships among believers.

TRANSLATION MATTERS: "MEMBERS OF THE CHURCH"

In order to use gender-inclusive language, the NRSV has chosen to translate the word ἀδελφοί as "members of the church" in 1 Tim 6:2. A more literal translation is "brothers," which I prefer because throughout the Pastorals the author views the groups of believers as members of a family.

In this verse it is the *slave-owners* who are called "brothers" and "beloved," not the slaves. The opposite labeling strategy appears in Paul's letter to Philemon. There he exhorts Philemon to receive the *slave Onesimus* as a "beloved brother" (v. 16). Of course, it depends on who is being addressed in each letter. However, in the Pastorals there are no corresponding teachings directed explicitly to "masters."[2]

2. For more on Christian slaveholders, see Powery's essay on Titus 2 below, p. 156.

Along with Titus 2:9-10, this passage gives explicit instructions to the slaves within the household of God. The author does recognize that this is an oppressive position: they are "under the yoke" (1 Tim 6:1). Yet rather than teaching them how to conduct themselves at a meeting of the assembly, how to think of themselves now as equals of other believers, or how to live out some kind of theological freedom, the author instead directs them to behave "appropriately" within their own actual domestic settings. His stated concern is that the community might be talked about negatively by outsiders (6:1; see also 1 Tim 3:7; 5:14; and Titus 2:5, 8, 10).

TRANSLATION MATTERS: "BENEFIT BY THEIR SERVICE"

The NRSV translation "benefit by their service" (1 Tim 6:2) represents the Greek phrase εὐεργεσίας ἀντιλαμβανόμενοι, which more literally reads those who "benefit by good service." The word for "good service" is different from the "good work" (ἔργον καλόν or ἔργον ἀγαθόν) urged many times in the Pastorals.[3]

Εὐεργεσία is most often used within the ancient system of patronage where a high-status person gives a benefaction, a special favor, or a material donation to a subordinate person, group, or city. It is difficult to say why the author chooses to apply this term to the service of a low-status slave, but I think that he is trying to give some higher spiritual significance to the demeaning work of a slave. He describes their "good service" as having benefits for their "believing masters," which may be thought of as benefiting their whole community.

The only *faithful* role for slaves in this particular conception is the kind of "good service" (1 Tim 6:2) expected of any loyal slave in the Roman Empire: to honor the master or mistress by submitting with respect, without contradicting them or stealing from them. In the words of Titus 2:10, this is what counts as "complete and perfect fidelity." It is acutely objectionable that the author subverts the very faith he has pressed on his audience by constructing a standard of faithfulness that is peculiar to slaves and basically replicates the values of his system of slavery.

Even though the author knows that some of the believing slaves have "believing masters" (1 Tim 6:2), one element absent from 1 Tim 6:1-2 (as well as Titus 2:9-10) is any instruction addressed directly to the slaveholders among the household of God. Such instructions can be found in the New Testament at Eph 6:9 and Col 4:1. Within the worldview of the Pastorals, as Jennifer A. Glancy states regarding 1 Tim 3:1b-5, "the leader

---

3. See above, "Translation Matters: 'Good Works,'" p. 58.

TRANSLATION MATTERS: "MASTERS"

The Greek word translated "masters" is the plural form of δεσπότης, which is the equivalent of "master" or "owner," a label for someone who held slaves. It could also mean "master of the house" more generally. When used for the Roman emperors, it conveys even more kyriarchic dominance: "tyrant," "despot," or "absolute ruler."

Although the word usually designated male authority figures, it could also apply to female slaveholders. The short letter *Theano to Kallisto* advises a newly married woman on how to supervise "her" household slaves. There the writer calls the mistress of the house by three interchangeable commanding titles: κυρία, δέσποινα, and δεσπότης. When reading 1 Tim 6:1-2, Titus 2:9-10, and any New Testament texts about slavery, it is essential to remember that both women and men were enslaved and that both women and men held slaves. This means that the intersections of gender, status, and power were complicated in the Roman world, and they remain no less so today.

of the house-church was identified as the quintessential householder: husband, father, and presumably slaveholder."[4] So, although the masters loom very large in the lives of the slaves (indeed, from a slave's perspective, the human masters might seem even more important than God or Christ), the author provides no specific principles for how slaveholders are to work with and live with their slaves. It is left to the reader to speculate whether, since the Pastor positions himself as a church leader, he too was a slaveholder.[5]

Interpretive Essay: Reflections on Engaging This Teaching Today

Every time I teach about slavery and the New Testament I hear questions like these:

> When Jesus or Paul talks about slaves, aren't they really talking about servants? Household help who are treated pretty well? Servants who sometimes even know how to read and write? Who are provided for and who work alongside the master in some business? They could even be educated as physicians or accountants, right? And isn't it also the

4. Jennifer A. Glancy, *Slavery in Early Christianity* (Minneapolis: Fortress Press, 2006), 146.

5. The presence of Christian slaveholders in the Pastorals audience is discussed more at length below: Powery, "Interpretive Essay," p. 156.

case that many slaves were set free in the Roman world? Slavery just really wasn't that bad back then, was it?

The students and parishioners asking the questions are mostly mainline and evangelical US Protestants, mostly middle-class, and from a range of ethnicities, people who have absorbed such ideas from a mixed bag of facts given in sermons, Sunday School lessons, and Bible translations. The notion that Roman slavery was different, and especially that it was somehow "easier on the slave," more lenient, less dehumanizing, is amazingly prevalent among the churchgoing population, both clergy and laity, in my experience. This is in spite of the proliferation of well-documented and creative social-historical studies of slavery in the Greco-Roman world that demonstrate without a doubt that, indeed, slavery was "really that bad back then."

Roman Slavery

According to Sandra R. Joshel, recent studies have defined a "slave society" using a few different criteria: the proportion of slaves in the population; the extent to which slave labor added to the larger economy, or phrased in the reverse, the extent to which the economy was dependent on slave labor; and cultural attitude that equated slave ownership with power and status. By all these standards, the Roman Empire qualifies as a "slave society."[6] Something above 10 percent of the total population were slaves, and the percentage was probably at least double that in the capital, Rome. The wealthy elite relied on slaves for working their agricultural estates, while slaves in their urban households tended to the masters' personal needs and added to their social reputation and political influence.

Slaves of differing ages, ethnicities, and occupations were especially to be found in every city in the empire. This is significant for the study of slaves in early Christianity because the Pauline mission moved from one city to another, and so Paul, his co-workers, and his co-believers were in regular contact with slaves on the streets and in the marketplace, at the baths and the gymnasium, and in their workshops as well as homes where they were offered hospitality. Encounters with slaves were so much a part of daily life in the first century CE that they were hardly

---

6. Sandra R. Joshel, *Slavery in the Roman World*, Cambridge Introduction to Roman Civilization (Cambridge: Cambridge University Press, 2010), 7–10.

remarked upon except in special circumstances. This ancient culture of slavery is an alien experience for those of us privileged to live in societies that promote, however unevenly, the freedom and rights of all human beings.

What can be gleaned from all the available sources about the actual experience of being "slaves under the yoke" (1 Tim 6:1a) within the Roman Imperial structure?[7] Significantly, the literary works from philosophers, biographers, historians, dramatists, and others speak from only one side of the master-slave "relationship," which is, of course, that of persons in the superior position over subordinated slaves. Such texts from the perspective of free males are almost the only sources we have about Greek and Roman slavery.

> We have very little direct testimony from the women and slaves of the ancient world and no voices raised in unmistakeable opposition to the dominant order. . . . The few texts authored by women and slaves that do survive are in highly conventional forms, such as epitaphs on tombstones, in which the dominant language of the culture tends to obscure individual testimony. . . . Meanwhile, the works of free men are deceptively full of details about women and slaves, but, as we have seen, these details *tell a story of men and masters.*[8]

The same state of affairs is true for New Testament writings about slaves and slaveholding, including the sections from 1 Timothy and Titus: they too are written by and from the viewpoint of free men, many of whom likely owned slaves and who, in any case, never speak against the slave system of their time. We possess no works at all from the hands and minds of slaves who were also members of early Christian communities. Slaves from antiquity have in effect been silenced, and so, in

---

7. Obviously, space considerations prohibit a full-scale description of Roman slavery in this volume. For the reader interested in further information, I recommend: Richard P. Saller, *Patriarchy, Property and Death in the Roman Family* (Cambridge: Cambridge University Press, 1994), esp. chaps. 4–6; Sandra R. Joshel and Sheila Murnaghan, eds., *Women and Slaves in Greco-Roman Culture: Differential Equations* (London: Routledge, 1998); Enrico Dal Lago and Constantina Katsari, eds., *Slave Systems: Ancient and Modern* (Cambridge: Cambridge University Press, 2008); and Joshel, *Slavery in the Roman World*. For situating the New Testament world within this larger culture of slave-owning, see Glancy, *Slavery in Early Christianity*, and J. Albert Harrill, *Slaves in the New Testament: Literary, Social, and Moral Dimensions* (Minneapolis: Augsburg Fortress Press, 2005).

8. Joshel and Murnaghan, "Introduction," in *Women and Slaves in Greco-Roman Culture*, 19; my italics.

order to make some small redress for that oppression, I have included here several testimonies from the American ex-slave narratives.[9] While the experience of slavery in the Mediterranean and the American South was not identical, at least these few American ex-slaves had a small opportunity to describe their remembrances of being enslaved. Their living memories of slavery can help to arrest the attention of the modern reader who might more typically skim over those New Testament passages that address the condition of slavery. We can learn from the powerful testimony of freed slave Henry Banner of Arkansas: "Freedom is better than slavery, though. I done seed both sides."

Legal Status of Roman Slaves

It is quite ironic to speak of the "legal status" of slaves, because these persons had no civil rights under Roman law. It is true that a few slaves had some privileges and skills gained from serving in the households of the elites or from supervising other slaves as an overseer on an estate, and a few could even entrust some earnings to their owners so that they could later buy their own freedom. However, under the law and as in other systems of chattel slavery, slaves remained "individual human beings [who were] owned as property and treated as commodities that [could] be used, bought and sold, willed, given, or lent."[10] Accordingly, within the confines of the law,

- Roman slaves could not marry
- their bodies were considered sexually available to the masters

---

9. Quotations from ex-slaves are taken from the more than two thousand oral histories collected by the Federal Writers' Project (1936–1938). These fascinating narratives are available in digitized (and searchable) form under the title "Born in Slavery: Slave Narratives from the Federal Writers' Project, 1936–1938," at the Library of Congress website: https://www.loc.gov/collections/slave-narratives-from-the-federal-writers-project-1936-to-1938/about-this-collection. In addition, some of the narratives are available in print anthologies: Benjamin Albert Botkin, *Lay My Burden Down: A Folk History of Slavery* (Chicago: University of Chicago Press, 1945; 1958); Norman R. Yetman, ed., *Voices From Slavery: 100 Authentic Slave Narratives* (New York: Holt, Rinehart, and Winston, 1970; 2nd ed., Mineola, NY: Dover, 2000); and in a complete collection, George P. Rawick, ed., *The American Slave: A Composite Autobiography*, 19 vols., Contributions in Afro-American and African Studies 11 (Westport, CT.: Greenwood, 1972). In 2003, some of these transcribed interviews were assembled in a documentary film, *Unchained Memories* (HBO production).
10. Joshel, *Slavery in the Roman World*, 7.

- their children were classed as slaves
- they could not make any legal transactions
- they could not own a business
- they could not own property, including land, buildings, tools, commodities, money, other slaves
- they could not transmit property upon death, nor inherit it from another
- they could be purchased, sold, traded, or even stolen
- slaves who tried to escape were labeled as thieves, for "stealing" from the master
- they were legally subject to physical punishment, symbolized in the concept of whipping
- slaves could be manumitted by their owners

In addition, contract laws regulated the sale of slaves, in particular what information needed to be disclosed about the origins and character of each slave. For example, the *Edict of the Aediles*, preserved by the Roman jurist Ulpian in the early third century CE, states, "Those who sell slaves should notify the purchasers if they have any diseases or defects, if they have the habit of running away, or wandering, or have not been released from liability for damage that they have committed. All of these things must be publicly stated at the time that the slaves are sold."[11]

Each of these lawful restraints reveals how slaves were treated as property, and while it is certainly true that enslaved individuals did not all have a coercive and/or abusive association with their own slaveholders, the underlying power differential inherent in the slave-master arrangement is decisively inscribed in the legal code. This officially authorized web of regulations restricted the lives of slaves at every turn, affecting their bodies, personal goals, family relationships, and acquisition of wealth. Moreover, the socio-historical context for the Pastoral Letters is founded on these very laws, so that the members (slave and free) of the early assemblies inhabited this system as if it were divinely

11. Translation by Peter Arzt-Grabner, "Neither a Truant nor a Fugitive: Some Remarks on the Sale of Slaves in Roman Egypt and Other Provinces," in *Proceedings of the Twenty-Fifth International Congress of Papyrology*, Ann Arbor, MI, 2007, American Studies in Papyrology (Ann Arbor, 2010), 22.

ordained. A corresponding legal situation for slaves existed in the American colonies, where, although slavery began to be abolished in the northern states in the late 1700s, the slave society of the South persisted for decades.

What did Roman slaves think about their lack of legal rights? We can only imagine that some of them felt like ex-slave Margrett Nillin of Texas: "What I likes best, to be slave or free? Well, it's this way. In slavery I owns nothing and never owns nothing. In freedom I's own the home and raise the family. All that cause me worriment, and in slavery I has no worriment, but I takes the freedom."[12]

Slaves and Their Families

Within the Roman legal system, family relationships for slaves were subject to painful disruptions. Even though Roman slaves could not legally marry, many still formed spousal relationships with other slaves, with whom they also had children. Inscriptional evidence shows that enslaved persons referred to each other as "husband" and "wife," no matter what the law allowed.[13] A similar approach by slaves and masters developed during American slavery, including informal ceremonies that recognized the marriage partnership. After emancipation, many of the ex-slaves reported that they were then able to marry "legally."

Roman female slaves were valued for "their biological capacities of reproduction and lactation."[14] Because "human milk was a valuable commodity in the ancient world," slave mothers of infants could be hired out as nurses for other infants.[15] As in many American slaveholding families, lactating slaves often served as nurses of their master's infants and then became child-minders as those children grew older.

Slave fathers had no lawful connection to their children, yet they too were essential to the "breeding program" that increased the wealth of the slaveholders.[16] Any children born of these unions belonged to the slaveholder because the children took on the legal status of their mother

12. Quoted in Botkin, *Lay My Burden Down*, 267.

13. For translations of such inscriptions, see Dale B. Martin, "Slave Families and Slaves in Families," in *Early Christian Families in Context: An Interdisciplinary Dialogue,* ed. David L. Balch and Carolyn Osiek (Grand Rapids, MI: Eerdmans, 2003), 207–30.

14. Glancy, *Slavery in Early Christianity*, 9.

15. Ibid., 18.

16. Joshel, *Slavery in the Roman World*, 125.

at the time of their birth. This entire state of affairs hindered the preservation of intimate bonds among slaves. Under the American slave system, similar familial interferences are recorded by the ex-slaves. Tines Kendricks of Georgia says,

> In the time of slavery another thing what make it tough on the n-----s [17] was them times when a man and he wife and their children had to be taken 'way from one another. This separation might be brung 'bout 'most any time for one thing or another, such as one or t'other, the man or the wife, be sold off or taken 'way to some other state like Louisiana or Mississippi. Then when marse die what had a heap of slaves, these slave n-----s be divided up 'mongst the marse's children or sold off for to pay the marse's debts. Then at times when a man married to a woman that don't belong to the same marse what he do, then they is liable to git divided up and separated 'most any day. They was heaps of n----r families that I know what was separated in the time of bondage that tried to find they folkses what was gone.

To those modern readers who assume that Roman slaves were not all that oppressed, it is important to understand that one of the most crucial legal and actual distinctions between the bodies of free Romans and those of enslaved Romans was that the slave body possessed no protection from physical retribution. Specifically, a body enslaved was lawfully susceptible to whippings. Not every slave was whipped on a regular basis, yet the legitimacy of this practice shaped even the lives of those slaves lucky enough to avoid it. This corporal punishment carried physical pain and suffering as well as the acute stigma of dishonor, serving to heighten in the minds of participants and observers the differences between slaves and free Romans.[18] Moreover, when the slave-free differentiation was combined with the typical gender ideology, it was only the "real man" who enjoyed immunity from whippings. Still, the enslaved man (and his family) knew the threat of physical punishment was a potential harm to his masculinity and social status. Richard Saller asserts that "the act of being whipped affected a Roman's status by

17. I have altered the quotations from the ex-slaves when they use the "n-word" to describe themselves and their compatriots. I choose not to use this word because, as a white person born in the United States, I do not want to re-institute any of the oppressive practices of the slave-owners.

18. A clear and compelling analysis of the multifaceted meaning of physical punishment in the Roman worldview is found in Saller, *Patriarchy, Property and Death in the Roman Family*, 133–53.

detracting from his honor through public humiliation and association with the lowest human form in the Roman world, the slave."[19] Those who have read books or viewed films that depict American slavery[20] will recognize that the threat of physical punishment served as a comparable practice of intimidation for enslaved people of African ancestry.

Slaves in the Pastorals

I have made this sketch of the lives of slaves in the Roman world in order to inform and, if necessary, reset the attitudes of modern readers of the Pastoral letters. Of course, not every believing slave endured every possible indignity at the hands of masters and mistresses, whether believers or not. However, these are the social contexts and legal structures within which every member of the Pauline communities lived. In those communities there surely must have been

- slaves who were "bred" at home or bought and sold at a marketplace
- female slaves who bore children to their masters, and male slaves who had been sexually abused
- slaves whose family members had been sold away from the household
- slaves whose daily drudgery wore down their bodies and spirits
- freed slaves whose only viable life-option was to remain in the master's business

Moreover, the Pastorals' advice reinforces the stereotypical depictions of Roman slaves: enslaved believers are to honor their masters, not be disrespectful, to provide "good service" (1 Tim 6:1-2), and, more specifically in Titus 2:9-10, to be subordinated to authority, "not to talk back, not to pilfer" (or "misappropriate" or "rob'), but to aspire "to show complete and perfect fidelity [πίστις]" required of the loyal slave.[21]

As with much of the teaching in the Pastorals, we do not know how the slaves in the audiences were actually conducting themselves. We

19. Ibid., 138.

20. A few examples: the miniseries *Roots* (1977), and the films *Amistad* (1997), *Beloved* (1998), *12 Years a Slave* (2013), and the stories that inspired them.

21. Emerson Powery discusses these commands at more length below, "Interpretive Essay," p. 156.

have only this one author's perspective of what was important for the communities to learn, and he consistently pronounces the opinions common to free men who were heads of their households. Certainly the deprivation of honor, the threat to one's family, and the hardships of life at the time could have convinced a Christian slave to take what they needed from a master or mistress. It is also probable that at least some slaves who joined these communities heard Paul's letters read aloud and latched onto a statement like "For freedom Christ has set us free. Stand firm, therefore, and do not submit again to a yoke of slavery" (Gal 5:1). Taken out of its original context where it refers to the "slavery" of circumcision, this declaration seems wholly unambiguous. What slave would not have rejoiced at those words and perhaps hoped for better times ahead?

Christian Readers Today

In addition to the lack of accurate information about Roman slavery, a few other factors have led to the defective impressions behind the questions I hear in classrooms and churches. First, there is the dilemma around the English translation of the Greek word for δοῦλος.[22] Ever since the revered King James Version chose to translate this as "servant" rather than "slave," the softer and perhaps more socially acceptable meaning became inscribed in Christians' understanding of both the parables and the Pauline teachings.[23] Influenced by various media, my twenty-first-century questioners tend to understand a "servant" either as a waiter at a restaurant or coffee shop or as someone who worked on an upper-class British estate, such as that depicted in the BBC production of *Downton Abbey*.

Second, and in a related step, it seems inconceivable to many that early church leaders who called themselves "*slaves* of God," "*slaves* of Christ," or "*slaves* of other believers" (e.g., Acts 4:29; Rom 1:1; 2 Cor 4:5; Phil 2:7; Titus 1:1; see also Gal 5:13) would actually mean to take on the role of *slave* rather than *servant*. In much of American Christianity, the thought that God would desire believers to act as *slaves*, obedient to divine commands, bumps up against modern ideas of human rights and individual freedoms.

---

22. See above, "Translation Matters: 'Slave,'" p. 70.

23. For the historical effects of this translation within the struggle to abolish slavery in the United States, see Harrill, *Slaves in the New Testament*, 167–68, 180–82.

Third, the institution of slavery in America, from its origins in the colonial period up to this very moment, broadly influences how Americans perceive slavery in the entire Bible, especially in the New Testament. Some white people think of how long ago in our history that was and deny any continued impact on African Americans today. Others, aware of the exceptionally race-based historical oppression in the United States, would prefer not to reflect on painful times of national racial division. Furthermore, many church people know that a "plain reading" of many New Testament texts was appealed to in order to support the practices of American slaveholders. Thus, the word "slave" in an English New Testament raises feelings of resentment, anxiety, guilt, and powerlessness for many white Americans. Since these are reactions that the readers of my acquaintance (including preachers and teachers) would rather deny, ignore, or explain away, biblical texts that refer to slavery are not handled with the care, the suspicion, and especially the creativity they require in order to be engaged with from a more critical standpoint.

Critical Readings

The First Letter of Timothy, as well as the letter to Titus and the First Letter of Peter, are New Testament writings that are not usually used in Latin American circles of community reading of the Bible. And when these letters are used, only the interesting texts are read, such as 1 Tim 4:12 "Let no one despise your youth, but set the believers an example in speech, in love, in faith, in purity," without taking into account the conflictive and apologetic context in which these words are found. We avoid, or just pass over, certain texts in the same letter that prejudice the excluded, such as women and slaves.

The reason these writings are avoided is obvious. The reading of the Bible from the perspective of the excluded does not find in this letter, or in some other biblical books, words of courage and hope that would animate people to overcome and resist the difficult life that confronts them in the midst of poverty and discrimination. Various verses in 1 Timothy can be singled out as contributing to this idea; the most problematic are those which speak about women, for example, 1 Tim 2:11-12. In our Christian communities and in neighborhood communities, for example, women are a very important axis. Women are the ones who direct, sustain, and animate the community most of the time. To read the letter of 1 Timothy and to obey it without discernment would be to take a step backward, to be silent and follow ideals that in everyday practice do not fit. We could say the same about the condition of exploitation and marginalization of men and women who are lucky enough to be employed or underemployed. Necessity obliges them to obey the boss quietly, even in minimal and sometimes indecent demands, as we have heard in so many testimonies. To read this letter without any critique—that

slaves consider their masters worthy of all honor and if the master is a believer they should serve them even more (see 6:1-2)—can be seen not only as biblical legitimation of inhuman situations but as a great absence of God, who is known to be in solidarity with the poor and in whom they have placed their hope for liberation.[24]

Elsa Tamez

African American Slavery and Scriptures

One of the strongest critiques against Christianity is the role that it has historically played in aiding and justifying major inequalities and social injustices. Not the least of these is the role that Christianity has played justifying slavery. In my experience as an African American minister, the issue of slavery often comes up from blacks and whites opposed to Christianity.

Interpreting 1 Tim 6:1-2, we can gain insight into this justification of slavery, while also developing an understanding of the text that accepts its veracity and importance in the Christian scriptural canon without adopting the same conclusions. Although slavery is defended in these two verses, American

chattel slavery does not have to be defended. Instead, the opposite can happen, that is, we can criticize it and offer new interpretations for this text.

One possible strategy is that we have the freedom to disregard this text altogether even though it remains in our canon. We can skip it and move on to the other less difficult issues presented in this letter. While this solution may not be the best, it is often the most popular. I have been in church for twenty-five years and I have never once heard a sermon preached on this passage or any other like it. While this strategy certainly has its perks, I think a real downside is that we miss something by not dealing with the Scripture that we have inherited. We may dislike this text, but we should really reconsider if we want to ignore it altogether.

24. Elsa Tamez, *Struggles for Power in Early Christianity*, trans. Gloria Kinsler (Maryknoll, NY: Orbis Books, 1970), xvii–xviii.

Another better possibility is to do what Elsa Tamez does by studying problematic texts closely and then dissenting from them.[25] Dissent is different from dismissing or ignoring them. As she dissents from it, she legitimately wrestles with it and fights with it. She engages it, teaches about it, and reconstructs it to show why she disagrees with it. This method is much more authentic and true to our history. It does not whitewash the teachings or pretend that some of our spiritual ancestors did not use this text to promote slavery in the Americas.

A final possibility is for us to engage the text on its own terms and see if it still has something to say to us beyond calling forth our anger or dissent. For example, Thomas C. Oden sees the phrase "under the yoke of slavery" as being very applicable to our own world. He does not freeze it in the antiquated world of our text but brings it to life for our time, saying that it applies to anyone who has had a low wage status of involuntary powerlessness.[26] Oden's interpretation allows us to be empathetic with the powerless slaves in Timothy's day while recognizing our own power. Oden also reminds us that slavery was a big deal to Paul and his followers in that they wrote about it often yet did not always outright affirm it. This should give us hope. It should also give us hope that Paul believed that the love of Christ could undermine slavery and all other oppressed and oppressor relationships.[27]

This text reminds me that the early church dealt with situations similar to ours, struggling with issues of church and state, of Christ and culture, and that their answers to these dilemmas were not always the best. I do not agree with this text at all, but I am guided by the paradox that the writer presents, and I am inspired to deal with my own ethical paradox. I am called by this text to think about the slave, or the low-wage powerless worker in my own time, and how I often compromise his and her humanity by reinforcing the customs of my day. While I believe that the teaching of 1 Tim 6:1-2 is not an endorsement of slavery by Christianity, it is instead something more complex, understandable, and still wrong. This pushes me to deeper levels of biblical literacy as well as more profound moral reflection. What I have learned, others can learn too, and we can be reminded that yes, my God is still on the side of the oppressed because "He has his eye on the sparrow and I know he watches me."

Elijah R. Zehyoue

---

25. Ibid., xix–xx.
26. Thomas C. Oden, *First and Second Timothy and Titus*, IBC 4 (Louisville, KY: Westminster John Knox, 1989), 100.
27. Ibid.

Campesinos and the Scriptures

As a member of a missionary congregation, I have had different experiences working with campesinos, many of whom live in situations that resemble the institution of slavery in the Roman Empire. Most campesinos are Mexican immigrants who pick vegetables and fruits from the fields of the central valley of California. The working conditions of these people are literally inhuman. They are paid by the job, and then in order to get a decent wage they have to work more than twelve hours in the hot weather under the sun. Campesinos live in groups of fifty or more in small houses. Since everything in the house is communal there is no privacy. Some campesinos have come to the United States under the direction of a coyote who connects them directly to the managers' fields. This "transaction" requires months of previous work in order to pay the coyote for his connection service. The lack of proper documentation to work in the United States makes their situation worse and there is no medical assistance, no opportunity for education, and no access to obtain a state ID or driver's license. Sexual harassment by their supervisors is often common, especially toward women who work along with men in the fields. Campesinos are susceptible to abuses of all kinds. Most of them

do not speak nor read English, some lack even an elementary education, and so often they ignore the basic rights this country grants them. Yet, campesinos have found ways to survive and to continue seeking to have a better life.

Making a comparison between Roman and such modern forms of slavery, we can say that thousands of campesinos share, in diverse ways and to varying degrees, the living and working conditions of slaves in the original audience of 1 Timothy. However, there are some essential differences: the campesinos working in California are in a sense free; they are not legally owned by anybody as were first-century slaves of the Roman Empire. Even though most of the campesinos are Catholic, their behavior, whether good or bad, would not jeopardize the teachings of the church, as the author of the Pastorals warns slaves in 1 Tim 6:1. Another critical difference is that slavery for Americans is not a standard in which all else in society is measured or judged, nor is slavery a way of thinking about society and social categorization. All kinds of slavery or subjugation are unacceptable in the United States. Modern slavery is strictly an economic institution and works clandestinely.

The proper question, then, is what to do with this. Is there something useful that any campesino can get out of 1 Tim 6:1-2? Without hesitation we should have a positive response.

Several years ago, the missionary group that I belong to launched a program that teaches people how to read the Bible. The target audience is campesinos working in the central valley of California. We have observed that they relate to the Scriptures as authoritative and without error. Our goal then is to teach ways of reading the Scriptures that will persuade them to get away from their oppressive or abusive situations. One of the methods used to accomplish the project is *desaprender*, "to unlearn," those principles of interpretation that do not necessarily help people reach another level of faith. It provides an explanation of who, why, and where the Bible was written, the myths in the Bible, and its symbolism, so that people can appreciate more objectively what the Scriptures say. This method draws from the teaching of Benedict XVI.

> Biblical revelation is rooted in history. . . . Revelation is suited to the cultural and moral level of distant times and thus describes facts and customs, such as cheating and trickery, and acts of violence and massacre, without explicitly denounc-ing the immorality of such things. This can be explained by the historical context, yet it can cause the modern reader to be taken aback, especially if he or she fails to take account of the many "dark" deeds carried out down the centuries, and also in our own day.[28]

In order to counteract an attitude of modern "enslavement" and "submission" among the campesinos, we invite people to make more sense out of 1 Tim 6:1-2 in contemporary times. In teaching on the passage, I would make these claims:

- the author in his own understanding and with the best intentions wrote his letter as he thought Paul would have done it
- the author had in mind a hierarchical society based on power and abuses
- ancient Roman society had different norms and therefore a different ethos that influenced the morality of the author's letter
- slavery was not itself a moral issue as it is today, but slavery was an economic reality of Roman society
- compared to other parts of Scripture, 1 Tim 6:1-2 betrays

28. *Verbum Domini* (VD) 42; italics original; this section is titled "The 'Dark' Passages of the Bible."

what Jesus would propose regarding equality before God

I would hope that the campesinos would completely change their understanding of 1 Tim 6:1-2 and that this new understanding would help them realize that their idea of submission should be set aside and help to convince them that they are not supposed to live and be treated as slaves. In this sense, the First Letter to Timothy should raise the awareness of their actual situation and provide hope for a better future for the thousands of campesinos who are facing modern slavery.

Eloy Escamilla

Our interpretive efforts cannot stop at simply gaining a better "understanding" of slavery in the Roman Imperial era. Americans must move on to consider the influences of slavery in their own national experience and to wrestle with the reality of Christian inspired texts that have been used to promote the deprivation, dependence, and dehumanization of the many human beings who have suffered—and continue to suffer—under such hierarchical domination. As a teacher and person of faith, I believe that exactly because every evocation of ancient slavery in the New Testament has the possibility of provoking a powerful encounter with American racisms, a parallel potential also exists for repentance, change, and healing, personally and culturally, to emerge from reading these biblical texts.

1 Tim 6:3-10

³Whoever teaches otherwise and does not agree with the sound words of our Lord Jesus Christ and the teaching that is in accordance with godliness, ⁴is conceited, understanding nothing, and has a morbid craving for controversy and for disputes about words. From these come envy, dissension, slander, base suspicions, ⁵and wrangling among those who are depraved in mind and bereft of the truth, imagining that godliness is a means of gain. ⁶Of course, there is great gain in godliness combined with contentment; ⁷for we brought nothing into the world, so that we can take nothing out of it; ⁸but if we have food and clothing, we will be content with these. ⁹But those who want to be rich fall into temptation and are trapped by many senseless and harmful desires that plunge people into ruin and destruction. ¹⁰For the love of money is a root of all kinds of evil, and in their eagerness to be rich some have wandered away from the faith and pierced themselves with many pains.

TRANSLATION MATTERS: "DISPUTES ABOUT WORDS"

The NRSV translation is actually one word in Greek, λογομαχίας, which could be translated "word-battles." This noun may have been created by the author of the Pastorals because the related verb is found in 2 Tim 2:14, and no other such word appears in the entire New Testament. Despite his critique of such practices, by writing these three letters, our author himself engages in "word-battles." Needless to say, Christian literature throughout history is disappointingly crammed with similar contests over truth and falsehood.

In terms and topics that echo his attacks on his opponents in 1 Tim 1, our author again turns his attention to what he views as their wrong teaching, using a verb he himself seems to have invented: "to teach otherwise" (ἑτεροδιδασκαλεῖν, 6:3). This word appeared first in 1 Tim 1:3, so we can assume that the author is returning to a key purpose of the entire letter, which is to distinguish true and false teaching. In this chapter the author is more interested in attacking the supposed immoral character and actions of his antagonists than in addressing their specific beliefs. As for the contents of *true* teaching and the characteristics of *true* teachers, the author has already established these by writing theology in the name of the revered apostle Paul and by setting up Timothy and other subsequent male church leaders as good examples to follow.

In 1 Tim 6:5 and 9-10, the author claims that the opponents' false teaching both emerges from and results in greediness. Their fundamental error is that they "imagine" that "godliness is a means of gain" (6:5).[29] Whether this was indeed the case for his adversaries, cannot be known for sure because we have only his single opinion about their motivations. Also, among classical orators, politicians, and philosophers, the charge of greed was a purely conventional way to discredit one's rivals. However, a valuable interpretation of the passage can be gleaned from presuming the accuracy of the author's assessment of the situation, as shown in these comments from Elsa Tamez.

---

29. See "Translation Matters: 'Godliness,'" p. 48.

The Gains of Godliness

The rich, for the author, have a false godliness; but why do they think that godliness is a means of gain? We do not find a satisfactory solution to this question. One of the answers could be that the rich, upon demonstrating godliness—in the religious sense, devoted and generous with their money—believed that they would receive honor and fame, as they would have in the patronage system. This reward from the clients (in this case the other members of the community) would reinforce the status and power of patrons. It could be that these rich persons would have in mind the Roman meaning of "godliness," which meant scrupulously following the rituals so as to find favor with the gods and honor from the religious authorities and their fellow citizens.

This last manner of understanding godliness as a means of gain is not foreign to our context of today's Latin America. There are television programs and large churches, driven by the so-called prosperity theology, in which it is demanded that the people make investments through offerings and donations in order to receive more money from God and to prosper economically. For the author of 1 Timothy this conception of godliness is a heresy, in that it does not follow the tradition of Jesus and the Hebrew Scriptures.

Going back to the wealthy in the Christian community of Ephesus, if godliness is a means of gain, then those who were rich would try to occupy spaces for leadership to obtain more power and status. We find, then, that there are struggles for power to occupy leadership positions in the Christian community.

As we have been able to observe, the position of the author is not a simple one. On the one hand, his radical attitude to women is disconcerting; on the other hand, we see an attractive position with regard to his critique of those who look for power because of their wealth and prestige. The rejection of controversy and disputes that oppose the simplicity of the words of the Gospel is also suggestive for our popular reading of the Bible. What is difficult to accept is the generalization of the exclusion of women, the assimilation of the values of the patriarchal household at the time of the Roman Empire, and the incapacity to enter into dialogue with new ideas.[30]

Elsa Tamez

---

30. Tamez, *Struggles for Power*, 24–25.

The godliness[31] that the author calls a "great gain" (1 Tim 6:6) has better benefits than the desire for materialistic acquisitions he ascribes to the opponents. He reminds the reader that, since we come into and go out of this world empty-handed (6:7), we ought to learn to be content with simple things, such as "food and clothing" (6:8). This verse evokes Jesus' teachings in Matt 6:25 and Luke 12:22 and also provides some specificity to the concept of "the sound words of our Lord Jesus Christ" (1 Tim 6:3). The effects of godliness and contentment extend beyond the present life since they allow people to avoid falling into temptation, "being trapped by many senseless and harmful desires," along with the final plunge into "ruin and destruction" (6:9; stated more positively in 4:8).

First Timothy 6:10 concludes the section with the well-known and powerful proverbial saying, "the love of money is a root of all kinds of evil." The King James Version of this verse has entered into many English-speaking cultures as "the love of money is *the* root of all evil." However, the Greek manuscripts do not have the definite article placed before the word ῥίζα ("root"). Similar hyperbolic statements about avarice are found in many philosophical sources, which may reveal our author's familiarity with that literature. Certainly he did not mean to argue that "love of money" is *the one cause* of every evil act. The NRSV translation rightly gives the sense of the vast power of greed without excluding other desires as sources of immorality.

Over the centuries, Christian thinkers have reflected on how to interpret this pithy saying within their own social locations. Some, like Augustine, Tertullian, and John Cassian, questioned the logic of this and other roots of vices, such as pride.[32] Others (Jerome, John Wesley, Pope Leo XIII) considered how the teaching might apply to believers who possess wealth,[33] a question the author also takes up later in this chapter. At the least, the declaration summons higher-status readers then and now to examine their relationship to and handling of money, and especially to ponder how this powerful entity influences their faith and actions.

31. See "Translation Matters: 'Godliness,'" p. 48.
32. Jay Twomey, *The Pastoral Epistles Through the Centuries* (Malden, MA: Wiley Blackwell, 2008), 97.
33. Ibid., 98–100.

[11]But as for you, man of God, shun all this; pursue righteousness, godliness, faith, love, endurance, gentleness. [12]Fight the good fight of the faith; take hold of the eternal life, to which you were called and for which you made the good confession in the presence of many witnesses. [13]In the presence of God, who gives life to all things, and of Christ Jesus, who in his testimony before Pontius Pilate made the good confession, I charge you [14]to keep the commandment without spot or blame until the manifestation of our Lord Jesus Christ, [15]which he will bring about at the right time—he who is the blessed and only Sovereign, the King of kings and Lord of lords. [16]It is he alone who has immortality and dwells in unapproachable light, whom no one has ever seen or can see; to him be honor and eternal dominion. Amen.

Suddenly shifting to a more direct address, the author speaks to Timothy as a "man of God" (1 Tim 6:11). The title serves to distinguish Timothy and other "men of God" from those in the previous section who are "teaching otherwise" and who exhibit avarice and other false desires and behaviors (6:3-10). The "man of God" ought to lead a different life, characterized by a list of virtues and progress toward morality (6:11-12). The author's serious intent is shown by his firm commands: "shun all this" (6:11), "pursue," "fight," "take hold" (6:12), followed by "I charge you" and the invoking of God and Christ Jesus as witnesses (6:13).

Since the content of 1 Tim 6:11-16 carries creedal and theological overtones, many interpreters believe they come from either a baptism or an ordination-type of setting. If drawn from a baptismal liturgy, the commands would apply to every believer, with Timothy simply standing in as a representative. Alternatively, Jouette M. Bassler argues for a connection to a ritual for commissioning church leaders:

> The epithet, "man of God" . . . is used in only one other place in the letters, where the "man of God" is assumed to be engaged in the tasks of teaching, reproof, correction, and training in righteousness (2 Tim 3:16-17). These, however, are the tasks of the church leaders, not the newly baptized Christian (2 Tim 2:24-25; Titus 1:9). . . .
>
> The origin of the title lies in the OT, where it refers to those engaged in special leadership roles in Israel: Moses (Deut 33:1), David (2 Chron 8:14), Samuel (1 Sam 9:6), and various prophets (1 Sam 2:27; 1 Kgs 13:1). In later usage, Philo of Alexandria refers to Israel's priests and prophets as "men of God." . . . (*Giants* 61; *Unchangeableness of God* 139). In the *Letter of Aristeas*, all Israelite men are called "men of God," yet they are given this title only insofar as they function as priests. . . . The persistent link . . . between this title and leadership roles in Israel strongly

suggests a similar link in 1 Timothy, which has a pervasive concern for qualified, orthodox leaders.[34]

Bassler also points to the solemn phrase "keep the commandment" (1 Tim 6:14), which sounds like other teachings to obey God's or Jesus' commandments found in the gospels and in John's letters. Here it seems to mean something more like "keep the *commission*," which indicates the "ordination charge" given to Timothy at his appointment.[35] The "good confession in the presence of many witnesses" would signify the statements he would have made at the ceremony (6:13).

It seems likely to me that Bassler is correct: these commands apply especially to the designated leaders who are divinely commissioned to their work and who are almost always male (although 1 Tim 3:11 has the ambiguous reference to women who might be deacons). Yet at the same time and throughout the letter, the author sets up these approved leaders as exemplary figures within the community, and this creates a problem. If, along with the historical Paul, Timothy, and all subsequent virtuous church officials—the *"men* of God"—are meant to be role models for "ordinary" believers, how can they be expected to act as examples for the *women* in the letters' audiences? Or, bluntly put: can a male apostle, overseer, or elder model faithful behavior for women? This question does not simply arise from modern feminist sensibilities; rather, it is a problematic situation perceived by the author himself, whose expectations of virtuous behavior are based on an ideological conviction that gender-differentiation results in distinct actions and roles for women and men. Since women are not allowed "to teach or to have authority over a man" (1 Tim 2:11-12), they can never perform the functions assigned to these male leaders. They cannot carry out Timothy's own ministry of "public reading of scripture," "exhorting," and" teaching" (4:13), and they will never receive "the gift" that Timothy received "through prophecy with the laying on of hands by the council of elders" (4:14). Today's reader of any gender might still be motivated to "pursue righteousness, godliness, faith, love, endurance, gentleness" (6:11), but our author implies that these possess a particular importance for the *"man* of God."

Echoing 1 Tim 1:17, a doxological "hymn" brings the section to a close (6:15-16). The descriptions of God arise from Roman political, philosophi-

---

34. Jouette M. Bassler, *1 Timothy, 2 Timothy, Titus,* ANTC (Nashville, TN: Abingdon, 1996), 113.
35. Ibid., 114.

[17] As for those who in the present age are rich, command them not to be haughty, or to set their hopes on the uncertainty of riches, but rather on God who richly provides us with everything for our enjoyment. [18]They are to do good, to be rich in good works, generous, and ready to share,[19]thus storing up for themselves the treasure of a good foundation for the future, so that they may take hold of the life that really is life.

cal, and Hellenistic Jewish contexts. For example, the title "Sovereign" (δυνάστης) was given to Zeus, while the emperor was call "lord" (κύριος). Rather than undermining a kyriarchal worldview, these strong monotheistic assertions place God in dominion over all idols and imperial rulers (6:15).[36] The assertion that only God is immortal, unapproachable, and invisible (6:16) places the Divine in a wholly different realm from all humankind, which could support a more egalitarian social order among humans. Yet our author has consistently endorsed hierarchical relationships in both civic and domestic settings.[37]

Having read the author's thorough critique of those adversaries who seek after wealth (1 Tim 6:5-10), we might imagine that he advocates for a "simple lifestyle," being content with owning just the basic necessities of life. However, he has already opposed an absolute asceticism (4:1-5), and he has indicated that there are rich people among the audience for his letters (women, 2:9-10; widows, 5:6; slaveholders, 6:2). Here, he gives teaching specifically for the rich, teaching that does not include divesting themselves of their possessions, unlike Jesus' words in response to the rich young man (Matt 19:16-30; Mark 10:17-31; Luke 18:18-30). Although wealth is an insecure and temporary thing (6:17), it is not evil in and of itself; rather, it is the "love of money" that leads one astray (6:10). The author appreciates personal riches as part of the good creation, given by God not just for subsistence living but to be enjoyed (6:17). The one who possesses riches ought to act just like this God who possesses "everything" by also giving and sharing abundantly (6:17-18).

The eighteenth-century English preacher John Wesley interprets 1 Tim 6:10 in light of 6:17-19: "'The love of money,' we know, 'is the root of all evil'; but not the thing itself. The fault does not lie in the money, but in

36. For further discussion about the patriarchal supremacy of God, see my comments on 1 Tim 2:1-7, pp. 10–13.

37. For example, 1 Tim 2:1-4, 11-14; 3:4-5, 12-13; 6:1-2.

them that use it. It may be used ill . . . but it likewise may be used well."[38] Wesley goes on to speak lyrically about the benefits of wealth: "in the present state of mankind, it [money] is an excellent gift of God, answering the noblest ends. In the hands of his children, it is food for the hungry, drink for the thirsty, raiment for the naked: It gives to the traveler and the stranger where to lay his head."[39] Yet Wesley knows that the teachings of 1 Tim 6 generated an ethical dilemma for rich believers for centuries after the letter was written. Stated bluntly, how much money may I legitimately keep for myself, and how much do I need to give away to others? Invoking the parable of the talents (Luke 19:12-27; Matt 25:14-30), Wesley outlines a practice of careful stewardship of God's resources, while stridently condemning anyone who gains wealth at the expense of one's own health or that of others. Another short excerpt gives the flavor of his sermon:

> We cannot, if we love everyone as ourselves, hurt anyone in his substance. . . . We cannot, consistent with brotherly love, sell our goods below the market price; we cannot study to ruin our neighbor's trade, in order to advance our own; much less can we entice away or receive any of his servants or workmen whom he has need of. None can gain by swallowing up his neighbor's substance, without gaining the damnation of hell!

This last sentence presents a harsh warning that is the complete opposite of the hopeful expectation of 1 Tim 6:19, where our author promises eternal rewards for generous wealthy believers. The stark contrast is due in part to differences in social location. The author of the Pastorals lived in a primarily static preindustrial, agricultural, and slave economy, whereas Wesley's powerful condemnation of unjust business practices emerges from his work during the Industrial Revolution in England. His perspective reflects a capitalist economy experiencing enormous technological and manufacturing changes, as well as the transformation of labor, working conditions, and urban migration. Since these upheavals continue to shape individual countries and the international economy to this day, the critiques of 1 Timothy by Wesley and, as discussed below, by the Rev. Dr. Martin Luther King Jr. provide a necessary correction to these more confident and even comfortable verses from the Pastorals.

About two hundred years after Wesley, Dr. King drew upon the teachings of 1 Tim 6 in order to rebuke another assemblage of believers.

38. John Wesley, "The Use of Money," Sermon 50; http://wesley.nnu.edu/john-wesley/the-sermons-of-john-wesley-1872-edition/sermon-50-the-use-of-money/.
39. Ibid. See also *Works* 6.126; cited in Twomey, *The Pastoral Epistles*, 99.

> ### Paul's Letter to American Christians: Excerpt from the Sermon Given at Dexter Avenue Baptist Church
>
> Montgomery, Alabama, November 4, 1956
>
> You have become the richest nation in the world, and you have built up the greatest system of production that history has ever known. All this is marvelous. But Americans, there is the danger that you will misuse your Capitalism. I still contend that money can be the root[40] of all evil. It can cause one to live a life of gross materialism. I am afraid that many among you are more concerned about making a living than making a life. You are prone to judge the success of your profession by the index of your salary and the size of the wheel base on your automobile, rather than the quality of your service to humanity.
>
> The misuse of capitalism can also lead to tragic exploitation. This has so often happened in your nation. They tell me that one-tenth of one percent of the population controls more than forty percent of the wealth.[41] Oh, America, how often have you taken necessities from the masses to give luxuries to the classes? . . . But you can work within the framework of democracy to bring about a better distribution of wealth. You can use your powerful economic resources to wipe poverty from the face of the earth. God never intended for a group of people to live in superfluous, inordinate wealth while others live in abject, deadening poverty. God intends for all of His children to have the basic necessities of life, and He has left in this universe enough and to spare for that purpose. So I call upon you to bridge the gulf between abject poverty and superfluous wealth.[42]
>
> *Martin Luther King Jr.*

40. Like John Wesley, Martin Luther King Jr. quotes from the KJV of 1 Tim 6:10: "the love of money is *the* root of all evil." The Greek lacks this definite article.

41. Unfortunately, these numbers have changed for the worse since Dr. King's sermon was preached in the 1960s. According to a September 2014 article in the *Wall Street Journal*, based on findings of the US government, "The top 3% held 54.4% of all wealth in 2013, up from 44.8% in 1989. The bottom 90% held 24.7% of wealth last year, down from 33.2% in 1989." Ben Leubsdorf, "Fed: Gap Between Rich, Poor Americans Widened During Recovery," *Wall Street Journal* (September 4, 2014); http://www.wsj.com/articles/fed-gap-between-rich-poor-americans-widened-during-recovery-1409853628.

42. According to the Martin Luther King Jr. Papers Project (Stanford University), this sermon was first preached by Dr. King at the seventy-sixth annual meeting of the National Baptist Conference in Denver in September 1956. See Martin Luther King Jr., "Paul's Letter to American Christians: Sermon Delivered to the Commission on Ecumenical Mission and Relations, United Presbyterian Church, U.S.A.," *Martin Luther King Jr. Papers Project* (Palo Alto, CA: Martin Luther King Research and Education Institute, Stanford University), https://swap.stanford.edu/20141218225624/http://

1 Tim 6:20-21

20 Timothy, guard what has been entrusted to you. Avoid the profane chatter and contradictions of what is falsely called knowledge; 21by profess-ing it some have missed the mark as regards the faith.

Grace be with you.

TRANSLATION MATTERS: "WHAT HAS BEEN ENTRUSTED"

By this phrase, the NRSV translates a single Greek word, παραθήκη, which more simply means "deposit," or, in Roman legal terms, "property entrusted to another." The noun is related to the verb παρατίθημι, which means "I hand over/give over/commend/entrust." In usual circumstances, such a deposit is still the property of the owner and could be retrieved from the "guardian" at any time. It is unclear whether the author is suggesting that "Paul," as the "property owner," might come again to Ephesus, although Paul does promise to return in 1 Tim 3:14-15.

The NRSV translation expresses the idea that Timothy is the "loyal" (1 Tim 1:2) and duly appointed (4:14) trusted recipient. But it fails to convey that the "deposit" is a substantial and valuable piece of property, which the author seems to understand to be Paul's *correct* teaching of the gospel.

First Timothy closes suddenly with another direct address to Timothy (6:11; see also 1:18) and in only two verses. We may safely assume that the author is mentioning his most important theme: that Timothy is Paul's authorized successor and has been entrusted with the "sound teaching." This *true* teaching is contrasted again with "what is falsely called knowledge," which is characterized by meaningless speech and "leads away from faith" (6:20-21). Since the final farewell is extremely brief (four words in both Greek and English), the end of the letter reemphasizes the persons of both "Paul" and "Timothy." These esteemed male church leaders remain conspicuously present to the reader, and that literary and canonical presence serves to authorize the many men who succeeded them for millennia.

mlk-kpp01.stanford.edu/primarydocuments/Vol6/3June1958Paul'sLetterto AmericanChristinas,SermonDeliveredtotheCommissiononEcumenicalMissions andRelations,UnitedPresbyterianChurch,USA.pdf.

The text of the sermon given at Dexter Avenue Baptist Church, Montgomery, Alabama, on November 4, 1956, can be read at http://www.thekingcenter.org/archive/document/pauls-letter-american-christians-0#. I am grateful to Jay Twomey, whose shorter quotes from the sermon in *The Pastoral Epistles Through the Ages* (99) led me to read the entire text.

2 Timothy 1

A Letter from "Father" to "Son"

Reading through the Second Letter to Timothy, we encounter an emotion-laden text that depicts a warm, longstanding, and quasi-familial relationship between the older Paul and the younger Timothy. The letter says that it was written by Paul[1] during his imprisonment in Rome (2 Tim 1:14-17), and, by reminiscing about Paul's experiences (1:15-18; 3:10-11; 4:10-14, 16, 19-21), the author suggests that the apostle is nearing the end of his life (1:12; 2:10-11; 4:6-8). Thus, the numerous commands given to Timothy convey the notion that "Paul" is writing one last set of reminders to his approved successor before he dies.

This letter falls into the category of "testamentary" literature—writing that expresses a person's last and best hopes and wishes for his family—which is found in both ancient and modern cultures. From the ancient world we have Jewish apocryphal works like the Testaments of the Three Patriarchs, of Job, and of the Twelve Patriarchs, that were perhaps inspired by the blessings given by Jacob to his sons in Gen 49. The American novel *Gilead* by Marilynne Robinson[2] is written as a letter

---

1. See my comments on the pseudonymous nature of the Pastorals in the introduction (pp. xlv–xlvii) and in 1 Tim 1 (pp. 1–3).
2. Marilynne Robinson, *Gilead* (New York: Farrar, Straus and Giroux, 2004).

from an ailing seventy-six-year-old pastor who believes he will not live long enough to pass on his life story and his wisdom to his seven-year-old son. In a powerful letter-memoir, *Between the World and Me*, Ta-Nehisi Coates writes an impassioned and challenging letter to his teenage son about America's long racial history, seeking to answer "the question of how one should live within a black body" within this country.[3] Second Timothy exhibits the personal tone and urgent instructions common to this kind of writing.

Yet this letter is not simply a private communication between the two men who were known to have worked together for decades. It was written and subsequently included in the New Testament canon because of its usefulness in at least three areas.

First, believers have found the letter's instructions applicable to their own faithful lives; there are several references to "we" and "us" (2 Tim 1:7, 9, 14; 2:11-13) that recognize the presence of a community—more than just the single recipient Timothy. That the author was reaching out beyond Timothy in order to address a broader audience is confirmed by the very last Greek word in the letter, ὑμῶν, a second-person plural "you all" (4:22).

Second, the letter's message authenticates the church supervisory functions of Timothy and all those men who, like him, continued to follow the true teachings and moral customs of Paul. The impassioned pleas of the near-death apostle emphasize his close relationship to Timothy, and through him to all other successors, so that the letter stands as one of the first pieces of explicit evidence that supports the church practice known as apostolic succession. This epistolary authorization of male leaders in the early church resulted in unjust restrictions on women's leadership roles, prohibitions that continue in many domestic and ecclesiastical arenas today.

Finally, this letter appears to be the "last word" of Paul, which makes it a very important document for the many communities founded and written to by that apostle. If we knew the author's original arrangement of the three Pastoral Letters, we would have some idea as to the order in which he intended for them to be read. However, as Paul's supposed "last word," 2 Timothy already carries a great deal of authority as a teaching text. When the author adopted the form of a "last word," he

---

3. Ta-Nehisi Coates, *Between the World and Me* (New York: Spiegel & Grau, 2015), 12.

2 Tim 1:1-5

¹Paul, an apostle of Christ Jesus by the will of God, for the sake of the promise of life that is in Christ Jesus, ²To Timothy, my beloved child: Grace, mercy, and peace from God the Father and Christ Jesus our Lord. ³I am grateful to God—whom I worship with a clear conscience, as my ancestors did—when I remember you constantly in my prayers night and day. ⁴Recalling your tears, I long to see you so that I may be filled with joy. ⁵I am reminded of your sincere faith, a faith that lived first in your grandmother Lois and your mother Eunice and now, I am sure, lives in you.

also made it possible for this letter, along with 1 Timothy and Titus, to be accepted as Pauline creations. In fact, the "finality" of 2 Timothy serves to position it as the capstone for *all* of the thirteen letters attributed to Paul in the NT, not just for 1 Timothy and Titus, as if it were a guarantee for the entire Pauline canonical collection.

The first two verses of 2 Timothy are similar to but longer than the opening of 1 Timothy. Here Timothy is called "my *beloved* child" (2 Tim 1:2), rather than "my *loyal* child" (1 Tim 1:2), a change that signals the affectionate relationship between the two men. Paul's fond feeling for Timothy continues through the next three verses, where the author describes his constant prayers, his longing and joy alongside Timothy's tears, his sincere faith, and his maternal forebears.

By referring to family members—"my beloved child," "my ancestors," "your grandmother," and "your mother"—the author points out that the faith is handed down through the generations. Paul's faith is derived from his ancestors just as Timothy's comes from the two older women in his life. The author sketches a scenario of Timothy's faith development: Timothy's biological father is not mentioned, perhaps due to the story that he was not a believer, as told in Acts 16:1. Instead, Paul now serves as Timothy's "father in the faith." It seems that grandmother Lois and mother Eunice acted as the faithful teachers and role models for Timothy while he was very young, a function that does not violate the author's prohibition on women teaching (1 Tim 2:12). In fact, the nurture of infants and young children was considered to be the responsibility of their mothers and nurses. However, as Timothy grew to manhood, it was the apostle himself who properly took over the mission of his moral and theological education. Their father-son relationship intensified through

[6]For this reason I remind you to rekindle the gift of God that is within you through the laying on of my hands; [7]for God did not give us a spirit of cowardice, but rather a spirit of power and of love and of self-discipline.

[8]Do not be ashamed, then, of the testimony about our Lord or of me his prisoner, but join with me in suffering for the gospel, relying on the power of God, [9]who saved us and called us with a holy calling, not according to our works but according to his own purpose and grace. This grace was given to us in Christ Jesus before the ages began, [10]but it has now been revealed through the appearing of our Savior Christ Jesus, who abolished death and brought life and immortality to light through the gospel. [11]For this gospel I was appointed a herald and an apostle and a teacher, [12]and for this reason I suffer as I do. But I am not ashamed, for I know the one in whom I have put my trust, and I am sure that he is able to guard until that day what I have entrusted to him. [13]Hold to the standard of sound teaching that you have heard from me, in the faith and love that are in Christ Jesus. [14]Guard the good treasure entrusted to you, with the help of the Holy Spirit living in us.

their work together of founding and caring for the churches,[4] so that nearing the end of his life, "Paul" conveys his farewell teachings to his son Timothy. Paul's "fathering" of Timothy has eclipsed the earlier activities of Lois and Eunice because it is he who has prepared Timothy for the highest levels of church supervision.

The main point of this section is for "Paul" to encourage "Timothy" to progress in the work given by God through the imposition of *Paul's* hands. It is unclear why the author says differently in 1 Tim 4:14 that the "gift" was given to Timothy through prophecy and the hands of elders. The genre of this letter leads to a supposed greater emphasis on Paul's role and influence in Timothy's life.

Certainly in this passage Paul is established as the prime model for his successor. *His* hands conveyed the gift of God, who appointed *him* to the threefold positions of "herald and apostle and teacher" (2 Tim 1:11). *His* presentation of the gospel is called "the standard of sound teaching" (1:13). In addition, Paul's experiences of suffering and his theological rationale to endure them in a courageous manner, without

---

4. See my comments on Paul's fatherly relationship to this "child" of his in 1 Tim 1 (p. 2).

shame, and in "a spirit of power and of love and of self-discipline" (1:7-8, 12) provide a notable example for Timothy, subsequent church leaders, and all other believers. The author portrays Paul as supremely confident in the power of a trustworthy God (1:8, 12), a gracious God who saves, calls, and acts with purpose (1:9). The divine purpose was eternally present in Christ Jesus (1:9, suggesting the idea of the preexistence of Christ) and has now been revealed through his "appearing" (1:10). Although it is the Christ who abolishes death and brings life and immortality (1:10), the earthly sufferings, crucifixion, and resurrection of Jesus are not explicitly mentioned here as a pattern for believers to follow. We read instead about *Paul's* exemplary grace under pressure, and Timothy is invited to "join" with *him* in suffering for the Gospel (1:8).

On the one hand, such encouragement to suffer with courage, love, and faith in God's power is a supportive message for peacemakers and justice advocates because it likens their actions to the divine acts of life-giving salvation. People dealing with chronic physical pain, broken relationships, or economic hardship might benefit from remembering Paul's assurances of the purposes of the God of grace and the human dignity Paul displayed while he was imprisoned and otherwise afflicted.

On the other hand, a tension around gender arises in these verses due to their social location in the Greco-Roman culture. Because the written advice comes from a supposed male author and is given to a male subordinate, the concepts of "cowardice," "power," "self-discipline," and "shame" need to be understood in light of ancient conventions about masculinity and femininity.[5] A foundational belief about gender was that a female was a "defective" male, so that any "feminine" characteristics displayed by a man showed him to be less than an ideal male. Philosophers, satirists, and historians severely critiqued men who cared too much about their personal appearances (too much oil in the hair, certain perfumes, or excessive jewelry), as well as those with high-pitched voices, mincing gaits, and unfounded anxieties. Men who did not practice self-control over angry outbursts, drunkenness, or gossipy speech were also accused of being effeminate. Such accusations were meant to shame them into better, that is, more manly, behavior. A man ought to be marked by appropriate self-assurance in public and private arenas, being not overly boastful but not shrinking back either. Throughout 2 Timothy, the author depicts Paul as a manly man; here he is boldly

---

5. The topic of masculinity in the Pastorals is addressed further in 1 Tim 2 (pp. 14–15).

confident in his proclamation of the gospel, brave in suffering, self-disciplined in his emotions, and therefore unashamed of his predicament. In addition, Paul urges Timothy to become what he is: a model of Christian manhood.

In the Imperial Era, it was thought that since women could not "escape" the features of their own bodies they could not be expected to live up to specifically masculine ideals. While a well-behaved woman—the wife or daughter of a free man—also ought to avoid displays of anger, intoxication, gossip, other loose speech, and excessive adornment (exotic jewels, make-up, and hairstyles), the ultimate moral objective for her was to remain discreetly in the background.[6] When going out to the agora, an activity that should not have been undertaken very often and preferably not when it was dark, she should have dressed modestly and spoken quietly, being accompanied by a chaperone (often a slave). If a wife behaved otherwise, then she opened herself, her husband, and her entire household to public shame. The stereotypical prescriptions for inconspicuous feminine demeanor stands in sharp contrast to the expectations for the poised and assertive men.

The effect of these cultural gender stereotypes is that when "Paul" tells "Timothy" not to be ashamed (1 Tim 1:8), then Timothy, like Paul, is supposed to stand strong when suffering and to speak boldly when testifying or teaching. The more modern commands "Be a man!" or "Man up!"[7] succinctly capture the gender-specificity of these verses. Since the discourse in 2 Timothy is based on such presumed sexual differentiation, the text pushes us to interpret the teachings from our own identity as either identified male or female. In his social location, the author does not grasp the existence of transgendered, gender-bending persons, or differently sexed bodies.

When we suggest that a male reader ought to adopt this teaching, then we find ourselves endorsing historical patriarchal expectations for male behavior in Western societies. Men ought not to show emotions, especially the "weaker" emotions such as fear, sadness, and confusion; they need, rather, to be bold, assertive, and strong. Even today parents of infant and toddler boys shame them for displaying normal human feelings, warning them, "Big boys don't cry." Other labels are applied to young males who lack athletic skill ("you throw like a girl"), who are

6. See "Translation Matters: 'Virtues for Women,'" p. 16.

7. Such commands are reminiscent of the author's address in 1 Tim 6:11: "But as for you, man of God!" Refer back to 1 Tim 6 (pp. 91–92) for my comments on limiting church teaching roles to men only.

not adept with machinery ("klutzes"), or who immerse themselves in intellectual pursuits ("nerds"). Epithets like "sissy," "fag," and "homo" are used to humiliate boys and men whose gestures, demeanor, and interests lie outside the restrictive stereotypes of manhood. Note that the main goal is still for males to avoid any behavior or characteristics associated with the "feminine."

Then too, how should a *female* reader apply this text to herself and her own difficult experiences? The author has put her in a quandary because he has given her conflicting advice about faithfulness. Should she, as the self-effacing woman of 1 Tim 2, bear her sufferings privately and quietly without histrionics or public displays? Then what of this example of Paul's confident endurance in the face of persecution and daily struggles? Would she be allowed to behave in ways that seem more masculine, publicly proclaiming her faith in word and action? In fact, beginning in the second century, we hear reports of persecuted Christian women who did indeed model their faithful courage after that of Paul, among them Thecla in Asia Minor, Perpetua and Felicitas in Carthage, and Blandina in Lyons. These women were noted for becoming man-like: Thecla donned a man's cloak; Perpetua miraculously "became a man" when she wrestled an Egyptian in the arena; and when tortured, Blandina "put on Christ, that mighty and invincible athlete."[8] Around 200 CE, Clement of Alexandria asserted that since women are human beings too, they could, like men, exhibit the virtue of supreme self-control.[9] In these ways female believers could live (and die) above their weaker sex, achieving the "higher standard" of godly masculinity.

Such tensions about appropriately gendered behavior—how to act as a truly good man or woman—persist in the Pastorals and other early Christian literature. Clement vacillates between an admiring defense of confident, strong women martyrs and his need to maintain that there is "some difference" between male and female. For him it seems that "biology is destiny" when he writes, "as there is difference as respects the peculiar construction of the body, she is destined for child-bearing and housekeeping."[10] His opinions about women's proper domestic roles are in complete agreement with those of the Pastorals.

8. *Acts of Paul and Thecla* 40; *Martyrdom of Perpetua and Felicitas* 3.2; *Letter from Vienne and Lyons.* These texts may be found online at https://cse.google.com.

9. Clement of Alexandria, "Women as Well as Men, Slaves as Well as Freemen, Candidates for the Martyr's Crown," *Stromata* 4.8.

10. Ibid.

2 Tim 1:15-18

¹⁵You are aware that all who are in Asia have turned away from me, including Phygelus and Hermogenes. ¹⁶May the Lord grant mercy to the household of Onesiphorus, because he often refreshed me and was not ashamed of my chain; ¹⁷when he ar-rived in Rome, he eagerly searched for me and found me ¹⁸—may the Lord grant that he will find mercy from the Lord on that day! And you know very well how much service he rendered in Ephesus.

In the last four verses of this chapter the author provides examples of other male believers who have either shown their shame over Paul or have stepped up boldly to honor Paul in his suffering. According to the fiction of the letter, Timothy is in the major city of Ephesus in the Roman province of Asia, so he is already "aware" of many people who have abandoned Paul. Presumably, Timothy and/or others in the author's audience know about Phygelus and Hermogenes, names that are not mentioned in the rest of the New Testament. The actions of these two men exemplify the entirely wrong response to Paul and his afflictions: by steering clear of him they have displayed shameful unmasculine behavior. In contrast, Onesiphorus actively looked for Paul in Rome and was "not ashamed" of his imprisonment (2 Tim 1:16-17). His confident masculine actions and concrete assistance to Paul and the Ephesian church (1:18) result in honor for him *and* for his household. Paul envisions that this honor comes in the form of the Lord's mercy in the present (1:16) and in the future (1:17).

By putting forward both honorable and shameful examples, the author paints a sharp disparity between those men who love Paul and those who shun him. His goal is for his audience to reject the behavior of Phygelus and Hermogenes and align themselves with the beliefs and works of Onesiphorus. Once again, among his original audience, male readers would have a clear picture of how they need to conduct themselves: they should hold to Paul's gospel message, especially the teachings in the Pastorals, and provide whatever assistance is needed to those who suffer for that gospel. It would be to their shame if they did not act in accordance with this masculine ideal, and the author wants to motivate them to avoid shame at all costs.

Our author clearly intends that his female readers will function only within the domestic feminine confines of marriage, childbearing, and household supervision (1 Tim 5:14; Titus 2:4-5). Yet stories of Christian women from its earliest times remind us that at least a few of them made unconventional life-choices beginning in the Roman Imperial Era. The martyr Perpetua is one example. She was imprisoned for her testimony of belief in Christ (ca. 202 CE), and her infant son was brought to her so that she could continue nursing him. When she was condemned to fight in the gladiatorial arena in Carthage, her father repeatedly begged her to renounce the faith so that her son would not be orphaned. She instead handed her son over to her father, renouncing the role of mother. Miraculously, her breast milk dried up, a sign, she thought, that God approved of her decision.[11] Granted, this situation is a far cry from women who work in the boardrooms of multinational corporations, but Perpetua's story exemplifies the persistent influence of the tensions around gender ideology that we find in the Pastorals.

11. *Martyrdom of Perpetua and Felicitas* 2.2.

2 Timothy 2

Manly Men

The chapter break between 2 Tim 1 and 2 does not indicate a distinct change in the topic, which continues to concentrate on the ideals of masculinity. The break signals instead a shift in "Paul's" focus: he turns from discussing his own situation and the help of the excellent Onesiphorus to addressing "Timothy" directly, giving him additional examples of how the younger man ought to behave. As before, there are good masculine examples to follow that will bring the honorable reward of salvation and bad ones to avoid that result in shameful infirmity and ruinous strife.

Re-emphasizing the father-son relationship between the two men ("my child"), the command in 2 Tim 2:1 upholds the masculine standard of strength-under-pressure. Verse 2 sketches the legitimate lineage of Paul the teacher: he taught Timothy, who now ought to teach other men, who will in turn continue to teach Paul's teaching.[1] The Mishnaic text, *Pirkei Avot* 1, describes a similar but much longer process of the patrilineal transmission of authorized teachings, beginning with Moses and proceeding through Joshua, the elders, the prophets, and "the men of the

---

1. The verb translated "entrust" (παρατίθημι) is related to the legal vocabulary of "deposit" found in 1 Tim 6:20 and 2 Tim 1:12, 14. See above, "Translation Matters: 'What Has Been Entrusted,'" p. 96.

¹You then, my child, be strong in the grace that is in Christ Jesus; ²and what you have heard from me through many witnesses entrust to faithful people who will be able to teach others as well. ³Share in suffering like a good soldier of Christ Jesus. ⁴No one serving in the army gets entangled in everyday affairs; the soldier's aim is to please the enlisting officer. ⁵And in the case of an athlete, no one is crowned without competing according to the rules. ⁶It is the farmer who does the work who ought to have the first share of the crops. ⁷Think over what I say, for the Lord will give you understanding in all things.

⁸Remember Jesus Christ, raised from the dead, a descendant of David— that is my gospel, ⁹for which I suffer hardship, even to the point of being chained like a criminal. But the word of God is not chained. ¹⁰Therefore I endure everything for the sake of the elect, so that they may also obtain the salvation that is in Christ Jesus, with eternal glory. ¹¹The saying is sure:

If we have died with him, we will
    also live with him;
¹²if we endure, we will also reign
    with him;
if we deny him, he will also deny
    us;
¹³if we are faithless, he remains
    faithful—
for he cannot deny himself.

great assembly." Later teachers are named as passing on the tradition down to Rabbi Shimon (first century CE), the son of Gamaliel. This is the kind of process of transmission of Paul's teachings envisioned within the Pastorals. Although the author does not name any male teacher except for Paul and Timothy—and, of course, we do not even know his own name—he certainly thinks of himself in reality as standing in an early and authoritative position of reception. One other difference between *Pirkei Avot* and 2 Timothy is that the rabbinic text tends to portray the lineage as a straight line, moving from one generation to another. The New Testament image is more like a tree, with Paul and Timothy near the roots and the trunk and other male church leaders representing different branches. What should not be forgotten is that in both texts these valuable teachings are inherited, passed along, and preserved by men, but not women.

Three male characters—soldier, athlete, and farmer—are set up as models for Timothy to follow. These also appear in 1 Corinthians, a letter known to be written by Paul himself: the soldier (1 Cor 9:7; also, Phlm 2); the athlete (1 Cor 9:24-27); and the agricultural worker (1 Cor 3:6-8; 9:7, 10). The soldier appears to represent endurance of rough conditions as well as the single-minded devotion that a "good soldier of Christ"

TRANSLATION MATTERS: "TO FAITHFUL PEOPLE"

In an effort to use more inclusive language for humans, the NRSV has chosen the translation "to faithful people" for the Greek πιστοῖς ἀνθρώποις in 2 Tim 2:2. Although the plural word may often mean "people/persons/human beings," in this case a more accurate translation of the phrase is "to faithful men." The NRSV's worthy goal of avoiding exclusive terms obscures the fact that, for the Pastorals, teaching as Paul did is a men-only profession. Women have been prohibited from the teaching (1 Tim 2:12), with the small exception that older women ought to teach younger women how to fulfill their household roles (Titus 2:3-5).[2]

ought to display. The athlete understands the self-discipline that is required for him to win a contest. And the farmer's hard work results in the reward of his produce. As I. Howard Marshall remarks, all three "indicate the need for commitment and readiness for acceptance of a demanding way of life by *the Christian leader*."[3] The words I have italicized at the end of Marshall's statement remind us that the soldier, athlete, and farmer symbolize ancient standards of masculinity: self-control, endurance of suffering, and even acceptance of proper authority. In the logic of this letter, the good "Christian leader" who embodies these ideals will, not surprisingly, be a man.

"Paul" continues to remind "Timothy" of things that he already knows, such as the two short creedal statements about Jesus Christ that were central pieces of Paul's proclamation of the gospel: he was raised from the dead and a descendant of David (2 Tim 2:8). Although Jesus' suffering and crucifixion are not explicitly mentioned, the author has implied that Jesus serves as an example of how to endure such trials (2:3). The memory of Paul himself "being chained like a criminal" (2:9) functions as a more vivid and present image for Timothy to imitate, and somehow undergoing that kind of suffering has a positive, even salvific, influence on God's people (2:10).

2. See also my comments on the authorization of male leaders at the beginning of 2 Tim 1 (p. 98).

3. I. Howard Marshall, *The Pastoral Epistles*, ICC (Edinburgh: T & T Clark, 1999), 728.

TRANSLATION MATTERS: "HIM"

In the parallel lines of 2 Tim 2:11-12, the NRSV and many other translations added the word "him" four times where it does not appear in the Greek. A more literal translation is: "If we have died with, we will also live with; if we endure, we will also reign with; if we deny, he will also deny us." Since this is poetic, and poetry often omits words for reasons of meter, sound, and mood, the NRSV is not necessarily wrong to insert the object "him" after the verbs, so that readers understand that the author is referring back to Christ Jesus (2:10).

However, in her comments on these verses, Jouette Bassler suggests the author may be expressing yet another image: "Without the pronoun, the text resembles a formula of friendship or loyalty. . . . Such a formula admirably fits the situation envisioned in this letter—the encouragement of Timothy to join Paul in 'dying,' that is, in suffering, for the gospel."[4] I find Bassler's idea compelling, because I can easily believe that the author intended for "suffering with" to point toward *both* Paul and Christ as examples for the youthful Timothy.

This section closes with a hymn-like affirmation that is introduced by the Pastorals' familiar phrase: "the saying is sure" (2 Tim 2:11a).[5] The affirmation consists of four short conditional statements (2:11b-13). The first two promise rewards for those who are faithful through suffering and death, while the third statement warns of a negative outcome for those who "deny." The fourth (2:13) is more complex, both grammatically and theologically. The faith*less*ness of people is contrasted with the faith*ful*ness of Christ Jesus, to which our author has added the explanation that the very nature of the Christ is always faithful.

In 2 Tim 2:11-13, it sounds as if the author has adapted lines from an early baptismal liturgy, in part because this section so closely follows Paul's reasoning about baptism, especially as explained in Rom 6:8. The repeated references to "we" indicate that 2 Timothy has a larger collective in mind, and we might assume this is the community of female and male believers. Yet the immediate context of naming of Timothy as "Paul's" child (2 Tim 2:1), along with the specific instructions to Timothy alone (2:1-3, 7-8, 14-16), once again make it difficult to discern what specific audience is being addressed.[6] The overall genre of this letter as

4. Jouette Bassler, *1 Timothy, 2 Timothy, and Titus*, ANTC (Nashville, TN: Abingdon, 1996), 145.

5. See "Translation Matters: 'The Saying Is Sure,'" p. 29.

6. See my comments on the relationship between Paul and Timothy on 2 Tim 1, pp. 97–100.

14 Remind them of this, and warn them before God that they are to avoid wrangling over words, which does no good but only ruins those who are listening. 15Do your best to present yourself to God as one approved by him, a worker who has no need to be ashamed, rightly explaining the word of truth. 16Avoid profane chatter, for it will lead people into more and more impiety, 17and their talk will spread like gangrene. Among them are Hymenaeus and Philetus, 18who have swerved from the truth by claiming that the resurrection has already taken place. They are upsetting the faith of some. 19But God's firm foundation stands, bearing this inscription: "The Lord knows those who are his," and, "Let everyone who calls on the name of the Lord turn away from wickedness."
20In a large house there are utensils not only of gold and silver but also of wood and clay, some for special use, some for ordinary. 21All who cleanse themselves of the things I have mentioned will become special utensils, dedicated and useful to the owner of the house, ready for every good work. 22Shun youthful passions and pursue righteousness, faith, love, and peace, along with those who call on the Lord from a pure heart. 23Have nothing to do with stupid and senseless controversies; you know that they breed quarrels. 24And the Lord's servant must not be quarrelsome but kindly to everyone, an apt teacher, patient, 25correcting opponents with gentleness. God may perhaps grant that they will repent and come to know the truth, 26and that they may escape from the snare of the devil, having been held captive by him to do his will.

a piece of testamentary literature seems to restrict the audience to those true heirs of Paul's gospel, whom the author has just described as "faithful men who will be able to teach others" (2:2). Bassler reminds us that in this chapter it is the "suffering of Paul and Timothy as church leaders that occupies [the author's] attention here, not their suffering as baptized Christians."[7] In that case, the creedal statement would have a more limited application, especially for the men who are supervising the community, and would therefore be less relevant to the lives of faithful women, or to the majority of male believers who are not leaders.[8]

7. Bassler, 1 Timothy, 2 Timothy, Titus, 148.
8. For more discussion of the audience for these teachings, see "Translation Matters: 'Them,'" p. 111.

TRANSLATION MATTERS: "THEM"

In 2 Tim 2:14, the pronoun "them" is only implied in the Greek and has been added by the translators in order to make better sense of the command "remind." This decision sharpens the interpretive question: to whom, exactly, is Timothy supposed to direct his reminders? I believe the author is looking back all the way to 2:2, to the "faithful *men* who will be able to teach others." But if one depends on the NRSV translation of that verse as "faithful *people*" then the whole community—male and female—is intended, which is quite often the way this command has been interpreted. While the author certainly wants all believers to "avoid wrangling over words," the wider context leads me to conclude that he is writing these commands expressly to the male leaders, Timothy included. Other evidence for this conclusion comes from the fact that the author claims that the reason "they" ought to avoid arguing is that it "only ruins those who are listening." We already know that one significant group of listeners is women, who are supposed "to learn in silence" (1 Tim 2:11) and "not to teach" (2:12). Therefore, these commands in 2 Tim 2:14-16 are given specifically to the faithful male teachers.

The NRSV translation presents these verses as two paragraphs, but because one specific issue recurs in both sections I have chosen to comment on them as one section. The recurring issue is that of proper speech (2 Tim 2:14-18, 23-24) and, in particular, proper *masculine* speech. As we have already seen, the author's advice appears in dualistic statements: some speech-acts are "good" and lead to positive rewards, while some are "bad," resulting in negative outcomes. He makes these value judgments based on his perception of what makes a man truly masculine. When he gives "Timothy" moral examples to follow and immoral examples to reject, the author relies on the acculturated responses from his audience: that they will be attracted to the "good" kind of manly behavior and disgusted by the "bad."

Jennifer A. Glancy's discussion, "Protocols of Masculinity," sketches out the Pastorals' teachings about the gendered manner and content of proper speaking, a topic the author returns to again and again. In 2 Tim 2:14-18, 23-25, he teaches about appropriately masculine speech, which, above all, ought not to be effeminate.

Protocols of Masculinity

In the Pastoral Epistles, we find a specification of what constitutes legitimate masculinity, ranging from the valorization of self-control as the epitome of virtue to an insistence that Christian men should exert a controlling influence over their wives and offspring. The Pastoral Epistles serve as a Christian hornbook of masculine propriety.

One strand of advice in the Pastor's writing suggests strongly that he is writing defensively, that is, that persons with opposing outlooks have become influential in the very circles over which he seeks (or seeks to maintain) influence. In his admonitions against these opponents, the Pastor focuses repeatedly on the character of their speech. He expresses a particular concern with those who insinuate themselves into other men's households and, through their words, enthrall the women of those households [2 Tim 3:6-7]. The Pastor delivers his straitlaced advice in order to undermine the authority of men whose seductive speech he views as symptomatic of their deviance from gender norms. The specter of men who violated conservative imperial gender norms threatened the Pastor's sense of order and excited his desire not only to control his own masculine self but also to define, more generally, a proper self for Christian men.

What clues do the Pastoral Epistles provide concerning the identity of those the Pastor views as agitators? Idle or frivolous talkers (*mataiologoi*), they disrupt entire households (Titus 1:10-11). At the same time, they do not understand what they are talking about (1 Tim 1:6-7). Their speech is empty sound (*kenophōnia*), their word a contagious disease (2 Tim 2:16-17). They spread "profane myths and old wives' tales," against which the Pastor urges Timothy to inoculate himself by a manly regimen of training himself for godliness (1 Tim 4:7-8). The Pastor sounds the same note repeatedly, warning Timothy to turn aside from "profane chatter [*bebēlous kenophōnias*] and the contradictions of what is falsely called knowledge" (1 Tim 6:20).

It was widely believed that a person's speech, delivery as much as content, conveyed his or her character. Quintilian asserted, "As a man lives, so he speaks" (Connolly, 132). The supposed babbling of women and slaves, for example, was at once a foil and a trap for free men whose rhetorical self-presentation often came dangerously close to employing the manipulative strategies associated with females and servile males.

The Pastor's invective against his enemies focuses precisely on their patterns of speech, insinuating that they use hollow, foolish, and ultimately effeminate modes of discourse to seduce women away from their proper roles and to corrupt young men such as Timothy. The setting of the Pastoral Epistles in a cultural milieu of contested masculinity inclines me to hear the Pastor's warnings as expressions of anxiety about the posture of masculinity proper for Christian men.

We can attach names to the characters whose speech the Pastor derides as weak and, by extension, womanish: Hymenaeus and Philetus [in 2 Tim 2:16-18]. The Pastor relies on vocabulary of disease to characterize his opponents' speech and thereby to dismiss their authority. While the Pastor expresses repugnance for what they represent, others in the community, notably certain women [2 Tim 3:6-7], find this rival's message more compelling than that articulated by the Pastor.[9]

Jennifer A. Glancy

Second Timothy 2:14-19 is dominated by warnings about unmasculine speech, which the author calls "wrangling over words" (2:14) and "profane chatter" (2:16). The wrong kind of talk will lead to ruin, impiety, and upsetting the faith of some listeners (2:14, 16, 18), and it will even spread infectiously like gangrene (2:17). Two men, Hymenaeus and Philetus, are named as contributing to such heretical teaching (2:17-18). Other than the assertion that the two men claim that "the resurrection has already taken place" (2:18), we learn nothing about the content of their heretical speech. The author describes their teachings more colorfully as "stupid and senseless controversies" that can be recognized because "they breed quarrels" (2:23).

In addition to avoiding *unacceptable* speech, Timothy and the other men in charge ought to apply themselves to *correct* ways of speaking. Verse 15 contains a brief positive description of proper speech as "rightly explaining the word of truth," which appears to refer to the teaching function of those designated leaders. We can also infer from two verses that another correct way of speaking is to "*call* on the name of the Lord/the Lord" (2:19, 22).

The good and bad kinds of speech are exemplified in the image of utensils found in a wealthy household (2 Tim 2:20-21). The idea that some are for special (literally, "honorable") use and some for ordinary (literally, "dishonorable") use evokes Paul's examples of honored and dishonored parts of the body in 1 Cor 12:22-25. Yet the author of 2 Timothy turns the

9. Jennifer A. Glancy, "Protocols of Masculinity in the Pastoral Epistles," in *New Testament Masculinities*, ed. Stephen D. Moore and Janice Capel Anderson, SemeiaSt 45 (Atlanta, GA: SBL, 2004), 249, 250–51, 252.

image into something different: the honorable utensils will become "dedicated and useful to the owner of the house,"[10] while the dishonorable utensils—which in 1 Cor 12 are said to be given "more honor"—are completely ignored by our author. The main point is that Timothy and other male leaders ought to make themselves into special, honored utensils "ready for every good work." Surprisingly, after castigating the so-called false teachers throughout these letters, the author urges that they now be "corrected with gentleness," even holding out some hope that they will come to the truth, as he understands it (2 Tim 2:25-26).

While concentrating so intently on honorable masculine conduct in this chapter, what did the author hope to communicate to female readers? Assuming that the women in his audience shared his perceptions of ideal masculinity, he appeals to them in two of their domestic roles. As wives, they ought to recognize such strength, self-mastery, and endurance in their husbands, and they ought to submit to male leadership in the family and in the community of faith. As with mothers like Lois and Eunice (2 Tim 1:5), the author expected believing women to be motivated not only to teach the content of faith but also to instill these masculine characteristics in their sons.

---

10. The Greek for "owner of the house" is δεσπότης, or "master." See above, "Translation Matters: 'Masters,'" p. 73.

2 Timothy 3

Insiders and Outsiders

Second Timothy 3 gives powerful descriptions of the wide differences between the teachers of truth, like Paul, Timothy, and other faithful men, and the teachers of falsehood, like Hymenaeus, Philetus, and others. The first half of the chapter describes and condemns more opponents of "Paul" while the second half rehearses Paul's sufferings and reminds Timothy of the characteristics of sound scriptural teachings.

The author returns to denigrating certain of his male opponents, linking their personalities and activities to the kind of moral deterioration that was thought to occur in "the last days" (2 Tim 3:1). Although the NRSV uses the word "people" in 2 Tim 3:2, the Greek once again is the plural noun ἄνθρωποι, which can mean either "people" or "men."[1] Since the author refers specifically to women later in this section (3:6-7), it seems perfectly logical to assume that he is thinking here of a number of *men* who oppose his own teachings and conduct.

Naming nineteen vices—the second longest list of such items in the New Testament after Rom 1:29-31—the author completely censures their inner and outer attributes (3:2-4). There is not much of a recognizable pattern for the inventory except that four traits beginning with the prefix

---

1. I discuss this issue in above, "Translation Matters: 'To Faithful People,'" p. 108.

2 Tim 3:1-9

¹You must understand this, that in the last days distressing times will come. ²For people will be lovers of themselves, lovers of money, boasters, arrogant, abusive, disobedient to their parents, ungrateful, unholy, ³inhuman, implacable, slanderers, profligates, brutes, haters of good, ⁴treacherous, reckless, swollen with conceit, lovers of pleasure rather than lovers of God, ⁵holding to the outward form of godliness but denying its power. Avoid them! ⁶For among them are those who make their way into households and captivate silly women, overwhelmed by their sins and swayed by all kinds of desires, ⁷who are always being instructed and can never arrive at a knowledge of the truth. ⁸As Jannes and Jambres opposed Moses, so these people, of corrupt mind and counterfeit faith, also oppose the truth. ⁹But they will not make much progress, because, as in the case of those two men, their folly will become plain to everyone.

TRANSLATION MATTERS: "YOU MUST UNDERSTAND THIS"

In the Greek, the phrase is much shorter, reading literally: "but know this!" (τοῦτο δὲ γίνωσκε). The NRSV has neglected to translate a conjunction δέ, meaning either "but" or "and," which indicates that 2 Tim 3:1 links back to the instructions given in 2:22-26. In addition, the second-person singular imperative parallels the similar verbal commands given in 2:22-23: "shun!"; "pursue!"; and "have nothing to do with!" This reminds the reader that the letter is addressed to just one (male) recipient. The English use of "you" for either the second-person plural or singular obscures the fact that, in the invented situation, the directive is given to Timothy alone.

---

for "love" (φιλ-) open and close the list. It includes nine words that begin with *alpha*, signifying that they are the negative opposite of a positive feature. In the English translation, a few of these appear with comparable prefixes (un-, in-, and im-). As was true in 1 Tim 1:9-10, the author does not explain what is wrong with the content of his opponents' teaching but relies instead on personal attacks as a means to undermine their authority and amplify his own.[2] By accusing the false teachers of socially reprehensible attributes, he also wants his audience to feel disgust toward them and thus to "shun" their teachings as well as their presence. Such an abusive approach seems to be quite at odds with the very advice he has just given to be "kindly toward everyone, . . . correcting opponents with gentleness" (2 Tim 2:24-25).

---

2. See my comments on 1 Tim 1 about how the author treats his opponents, pp. 3–7.

TRANSLATION MATTERS: "SILLY WOMEN"

Translators struggle to find a good English equivalent for the Greek word γυναικάρια, a diminutive (plural) from the word γυνή.[3] Several choose "weak women" (ESV, GNT, NASB, RSV), while the NIV opts for "gullible women." Eugene Peterson's paraphrase in *The Message* expands this to "unstable and needy women." Although the word somewhat literally means "little women," it almost always has belittling connotations in Greek literature, referring to women who are easily deceived. The NRSV has tried to capture that meaning with "silly women," which conveys to some extent the sexist ridicule inherent in this word.

As if further evidence was needed for the falsity of the opponents' ideas and the hypocrisy of their motivations, the author states that some of the opponents and their teachings have proved attractive to a particular group of people: some "silly women" (2 Tim 3:6). In the author's view, a disreputable relationship has developed between the false male teachers and their duped female learners. The fallacy and immorality of the teachers are demonstrated by the fact that they have persuaded members of the "weaker sex" to follow them. Presumably, if they were really manly teachers like Paul and Timothy, they would obtain a proper audience composed of other good men, and they would not "sneak into the households" in search of simple-minded female students. Meanwhile, the supposedly more fragile nature of the "silly women" makes them especially susceptible to the "counterfeit faith" of the teachers. These γυναικάρια are said to be affected by their sins, unpredictable in their desires, and not able to learn much of the truth. It is not surprising that the author would express the strong opinion that women have little aptitude for learning since he has already commented on the unfruitful learning of the younger widows (1 Tim 5:13) and has ordered absolutely that women ought to learn in silence (1 Tim 2:11-12).

The Pastorals author's repressive and gendered attitude toward educating women is typical of those in the Greco-Roman world who believed that a female *by nature* was neither capable of, nor destined for, learning. By straying into such masculine territory, an educated woman would appear not just less feminine but even alarming to others because of her acquired knowledge. A popular saying from Menander, a source of maxims often used by ancient educators to teach composition, illustrates this

3. See my comments on translation options for γυνή above, pp. 35–36.

fear: "He who teaches a woman letters well provides a frightening snake with additional venom."[4] In spite of such withering social commentary, some women within the Roman Empire, primarily from well-to-do families, did indeed learn to read and write Greek. Many of them were seemingly proud of the level of literacy they had acquired, even if it was only to sign their own names to legal documents.[5]

Among such women, the number who received more than a primary education must have still been so small as to be remarkable. In general, educated women would know how to read some literature and be able to write correspondence to their families and to keep track of their property, but they would not have been trained in the more advanced Roman customs of education. No one would have imagined that a girl needed to be taught the more advanced skills that occurred at upper levels of schooling: the close reading, memorization, and imitative composition of classical Greek authors.[6] Similarly, there appeared to be no necessity for her to study rhetorical texts and strategies or to write sample speeches and to practice their delivery as in the training of elite young men for their visible societal roles.

In his negative and belittling claims about female learners, the author of the Pastorals shows an affinity for Menander's maxim about the "frightening" results of teaching literacy to a woman. Even though he himself has benefited from a generous measure of Greek *paideia* and has employed his grammatical and rhetorical training throughout the composition of the letters, he intends to restrain female believers from any unconventional, "unfeminine," and therefore immoral participation in education. Rather than prescribing how girls and women could or would become functionally literate or more learned in biblical interpretation, he focuses instead on training women for their traditional "feminine" domestic roles.

The author of the Pastorals is suspicious about what educated women might learn and how they might then behave in society. Modern studies of the value of educating girls and women would probably confirm his suspicions that such females would be empowered to step outside of restrictive cultural standards for femininity. We do not need to support every

---

4. Patricia A. Rosenmeyer, trans., *Ancient Epistolary Fictions: The Letter in Greek Literature* (Cambridge: Cambridge University Press, 2001), 27.

5. Raffaella Cribiore, *Gymnastics of the Mind: Greek Education in Hellenistic and Roman Egypt* (Princeton, NJ: Princeton University Press, 2001), 76, 86.

6. Ibid., 187.

initiative of the World Bank in order to appreciate its work on promoting gender equality, which is based on the following undeniable evidence:

> Girls' education is more than just about getting girls into school. It is also about ensuring that girls feel safe and learn while in school, complete all levels of education with the skills and competencies to secure jobs, make decisions about their own lives, and contribute to their communities and the world.
>
> Girls' education is a strategic development priority. Better educated women tend to be healthier than uneducated women, participate more in the formal labor market, earn higher incomes, have fewer children, marry at a later age, and enable better health care and education for their children. All these factors combined can help lift households out of poverty.[7]

The effects of educating girls and women seem only fair and even positively constructive to many people and societies in the twenty-first century, but within certain cultures the struggle continues.

One recent and vivid example of a young girl who fiercely loves to learn is Pakistani teenager Malala Yousafzai. Her memoir tells of her and her family's commitment to education for girls, which resulted in her being shot by the Taliban in 2012 in northwest Pakistan.[8] Along with the Indian children's rights advocate Kailash Satyarthi, Malala won the Nobel Peace Prize in 2014. Later that year, Malala gave a speech at "Girl Summit," a conference co-sponsored by the government of the United Kingdom and UNICEF and dedicated to ending child marriage and female genital mutilation.[9] She asserted, "Education is the best way we can fight all the problems we're discussing now. . . . Traditions are not sent from heaven, they are not sent from God. [It is we] who make cultures. We have the right to change it and we should change it. Those traditions that go against the health of girls, they should be stopped."[10]

7. "Girl's Education," http://www.worldbank.org/en/topic/education/brief /girls-education.

8. Malala Yousafzai, with Christina Lamb, *I Am Malala: The Story of the Girl Who Stood Up for Education and Was Shot by the Taliban* (New York: Little, Brown and Company, 2013).

9. "Girl Summit 2014: A Future Free from FGM and Child and Forced Marriage," GOV.UK Government Digital Service, https://www.gov.uk/government/topical -events/girl-summit-2014.

10. Emma Batha, "Malala Tells Girl Summit Education Is Key to Ending Child Marriage," *Thomson Reuters Foundation News* (July 23, 2014), http://news.trust.org //item/20140723034658-8zyt6.

Malala's view that human traditions are not divinely ordained challenges the entrenched opinions of the Pastorals about women, for instance, when the author draws on Gen 2–3 to make the claim that women share in the earliest female sin of mother Eve (1 Tim 2:13-14).

The educational journey of another woman has intersected with mine in more immediate ways. I met Ekram Kachu when she was a master of divinity student at the University of Dubuque Theological Seminary. I am honored to include here her reflections on her life and calling and especially on the central role that learning has played in her development. The Pastorals' views on female learners and teachers have been employed as obstacles to her own education.

Learning to Serve God

My name is Ekram Komikela Kachu. I am the organizing pastor of the First Arabic Presbyterian Church of Des Moines, Iowa. I am from the Heiban people of the Nuba Mountains area of Sudan.

In my clan, communal life is an important part of the culture. A family includes aunts, uncles, cousins, and other relatives. Marriage is considered a family and community affair. The wife must be good to her parents, the in-laws, and friends as well as the people of the village. Relatives and the community at large support widows and orphans, who are treated as family and not strangers. We have a saying, "A person exists because the community exists."

My childhood in Sudan was simple but also tough. I am a middle child from a family of twelve children, six boys and six girls. Our family was totally dependent on agriculture. We farmed about ten to fifteen acres and raised cattle, goats, and chickens. My father also worked in the housekeeping department of the hospital. We are a Christian family and my father and uncles were elders in the church. My siblings and I went to primary school, but we were looked down on and bullied because we didn't have new clothes or school supplies. The population in the town was mostly Muslim, and the Christians were a minority. This is where I learned Arabic, and we also studied Islam every day in the public school from elementary through high school.

My Daddy wanted to provide only for my brothers' education, but my mother wanted her daughters to be educated too. She did housework for other families to raise money for our supplies, and every evening she would check that we were studying. Mother told me many times, "Don't quit school, no matter what!" Her hope was that we girls would become nurses or teachers. It still makes me very sad that she never knew how to write her own name, but I am thankful that she knew that education could be so important for a girl.

When my mother passed away in childbirth when I was twelve, my life became more difficult and dark because she was the only person who encouraged me and took care of us. In my culture, when a girl turns twelve years old, her parents look for a man to marry her. Once married, the wife is responsible for all the cooking, cleaning, and childcare. If she is unable to have children, or if she has female rather than male children, her husband sometimes divorces her. My uncles thought it was time for me to quit school and get married and that it was foolish to spend money on educating a girl.

In this dark time, I cried out to Jesus, and I kept asking my father to send me to school anyway, and he agreed. When civil war broke out in Sudan in the late 1980s, my father chose me of all his children to be evacuated to a safer place where I could continue to go to high school. That is why I am the first woman in my family to get a good educational background. My mother and my aunts never went to school, and my sisters dropped out from elementary or high school. This was because of the cultural opinion that God created women to get married and be good wives and mothers.

Now my life and the lives of females in my family have been changed.

It is a custom of the church in Sudan for young women to teach in Sunday School. I started doing this when I was twelve years old. I took care of the children, read Bible stories to them, and taught them hymns in the church. This gave me a lot of knowledge about faith in Jesus and made me interested in studying theology. I had a strong vision that, instead of teaching children only, I needed to serve the whole church. I began to lead services in the church for children, youth, and other women, but not for the men, because we were taught women were not supposed "to teach or have authority over a man" (1 Tim 2:12).

Still I hungered for more education in order to become a more professional servant of the Lord. First I studied at a West Al-Jarif Bible School, which is Evangelical Presbyterian in Khartoum, Sudan, from 1993 to 1995, and went on from there to the Arab Baptist Theological Seminary in Lebanon (1995–1998). After graduation I returned to Sudan and served in the Evangelical Presbyterian Church as an evangelist and teacher. I preached at worship services, trained Sunday school teachers, worked among women, and taught at summer conferences. Even though the church taught that women could not become pastors, the people recognized the gifts I had been given for preaching and teaching. In 2000 I left for Egypt to minister to Sudanese refugee girls ages twelve to eighteen through a Korean mission.

Many members of my family moved to the United States as refugees from the Sudanese civil war. My husband and I arrived to live in Des Moines, Iowa, in January 2001. We raised our four children in the United States and we are now American citizens. A large Arabic-speaking community lives in Des Moines, and I have been ministering among Sudanese refugees there and all over the country.

Our family became members of the Presbyterian Church (USA), which does ordain women as pastors. I began to see that God was calling me to become a pastor who could freely teach, preach, baptize, and celebrate Communion. That is why I went back to school again: to work on a master of divinity degree. Even though it takes so long for me to read and write in English, I love learning, especially about the Bible and pastoral care. I now speak three languages: a Nuba language called Aboul, Arabic, and English; and I have studied biblical Greek and Hebrew, as well as French. I was happy to discover that biblical Hebrew is very close to the Arabic that I know very well.

When I graduated in May 2015, I became the first woman in my tribe to achieve a master's degree. Soon after that I will be the first woman from the tribe to be ordained. As my husband and I constantly encourage our own sons and daughters in their education, I have plans to begin doctoral studies in the Hebrew Scriptures so that I can become a professor able to train ministers for Christ's church. My Daddy, an elder in the church, has memorized much of the New Testament, and did not think women should lead a church. But he now supports me in my work and says that he "sees God in me." God continues to work in me through my mother's advice: "Don't leave school, no matter what!"

Ekram Kachu

The flourishing lives of Ekram and Malala and others like them speak prophetically against the negative assessments of the results of women's education found in the Pastorals. These are not "silly women" who have fallen under the spell of some male charlatans. They are determined and powerful women whose commitment to learning consistently leads them to a knowledge of the truth.

[10]Now you have observed my teaching, my conduct, my aim in life, my faith, my patience, my love, my steadfastness, [11]my persecutions and suffering the things that happened to me in Antioch, Iconium, and Lystra. What persecutions I endured! Yet the Lord rescued me from all of them.[12]Indeed, all who want to live a godly life in Christ Jesus will be persecuted. [13]But wicked people and impostors will go from bad to worse, deceiving others and being deceived.

[14]But as for you, continue in what you have learned and firmly believed, knowing from whom you learned it,[15]and how from childhood you have known the sacred writings that are able to instruct you for salvation through faith in Christ Jesus. [16]All scripture is inspired by God and is useful for teaching, for reproof, for correction, and for training in righteousness, [17]so that everyone who belongs to God may be proficient, equipped for every good work.

TRANSLATION MATTERS: "FOLLY"

The Greek word translated as "folly" is ἄνοια, a compound of *a* + *noia*, meaning, very basically, "lack of understanding." Terms with the root *no-* refer to the mind, mental processes, understanding, and perception. For medical writers, this word ἄνοια conveys a problem more profound than "folly." The Roman physician Galen described this as "a state of complete mental deficiency . . . a *paralysis* of the thinking faculties."[11] The author of the Pastorals is in fact denouncing the opponents as suffering from mental illness.

The author's critique turns away from the γυναικάρια back to male "counterfeit" teachers (2 Tim 3:8-9). In 2 Tim 3:8, the NRSV yet again uses the word "people" for the Greek ἄνθρωποι[12] when the word ought to be translated "men." That the sex of these false teachers is male is underscored by two things: the allusion to the men Jannes and Jambres, legendary opponents of Moses, and the accusations that their minds are defective. A virtuous man, a model of true masculinity, possesses a sound mind (2 Tim 1:7) and would be able to reason after the example of Paul.

11. Quoted in Patricia A. Clarke and M. Lynn Rose, "Psychiatric Disability in the Galenic Medical Matrix," in *Disabilities in Roman Antiquity: A Capite ad Calcem*, ed. Christian Laes, C. F. Goodey, M. Lynn Rose (Leiden: Brill, 2013), 64.

12. See my comments on 2 Tim 3:2 above (p. 115), and in "Translation Matters, 'To Faithful People,'" p. 108.

In a move we have already observed several times in both 1 and 2 Timothy, the author shifts his attention away from describing and condemning the false teachers back to establishing a constructive role model for the young Timothy. Beginning with a list of nine items, this section highlights the ways in which Paul endured throughout difficult times. While the term "my teaching" probably refers to both the content and the method of the apostle's instruction, the rest of the list focuses on external expressions of Paul's steadfast faith: his acts demonstrate his beliefs. His perseverance under pressure is confirmed when he is "rescued" by the Lord.

The author then states categorically that "*all* who want to live a godly life in Christ Jesus will be persecuted" (2 Tim 3:12). Reading such a claim in the context of ancient gender perspectives once again raises the tension inherent in the text: after so many good (and bad) *masculine* examples have been given, what is the position of women?[13] The author has confined them to domestic roles and has given them a subordinate status to men. He does not think of female believers as able—due to their very nature—to teach or even to learn, to act publicly in the world, or to endure in a truly masculine fashion like Paul, Timothy, and other male leaders. How, then, can a woman put this advice into practice? Should she also expect to experience persecution? In what ways might she know suffering as well as the ultimate liberation from it by "the Lord"?

Second Timothy 3:14-17 needs to be examined within this same gendered context. As a male leader, Timothy has benefited from instruction in the "holy writings"; here the author is referring to the Jewish scriptures. He has supposedly come to know that these texts are "inspired by God and useful" to him for guiding the community and for opposing the false teachers. Scripture is a resource for Timothy in his various leadership roles. Knowledge of the Scriptures makes "the man of God" proficient and equipped. On the other hand, the author believes that females have a gender-specific involvement with such scriptural education. They need to receive instruction as "silent learners" (1 Tim 2:11-12) so that they can embody feminine virtues and fulfill their domestic functions (1 Tim 2:9-10, 15; 5:14; Titus 2:3-5). For them, the benefit of learning Scripture does not lie in developing a capacity to use it while performing tasks like teaching, reproof, correction, or training in righteousness. Instead, as recipients of these educational tactics at the hands of male leaders, the believing women will grow into feminine exemplars who

13. See my comments on 2 Tim 1 on this issue, pp. 102–3.

TRANSLATION MATTERS: "EVERYONE WHO BELONGS TO GOD"

The NRSV translation in 2 Tim 3:17 completely obscures the fact that the Greek says ὁ τοῦ θεοῦ ἄνθρωπος, which is literally "the man of God."[14] In both 1 and 2 Timothy, "man of God" reinforces the idea that the author is addressing Timothy as a male church leader.

are decidedly different from the masculine men in the community. In this passage, the author is not particularly interested in any woman's understanding or application of the Scripture. His thoughts reiterate instead his fixation on the leadership positions of Timothy and the men who will succeed him.

14. On this designation, see my comments on 1 Tim 6, pp. 91–92.

2 Timothy 4

Take It Like a Man

The author brings a solemn resolution to the fore in 2 Tim 4, the last chapter of the letter. He depicts Paul near the end of his life, giving the culmination of his advice to Timothy while expressing a strong sense of fulfillment over his own life's work. In order to build verisimilitude, the letter ends with a number of short messages to, from, and about other (mostly male) co-workers, friends, and acquaintances, some of whom have caused Paul more suffering.

In a serious mood, the author imagines a courtroom scene in front of God and Christ Jesus (who is the future judge) and with two additional witnesses: "his appearing and his kingdom" (2 Tim 4:1). The whole arrangement evokes the day of judgment at the end of time, when Christ Jesus will appear again and his kingdom will be revealed. This image provides an imposing context for the nine short commands given to Timothy (4:2, 5); at the last day, he will be judged based on his satisfactory completion of these orders.

As I have noted before about this letter, the commands in 2 Tim 4:2 and in 4:5 are in the second-person singular, a detail unclear from the English pronoun "you." Modern readers, especially those in Protestant traditions, might hear these verses as addressed to all individual believers, no matter their social location, charging them with implementing

[1]In the presence of God and of Christ Jesus, who is to judge the living and the dead, and in view of his appearing and his kingdom, I solemnly urge you: [2]proclaim the message; be persistent whether the time is favorable or unfavorable; convince, rebuke, and encourage, with the utmost patience in teaching. [3]For the time is coming when people will not put up with sound doctrine, but having itching ears, they will accumulate for themselves teachers to suit their own desires, [4]and will turn away from listening to the truth and wander away to myths. [5]As for you, always be sober, endure suffering, do the work of an evangelist, carry out your ministry fully.

[6]As for me, I am already being poured out as a libation, and the time of my departure has come. [7]I have fought the good fight, I have finished the race, I have kept the faith. [8]From now on there is reserved for me the crown of righteousness, which the Lord, the righteous judge, will give me on that day, and not only to me but also to all who have longed for his appearing.

these practices. The earliest Greek-speaking audiences would have recognized the singular pronoun, so that the hearers would need to consider more carefully whether they too are included as direct recipients of the instructions. After all, the actions to be done are the tasks of male church leaders: proclaiming, convincing, rebuking, and encouraging, as well as the work of an evangelist, all summed up in the phrase "carry out your ministry [διακονία] fully." Since the Pastorals put forward male heads-of-households as leaders of the believers, it would require an intuitive leap for a lower-status male—a slave or freedman—or any female to figure out how these commands might apply to their own lives of faith. Certainly throughout the history of the church, the instructions were understood as addressed specifically to Timothy and then to the male ministers and priests who followed him.

Two other elements sustain the solemn atmosphere evoked by the judicial scene. First, the prediction of apostasy shows "Paul" as a prophet. In this role, he has even foreseen the conflicts with false teachers and their followers (2 Tim 4:3-4) encountered in the author's own time and place. By warning that such troubles will occur in the time to come, the author stresses the seriousness of forcefully opposing the deceivers and their deceptions. We remember that in 2 Tim 3:1-9 such opponents are critiqued as unmanly men whose teachings and practices are successful at deceiving "silly women."

Second, the moving depiction of a tired and aging yet ultimately triumphant Paul (2 Tim 4:6-8) invests the words with a lofty formality. They become his last testimony, handed over to his trustworthy and beloved "child," who now "must carry out his ministry not only in imitation of Paul, but in place of Paul."[1] All three Pastorals draw on various sources of information about Paul, including his earlier letters and the stories and legends about his mission, but because 2 Timothy finds "Paul" closer to his death, this letter, more than 1 Timothy and Titus, conveys the authoritative influence of the apostle Paul. Whatever "Paul" teaches here carries the power of supreme truth.

The Roman masculine ideal of the endurance of suffering with patience and discipline resurface in 2 Tim 4:1-8, with Paul himself again serving as the prime exemplar. It is notable, then, that throughout the Pastorals the depiction of Christ does not emphasize his endurance of suffering. Colleen M. Conway articulates the connections between our author's masculine ideals and his christological thinking.

Manly Suffering

The [Pastorals] take the form of instructions from Paul to Timothy and Titus on proper leadership and conduct in the Christian community. In this sense, as Mary Rose D'Angelo notes, the letters are essentially "man-to-man counsel." This counsel is based on the normative household codes of the Greco-Roman elite, in which man [sic], women, children, and slaves all have their proper place. By advocating for this household structure, the "Paul" of these letters defines a masculinity that affirms Roman family values. Not only that, but the author makes clear that the benefits of salvation include a Christian *paideia*, or education in proper masculine deportment. The saving grace of God, according to the author, "teaches us [παιδεύουσα ἡμᾶς] to renounce impiety and worldly passions, that we may live self-controlled, just and pious lives in the present age" (Titus 2:12, my translation). Thus, in these later letters there is a continuation of the idea that belief in God through Christ enables one to achieve a virtuous, manly status.

The Christology of these letters adds to this impression. While there are some familiar Pauline themes to be found, others have gone missing in these later letters. What is present, for instance, is the

---

1. Jouette Bassler, *1 Timothy, 2 Timothy, Titus*, ANTC (Nashville, TN: Abingdon, 1996), 170.

notion of vicarious death. Christ is called a ransom for all (1 Tim 2:6) who "gave himself for us" (Titus 2:14). Christ also appears as one who is merciful and patient, much like the Christ who shows clemency in Corinthians (1 Tim 1:13-16). The virtue of endurance is evident as well. The author urges his reader to be a "co-sufferer" like a good soldier of Christ (2 Tim 2:3). Those who live in Christ are guaranteed persecution (3:12), but they are also promised that endurance will bring the reward of ruling with Christ (2:11, 4:8).

What is missing, however, in spite of the emphasis on suffering, are references to the cross or crucifixion. It is as though the author, in his earnestness to both promote proper gender deportment and defend against gender attacks, wants to avoid the complicated issue of Christ's death. In fact, shame seems to be on the author's mind throughout the letters, including the acknowledgment of the possible shame involved in following Christ. If the Paul of Romans declares that he "is not ashamed of the gospel," the Paul of the Pastorals urges Timothy not to be ashamed "of the testimony about our Lord" (2 Tim 1:8). He further insists that he is not ashamed of his own suffering, suggesting that the treatment he has received would be viewed by others as emasculating (2 Tim 1:12). By the second century, this concern about looking shameful is understandable in light of the opposition that was voiced by opponents such as Celsus. Thus, in the Pastoral Epistles one finds traditions of Jesus' vicarious self-sacrifice interwoven with assertions against the shamefulness of Christ or his followers and detailed exhortations to conform to normative gender scripts as closely as possible.[2]

Colleen M. Conway

2. Colleen M. Conway, *Behold the Man: Jesus and Greco-Roman Masculinity* (New York: Oxford University Press, 2008), 86–87. Conway quotes D'Angelo, "The ANHP Question in Luke-Acts: Imperial Masculinity and the Deployment of Women in the Early Second Century," in *A Feminist Companion to Luke*, ed. Amy-Jill Levine and Marianne Blickenstaff (London: Sheffield Academic Press, 2002), 44–69. However, I have not been able to verify the quotation.

2 Tim 4:9-22

⁹Do your best to come to me soon, ¹⁰for Demas, in love with this present world, has deserted me and gone to Thessalonica; Crescens has gone to Galatia, Titus to Dalmatia. ¹¹Only Luke is with me. Get Mark and bring him with you, for he is useful in my ministry. ¹²I have sent Tychicus to Ephesus. ¹³When you come, bring the cloak that I left with Carpus at Troas, also the books, and above all the parchments. ¹⁴Alexander the coppersmith did me great harm; the Lord will pay him back for his deeds.¹⁵You also must beware of him, for he strongly opposed our message.

¹⁶At my first defense no one came to my support, but all deserted me. May it not be counted against them!

¹⁷But the Lord stood by me and gave me strength, so that through me the message might be fully proclaimed and all the Gentiles might hear it. So I was rescued from the lion's mouth. ¹⁸The Lord will rescue me from every evil attack and save me for his heavenly kingdom. To him be the glory forever and ever. Amen.

¹⁹Greet Prisca and Aquila, and the household of Onesiphorus. ²⁰Erastus remained in Corinth; Trophimus I left ill in Miletus. ²¹Do your best to come before winter. Eubulus sends greetings to you, as do Pudens and Linus and Claudia and all the brothers and sisters.

²²The Lord be with your spirit. Grace be with you.

Second Timothy ends with something of a barrage of names and places associated—for good or for ill—with Paul and his mission. Many of these characters appear in other New Testament texts and in noncanonical early Christian literature, but some are completely unknown to present-day readers. In spite of the large number of persons named—seventeen in all, not to mention "all the brothers and sisters" of 4:21—it is Paul himself who stands as the central figure. All the other persons are important only because of their relationship to the apostle. Some have abandoned or simply gone away from Paul (4:10, 16). Luke has staunchly remained with him (4:11). Timothy needs to go to Paul, taking Mark with him (4:9, 11). Alexander strongly opposed Paul and his proclamation (4:14-15). Other members of the Pauline mission organization are stationed at various cities. Another group of believers sends greetings along with Paul. The author sets up each person as an example either to follow or to reject based on how he responds to Paul. Above all, it is "the Lord" who remains faithful to Paul (4:17-18) and who will thereafter stand by and rescue all those who are in a "right relationship" with Paul.

This passage underscores the fact that the world of the Pastorals is mostly populated by male actors. Of the seventeen people brought up in the passage, it is notable that only two women are named: Prisca and Claudia. In fact, there are only three other female proper names in the

Pastorals: Eve (1 Tim 2:13) and Lois and Eunice (2 Tim 1:5). Twenty-seven men's names are used,[3] six of them more than once: Timothy, Hymenaeus, Alexander, Onesiphorus, Titus, and Tychichus. All of the named opponents in the Pastorals are men: Hymenaeus and Alexander (1 Tim 1:20); Phygelus and Hermogenes (2 Tim 1:15); Hymenaeus and Philetus (2 Tim 2:17); Demas (2 Tim 4:10); Alexander (2 Tim 4:14). That the majority of these names, both male and female, appear in 2 Timothy rather than 1 Timothy or Titus emphasizes the more personal nature of this communication from Paul to Timothy.

Along with 1 Timothy and Titus, the entire letter rests on the patriarchal perspective that men ought to be in charge of their households and likewise that they ought to manage the communities of believers. Therefore, because Paul is depicted as the original and continuing head-of-the-household-of-God, he functions as the role model for his male successors. Finally, loyalty to Paul and adherence to his teaching serve as litmus tests for determining genuine male leaders, so that judgment falls on those who oppose him (e.g., Alexander, 2 Tim 4:14) while his supporters are "useful" in his ministry (e.g., Mark in 4:11).

Four of the five named women represent traditional feminine roles. Lois and Eunice function as mother and grandmother, while Prisca is well-known as the wife of Aquila. In both Acts 18:24-28 and in Paul's letters (Rom 16:3; 1 Cor 16:19), Prisca functions as a teacher and co-worker of the apostle, but our author does not want to emphasize that aspect of her ministry. It may be that Claudia also was recognized as a wife (perhaps of Linus?), but nothing more is known of a believer by that name. The most (in)famous name is that of Eve, the mother of all women, who, due to her female nature, was easily deceived.

Female readers then and now who seek insights from this letter for living faithful lives are obstructed when confronted with the full-on propagation of male examples, the Roman ideals for masculinity, and even the straightforward catalogue of men's names. Where do women fit into this patriarchal depiction of the assembly of the faithful? What

3. Compare these five total to the twenty-seven men's names in the Pastorals: Timothy; Hymenaeus (1 Tim 1:20; 2 Tim 2:17); Alexander (1 Tim 1:20; 2 Tim 4:14); Adam (1 Tim 2:13-14); Phygelus (2 Tim 1:15); Hermogenes (2 Tim 1:15); Onesiphorus (2 Tim 1:16; 4:19); Philetus (2 Tim 2:17); Jannes (2 Tim 3:8); Jambres (2 Tim 3:8); Moses (2 Tim 3:8); Demas (2 Tim 4:10); Crescens (2 Tim 4:10); Titus (2 Tim 4:10; Titus 1:4); Luke (2 Tim 4:11); Mark (2 Tim 4:11); Tychicus (2 Tim 4:12; Titus 3:1); Carpus (2 Tim 4:13); Aquila (2 Tim 4:19); Erastus (2 Tim 4:20); Trophimus (2 Tim 4:20); Eubulus (2 Tim 4:21); Pudens (2 Tim 4:21); Linus (2 Tim 4:21); Artemus (Titus 3:12); Zenas (Titus 3:13); and Apollos (Titus 3:13).

situations might they encounter where, as with Paul in 2 Tim 4:18, the Lord will need to "rescue [them] from every evil attack and save [them] for his heavenly kingdom"? Perhaps the author and other male officials would have said that they were protecting women from the heavy burdens of leadership (2:20); from the insinuating teachings of the opponents (3:6-7); and from the harsh treatment of opposition, arrest and imprisonment, and various other sufferings (1:8, 12; 2:3, 9; 3:10-12; 4:16-18). Whatever their intentions, the author's ancient perspective on gender continues to influence ecclesial structures and has restricted the aspirations and activities of faithful women and men.

Titus 1

Rungs on the Social Ladder

The letter to Titus is a compact text that employs many of the words (e.g., "godliness," "savior," "greed," "self-control," "truth") and themes (church leadership, opponents, women, and slaves) of the other two Pastorals. Here again the author urges the audience to remain loyal to Paul's proclamation of the faith and to live a virtuous life within household, community, and society. He discusses (male) church leadership, proper household relationships, and true and false teaching/teachers. The first chapter of Titus contains topics familiar to the readers of 1 and 2 Timothy in three sections: opening greetings, directions for Titus' ministry in the churches, and a condemnation of some opponents.

In fact, if you have read previous chapters of this commentary, you may be wondering what new ideas and location-specific advice arise in the letter to Titus. You may be asking why the author wrote letters that are so similar in style and contents. At least, these are questions that occur to me in the process of studying and interpreting the Pastorals. I believe that the author intended to add authoritative weight to his opinions by *repeating* his teachings in more than one text. By writing these letters under the pseudonym "Paul," he could accomplish three things: a reworking of some of Paul's more socially controversial teachings, such as Paul's claim that everyone ought to remain single (1 Cor 7:7); a recasting of the roles of women in the Pauline mission and churches; and a powerful

Titus 1:1-4

[1]Paul, a servant of God and an apostle of Jesus Christ, for the sake of the faith of God's elect and the knowledge of the truth that is in accordance with godliness, [2]in the hope of eternal life that God, who never lies, promised before the ages began— [3]in due time he revealed his word through the proclamation with which I have been entrusted by the command of God our Savior,

[4]To Titus, my loyal child in the faith we share:

Grace and peace from God the Father and Christ Jesus our Savior.

TRANSLATION MATTERS: "SERVANT OF GOD"

One phrase that deserves special attention is "servant of God." The label "servant" is actually the Greek word δοῦλος, which I much prefer to translate as "slave." I have already discussed this issue,[1] but here it is important to note that the NRSV has chosen "servant" instead of "slave." For English readers, the NRSV's inconsistency is bothersome because it obscures the author's intentions. He may be trying to emphasize Paul's utter submission to God's power and will. Or he may want to depict Paul as an unquestioned agent of God. The author has employed the legal, economic, and cultural position of a slave as a powerful rhetorical device, and the NRSV has watered down its meaning by using the word "servant."

---

duplication of his own beliefs about the proper organization for households and house-churches. As a result, when the three Pastorals are read in light of the larger collection of Pauline letters, each Pastoral does not seem so very unusual because the other two provide supportive evidence: this is how Paul instructed his younger subordinates to encourage right thinking and respectable relationships within their communities.

As is often noted, the opening verses of Titus give a longer-than-usual depiction of Paul and his beliefs. Yet similar ideas have already been conveyed by the letters to Timothy: faith, the "elect," knowledge of the truth, godliness,[2] revelation of the word, and Paul's proclamation under God's commission. One word that is especially important in the letter to Titus is that of "savior" (σωτήρ); the related adjective and verb appear

---

1. See above, "Translation Matters: 'Slave,'" p. 70.
2. See above, "Translation Matters: 'Godliness,'" p. 48.

in Titus 2:11 and 3:5. This title, which was frequently bestowed on God in the Old Testament and also on emperors and other great military victors, is used three times for God (Titus 1:3; 2:10; 3:4) and then three times for Jesus Christ (1:4; 2:13; 3:6) in an alternating pattern. This usage shows that the author participates in a historical development: "By placing [savior] regularly in tandem with both God and Christ, these texts are doing with *sōtēr* what had been done with *kyrios* in the first Christian generation. Jesus the Christ is to be addressed by the same titles as those which could be given to the God of Israel."[3] The deep reverence for God and Christ shown by these jointly held titles testifies to the author's kyriarchical theology.[4]

Such an assertion of the rule of lords and the submission of subordinates intersects with the belief that male figures are rightly positioned at the top of the hierarchy. In the case of the letter to Titus, the personages at the apex are "God the Father and Christ Jesus our Savior" (Titus 1:4). As in 1 and 2 Timothy, the next male in the chain of command is the apostle Paul, who in this case has designated Titus as his faithful deputy in Crete. The author also addresses Titus as "loyal child," exactly as he addresses Timothy (1 Tim 1:2), which means that Titus functions as another son for "father" Paul. Therefore, the process of authorizing Titus' ministry in Crete follows the same pattern as I outlined for Timothy: the author wants to persuade the audience that the rightful leadership structure for the community derives from God, who entrusted Paul with an apostolic role, which power Paul then delegated to the younger man Titus (and Timothy), and from him to other male leaders.

For those familiar with 1 and 2 Timothy, this male predominance is nothing new. The author has repeatedly asserted that the community ought to be structured as a proper patriarchal household and that its members ought to perform only within their social stations. Still, it is worthwhile to consider how these teachings stand in tension with some of the reasoning found in the letters that most every scholar believes to be written by Paul himself.

One example is that the author of the Pastorals only rarely uses sibling language in his descriptions of the family and the community. Many ancient sources articulate how some of the most intense familial bonds in a Roman family are those between brothers and sisters. That is prob-

3. Jerome D. Quinn, *The Letter to Titus*, AB 35 (New York: Doubleday, 1990), 309.
4. This theology has been described in "Interpretive Essay: Roman Imperial Religion," pp. 11–13.

ably why the apostle Paul often uses sibling terminology to describe his relationship with other believers, including Timothy (1 Thess 3:2) and Titus (2 Cor 2:13), and urges the churches to treat each other as siblings (e.g., Rom 14:10; 1 Cor 11:33-34; 1 Thess 4:6, 9-10; Phlm 15–16). Raymond F. Collins has analyzed how Paul's letters differ from the Pastorals on the subject of sibling language and states:

> Given Paul's predilection to call Timothy his brother, it is striking that neither the author of First Timothy nor the author of Second Timothy uses the vocative ἀδελφέ ["brother"] in appealing to "Timothy," the purported recipient of these missives. The absence of ἀδελφέ from these relatively long texts stands in marked contrast with the much shorter Letter to Philemon where the vocative ἀδελφέ emphasizes the close relationship that exists between the apostle and the recipient of the letter, making it possible for Paul to exploit that relationship when he urges Philemon to accede to his request.[5]

Neither does the "Paul" of the Pastorals call Titus "brother" in 2 Tim 4:10 or Titus 1:4, even though the real Paul laments in 2 Cor 2:13, "my mind could not rest because I did not find my brother Titus there." About the Pastorals, Collins exclaims,

> What a far cry from ἀδελφοί ["brothers"] being "far and away Paul's favorite way of referring to the members of the communities to whom he his writing,"[6] and the apostle's frequent use of ἀδελφός to describe Timothy and other Christian evangelists, including Titus (2 Cor 2:13)! The apostle could well have asked, "Where have all the siblings gone?"[7]

In partial answer to Collins's plaintive question about the absence of siblings in the Pastorals, I would say that the author is more concerned with shoring up Paul as the foremost father of the churches than in depicting him as one of many faithful brothers and sisters. The author cannot even allow "Paul" to call Timothy and Titus "brother" but instead identifies them as "loyal/beloved children" (1 Tim 1:2; 2 Tim 1:2; Titus 1:4). In the face of the opposition perceived by our author, he declares that the male leadership hierarchy must be maintained so that his vision

---

5. Raymond F. Collins, "Where Have All My Siblings Gone? A Reflection on the Use of Kinship Language in the Pastoral Epistles," in *Celebrating Paul: Festschrift in Honor of Jerome Murphy-O'Connor, O.P., and Joseph A. Fitzmyer, S.J.,* ed. Peter Spitaler, CBQMS 48 (Washington, DC: Catholic Biblical Association, 2011), 326.

6. Collins, "Where Have All My Siblings Gone?," cites Robert J. Banks, *Paul's Idea of Community: The Early House Churches in Their Historical Setting* (Grand Rapids, MI: Eerdmans, 1980), 50–51.

7. Collins, "Where Have All My Siblings Gone?," 335.

⁵I left you behind in Crete for this reason, so that you should put in order what remained to be done, and should appoint elders in every town, as I directed you: ⁶someone who is blameless, married only once, whose children are believers, not accused of debauchery and not rebellious. ⁷For a bishop, as God's steward, must be blameless; he must not be arrogant or quick-tempered or addicted to wine or violent or greedy for gain; ⁸but he must be hospitable, a lover of goodness, prudent, upright, devout, and self-controlled. ⁹He must have a firm grasp of the word that is trustworthy in accordance with the teaching, so that he may be able both to preach with sound doctrine and to refute those who contradict it.

TRANSLATION MATTERS: "ELDERS" AND "BISHOP"

Unlike in English, where the word "elders" can be applied to either older women or older men, the Greek word here undoubtedly refers to male elders. As we have already seen in 1 Timothy, especially in 5:17-19, the author allows church leadership to be held only by men. Even though the Greek adjectives in Titus 1:6 are all in the masculine gender, the NRSV translation makes this gender restriction indistinct by not using the male pronoun "he" until verse 7. Other exclusively masculine titles in this section are "bishop" and "steward."[8]

of the Pauline teaching and way of life will be preserved. By defending a patriarchal structure, he reinforces the social ideology that consigns persons to lower status positions. In the churches, as in society, he suppresses equal respect, relationships, and functions for women, children, the poor, those who do manual labor, those who had been freed, and those who are still enslaved.

The body of this letter opens with a short explanation of the situation: "Paul" has apparently left "Titus" on the Mediterranean island of Crete and delegated the completion of a few tasks to him. The first of these is to choose elders (literally, "older men") for every town. Two other masculine titles, "bishop" (ἐπίσκοπος, "overseer") and "steward" (οἰκονόμος), are also used, both of which seem to describe the function of the elder as a subordinate of God and a leader of a church. It is unclear how these

---

8. See also "Translation Matters: 'Office of Bishop,'" p. 32, and "Translation Matters: Older Man," p. 50.

[10]There are also many rebellious people, idle talkers and deceivers, especially those of the circumcision; [11]they must be silenced, since they are upsetting whole families by teaching for sordid gain what it is not right to teach. [12]It was one of them, their very own prophet, who said,

"Cretans are always liars, vicious brutes, lazy gluttons."

[13]That testimony is true. For this reason rebuke them sharply, so that they may become sound in the faith, [14]not paying attention to Jewish myths or to commandments of those who reject the truth. [15]To the pure all things are pure, but to the corrupt and unbelieving nothing is pure. Their very minds and consciences are corrupted. [16]They profess to know God, but they deny him by their actions. They are detestable, disobedient, unfit for any good work.

three terms relate to each other, although they were later interpreted as supporting the position of one regional bishop who supervised elders in individual churches. What is more obvious is that the audience is supposed to perceive the leadership succession as exclusively male, consisting of Paul first, Titus second, and followed in an orderly fashion by the elders acting as bishops and stewards. The patriarchal structure envisioned by the author builds on the male domestic roles, presuming that an elder's respectable administration of his household gives him the experience necessary for leading a church. This elder ought to be a "one-woman man."[9] and his young adult children ought to be believers who behave in an honorable manner. A list of typical virtues to display and vices to shun fills out the job qualifications for the elder-bishop who will then be approved for teaching "sound doctrine" and for countering the opponents.

The author turns to attacking those he calls "rebellious people" using the Greek word ἀνυπότακτοι, which more neutrally means "independent" but may also be translated as "disobedient" or "undisciplined."[10] He describes their behavior in several strongly negative ways; in particular he condemns their speaking and teaching for "upsetting whole families." Rather than taking up their proper position within a social hierarchy, he thinks that they are overturning the community order. Since these kinds of overstated criticisms are regularly found in the Pastorals and in other

9. See above, "Translation Matters: 'Married Only Once,'" p. 33.
10. For a brief discussion of this word family, see "Translation Matters: 'Disobedient,'" p. 5.

literature of the time, we cannot be sure that his adversaries are actually guilty of the accusations. On the other hand, he plainly believes they are a danger to the faith and practice of his audience.

One of his most offensive tactics is to put into writing an ethnic insult: "Cretans are always liars, vicious brutes, lazy gluttons."[11] He even asserts, "That testimony is true." Along with many modern commentators, Jouette Bassler states:

> Throughout these three letters the author addresses the problem of these opponents, but nowhere is his condemnation as harsh as in this passage. This is due in large part to the tone of the quotation he cites, which repeats a familiar racial slur in a particularly virulent form. Through it the opponents are dehumanized (Gk. *kaka thēria*; NRSV: "vicious brutes"), and the accompanying instructions are to muzzle or gag them (Gk. *epistomizein*; NRSV: "silence"). Moreover, all Cretans are included in this brutal condemnation.[12]

The author expresses more ethnic bigotry when he links the opponents to "those of the circumcision" (Titus 1:10) and derides "Jewish myths" (1:14). We have read similar verbal abuse of women when he maligns "old wives' tales" (1 Tim 4:7) and the "silly women" (2 Tim 3:6-7). Wolfgang Stegemann analyzes these statements in his essay "Anti-Semitic and Racist Prejudices in Titus 1:10-16."

Race and Ethnicity in Titus

Titus 1:10-16 is a single polemic against a group and its protagonists, whom the author of the letter understands as a sort of "party" (cf. Titus 3:10) within the Christian communities of Crete. He does not use a group label, but on the other hand we find in the text a conglomeration of terms of abuse and slogans. These relatively general labels are interwoven with two fundamental identifications. On the one hand it is maintained that these negative characteristics are particularly or primarily (μάλιστα) applicable to "those of the circumcision" (οἱ ἐκ τῆς περιτομῆς). Shortly afterwards a warning is given not to subscribe to Jewish fables (Ἰουδαϊκοὶ μῦθοι). On the other hand the "opponents" are also identified with negative prejudices concerning the Cretans.

11. The saying is often attributed to Epimenides of Crete (sixth century BCE).
12. Jouette Bassler, *1 Timothy, 2 Timothy, Titus*, ANTC (Nashville, TN: Abingdon, 1996), 190.

Two polemical strategies of argumentation are intertwined: on the one hand the author labels the deviant group with various derogatory terms. On the other hand he is concerned to identify them with Judaism or the Cretans, whereby certain prejudices are clearly intended to be transferred to the deviant group.

Titus1:10-16 represents a strategy of negative labelling which is intended to highlight the deviance of the opposing group. This polemic, characterized as "deviance accusations," makes use of stereotypes and generalizing suspicions. The strategy of identifying the deviants with Judaism is part of it. The author does not flinch even from evaluating the apostates as abnormal, or "evil animals" (κακὰ θηρία), in the context of the "Cretan" quotation and thus to place them outside the human species. The author's concern is doubtless by these accusations to undermine the position and role of the opposing group within the Christian community. The derogatory labelling of the deviants corresponds to severe treatment. Disputes with them on matters of substance should be avoided (3:9). The aggressive rejection of an intra-Christian deviance group is not only a feature of Titus 1:10-16. It is typical of the Pastoral Epistles as a whole. However, it is particularly striking in our text that the rejected group is connected with implicit prejudices about Judaism and explicit prejudices about the Cretans.

In my view, our text reflects an ancient form of racism. For in the dreadful proverb about the Cretans their ethnic origins are linked with negative quasi-biological features. It assumes that all members of the ethnic group of the Cretans have negative characteristics, which disqualify them morally and in the end place them outside the human race. And neither the historical situation of the letter to Titus, nor the general mentality of Mediterranean culture, which presumably took little offence at the text's anti-Semitic and racist prejudices, can "justify" its prejudice structure. In any case the ancient situation and mentality can be no criterion for its reception today. It is not, however, simply a question of a critique of the New Testament text and of its Christian exegesis. Rather, historical criticism is always also a criticism of the present, in which, as always, in church and theological discourses anti-Semitism and racism are encountered and are not infrequently justified on the basis of biblical texts.[13]

Wolfgang Stegemann

13. Translated from the German by David E. Orton, in *Ethnicity and the Bible*, ed. Mark G. Brett (New York: Brill, 1996), 271–94.

We could just possibly ignore the author's racist and anti-Semitic statements as a random fragment of a long-ago culture, except that it has ended up in our own scriptures under the name of the famous apostle. What I, along with Stegemann, find especially troubling is that the negative assessments of Jews, Jewish traditions, and the ethnic Cretans seem to have influenced several modern commentators to adopt a similar prejudice, which then leads to a tendency to read the rest of the letter as if it were written to a culturally and morally backward community. Here are a few examples:

- I. Howard Marshall speculates on Titus 1:8: "It is . . . possible that the emphasis on *elementary* qualities, just as the prohibition of certain behaviour patterns that would have seemed *too obvious to mention*, spoke to an *immature* church struggling to break free from *depraved patterns of behaviour, such as were widely associated with Crete.*"[14]

- Philip H. Towner characterizes the opponents who are "upsetting whole families" (1:11) in this way: "The household was, after all, a typical setting for philosophical recitations and rhetorical performance. *Dangerous teaching that was tinged with Cretan permissiveness (and other elements more Jewish perhaps)* would thus 'disrupt' household first."[15]

- Luke Timothy Johnson seems to concur with the prophet from Crete: "the *unsavory* character of the local population that was already suggested by [Titus] 1:6-9 here becomes explicit: even a native Cretan prophet testified truly to their *coarse and evil ways.*"[16]

The value judgments of Cretan culture as untruthful and gluttonous (and thus, rudimentary, corrupt, savage, uncivil, etc.) do not arise from any "sociological" studies of the population but rather from the simple proverbial sayings and ancient reports. It is impossible for later readers to tease out the facts about life on Crete during the Roman Empire, and we cannot know the cultural realities for various people and groups when they are framed in such polemical and stereotypical ways. The

14. I. Howard Marshall, *The Pastoral Epistles*, ICC (Edinburgh: T & T Clark, 1999), 165; my italics.

15. Philip H. Towner, *The Letters to Timothy and Titus*, NICNT (Grand Rapids, MI: Eerdmans, 2006), 697; my italics.

16. Luke Timothy Johnson, *Letters to Paul's Delegates: 1 Timothy, 2 Timothy, Titus* (Valley Forge, PA: Trinity Press International, 1996), 228; my italics.

author of this letter has simply adopted the common perceptions about Cretans that designate them as the "other." Such strident rhetoric serves to set them apart from "good" Greeks and "good" Romans and now excludes them from the category of "good" Pauline Christians.

Turning to Titus 1:15, we might puzzle over the ambiguous saying that "to the pure all things are pure." Here the author seems to assert that each person may determine what behavior is right for them based on their own perception of rightness. However, when read in the context of this passage, it is obvious that he assumes that his audience will agree with his depiction of his opposition ("those of the circumcision," Cretans, and others) as belonging to the broad category of "corrupt and unbelieving . . . detestable, disobedient, unfit for any good work." While our author does not intend to allow for unconventional readings of 1:15, he has nonetheless opened a door to an incredible freedom of interpretation for many readers, as can be found in this excerpt of Jay Twomey's discussion of Jeanette Winterson's novel *Oranges Are Not the Only Fruit.*

"To the Pure" an Opportunity

The novel [*Oranges Are Not the Only Fruit*] tells the story of a young, evangelical lesbian named Jeanette who must come to grips with conflicts between her sexual identity and her religious faith, conflicts that she neither understands nor accepts. When her relationship with her first lover, Melanie, is discovered, she is hauled before the congregation.[17]

The church was very full as usual, and every time I caught someone's eye they smiled or nodded. It made me happy. There was nowhere I'd rather be. When the hymn was over I squeezed a bit closer to Melanie and tried to concentrate on the Lord. "Still," I thought, "Melanie is a gift from the Lord, and it would be ungrateful not to appreciate her." I was still deep in these contemplations when I realised that something disturbing was happening. The church had gone very quiet and the pastor was standing on his lower platform, with my mother next to him. She was weeping. I felt a searing pain against my knuckles; it was Melanie's ring. Then Miss Jewsbury was urging me to my feet saying, "Keep calm, keep calm," and I was walking out to the front with Melanie. I shot a glance at her. She was pale.

"These children of God," began the pastor, "have

17. Twomey, *The Pastoral Epistles Through the Centuries*, 200.

fallen under Satan's spell."

His hand was hot and heavy on my neck. Everyone in the congregation looked like a waxwork.

"These children of God have fallen foul of their lusts."

"Just a minute . . .," I began, but he took no notice.

"These children are full of demons."

A cry of horror ran through the church.

"I'm not," I shouted, "and neither is she."

"Listen to Satan's voice," said the pastor to the church, pointing at me. "How are the best become the worst."

"What are you talking about?" I asked, desperate.

"Do you deny you love this woman with a love reserved for man and wife?"

"No, yes, I mean of course I love her."

"I will read you the words of St Paul," announced the pastor, and he did, and many more words besides about unnatural passions and the mark of the demon.

"To the pure all things are pure," I yelled at him. "It's you not us."

He turned to Melanie. "Do you promise to give up this sin and beg the Lord to forgive you?"

"Yes." She was trembling uncontrollably. I hardly heard what she said.

"Then go into the vestry with Mrs White and the elders will come and pray for you. It's not too late for those who truly repent."

He turned to me.

"I love her."

"Then you do not love the Lord."

"Yes, I love both of them."

"You cannot."

"I do, I do, let me go." But he caught my arm and held me fast.

"The church will not see you suffer, go home and wait for us to help you."

I ran out on to the street, wild with distress.[18]

In Winterson's novel, the idea of purity does not produce divisive options, but rather a relatively decentralized view of religious authority according to which the minister, and others like Jeanette's mother, who oppose the young love affair, and the two young women, could, ideally, coexist.[19]

Jay Twomey

---

18. Jeanette Winterson, *Oranges Are Not the Only Fruit* (New York: Grove, 1985), 105. I have excerpted a longer passage from the novel than does Twomey in order to give more of the narrative substance.

19. Twomey, *The Pastoral Epistles Through the Centuries*, 200.

Of course, the author of the Pastorals would be opposed to such "a relatively decentralized view of religious authority" and even horrified at this particular use of his writings. But as a biblically literate Protestant evangelical, "Jeannette" has been trained to read and to interpret the scriptures on her own. In so doing, she has found a weak spot in the Pastorals' teachings, one that authorizes her own moral and relational development.

By the end of Titus 1, our author has set forth these core teachings that have already been asserted in 1 and 2 Timothy:

1. Male heads-of-households are the most suitable leaders in the communities (e.g., 1 Tim 3:1-10, 12; 4:14; 5:17-19; 2 Tim 2:2; Titus 1:5-9).

2. Loyalty to Paul's beliefs and endurance in suffering is highly regarded (e.g., 1 Tim 1:6-7, 18-20; 2:7; 4:10; 5:21-22; 6:3, 20-21; 2 Tim 1:8-14; 2:8-10; 4:16-17; Titus 1:9; 2:1).

3. Opponents to Paul's teaching (as found in these letters) are to be dealt with unsympathetically (e.g., 1 Tim 1:19b-20; 5:8, 20; 6:17; 2 Tim 2:14, 17-18; 3:8-9; 4:14-15; Titus 1:10-14; 3:10).

4. Men, especially Paul, Timothy, and Titus, serve as exemplary figures (e.g., 1 Tim 1:12-16; 4:11-16; 6:11-14; 2 Tim 1:8-14; 2:1-15; Titus 1:7-9; 2:6-8)

5. Other men are vilified for failing to demonstrate manly virtues (e.g., 1 Tim 1:8-10; 6:3-5; 2 Tim 2:17b-19; 3:1-9; Titus 1:10-16).

This by-now-familiar advice about the high standing of free male citizens in the community is followed in the very next chapter by the author's stereotypical instructions for women and other subordinated persons. These two chapters characterize the patriarchal educational program he has in mind for community members.

Titus 2

Staying in Your Place

W*hat*, exactly, is Titus supposed to teach? *Who* is he supposed to teach it to? And *how* should he go about the task of teaching? Turning away from the sharp criticisms of the opponents at the end of Titus 1, the letter's next chapter begins to answer these questions very directly.

Commentators often read Titus 2 through the lens of the stereotypes propagated in Titus 1:10-16 by adopting the author's prejudices about Jews and Cretans so that all the instructions in Titus 2 are understood as descriptions of and remedies for the actual behavior of people in the assemblies on Crete. As just one example, Philip H. Towner believes that the churches there "are being urged to sink healthy roots deep into the *uncertain Cretan soil* and to *shake loose the cultural elements* that have attached to the Christian message, and they are to be as salt and light in this *wild frontier*."[1] I have already disagreed with this perspective on the letter to Titus, stating that the strident polemics of the author's arguments make it difficult to discern the real and complex social-historical situation of the believers on Crete. When he takes up such troubling views on

---

1. Philip H. Towner, *The Letters to Timothy and Titus*, NICNT (Grand Rapids, MI: Eerdmans, 2006), 717; my italics.

¹But as for you, teach what is consistent with sound doctrine. ²Tell the older men to be temperate, serious, prudent, and sound in faith, in love, and in endurance. ³Likewise, tell the older women to be reverent in behavior, not to be slanderers or slaves to drink; they are to teach what is good, ⁴so that they may encourage the young women to love their husbands, to love their children, ⁵to be self-controlled, chaste, good managers of the household, kind, being submissive to their husbands, so that the word of God may not be discredited.

⁶Likewise, urge the younger men to be self-controlled. ⁷Show yourself in all respects a model of good works, and in your teaching show integrity, gravity, ⁸and sound speech that cannot be censured; then any opponent will be put to shame, having nothing evil to say of us.

ethnicity and then advises people to avoid particularly objectionable vices, we cannot trust his portrayal to be accurate, whether he is describing Titus, the opposition, or any of the ordinary folks. In fact, our suspicions may only increase as we consider the author's depictions of younger and older, men and women, and enslaved persons.

In Titus 2:1, the author abruptly shifts his attention away from the opponents toward Titus, giving a short and clear command: "teach!" The "you" in this verse is Σύ, a singular form in Greek. The content of Titus' instruction must match up with what is called "sound doctrine" (2:1), but the teachings that follow in the rest of the chapter are not really the sort of topics that most modern Christians would consider to be "doctrine." The author does not insert any creedal sayings or Scripture verses, such as we read in 1 Tim 2:5-6. Instead, Titus must teach the believers about right actions, especially in fulfilling their household roles and in proper moral behavior.

TRANSLATION MATTERS: "SOUND DOCTRINE"

The Greek word-family translated as "sound" and "to be sound" appears nine times in the Pastoral Letters and, remarkably, three times in this chapter alone. No other New Testament author uses these terms. Both the adjective and the verb begin with the syllable ὑγι- which comes into the English words "hygiene" and "hygienic." Alternative translations are "healthy/to be in good health" and can be used for either physical or metaphorical health. The Greek word is occasionally translated as "right" (TEV, NLT), which stresses the author's belief that his version of Pauline teaching is the correct one.

In the Pastorals, there is always an object being described as "sound" or "healthy": "doctrine/teaching" (διδασκαλία; 1 Tim 1:10; 2 Tim 1:13; 4:3; Titus

1:9; 2:1), "faith" (πίστις; Titus 1:13; 2:2), and "word/speech" (λόγος; 1 Tim 6:3; Titus 2:8).

Abraham J. Malherbe explains how the author uses such images of health and illness to define the differences between true and false teachers:

> The author describes them [the opponents] as intellectually inferior, having diseased minds that produce violent preaching and contaminate those who accept their teaching. They are antisocial and upset the social order by their preaching. . . . Contrasted to the heretics are the orthodox who have knowledge and hold to sound teaching, who are generally mild in their own teaching, yet know to be severe when the occasion demands severity, who are socially responsible, give constant attention to their own moral progress, and always have the benefit of others at heart.[2]

Accusing the opponents of mental illness is part and parcel of the author's attacks on their persons and establishes them as negative examples for his audience.[3]

The Pastorals' emphasis on "sound doctrine" (Titus 2:1) or "healthy teaching" echoes the ideas of ancient philosophers who present themselves as physicians of the soul and their instructions as good "medicine." The philosophical movements of Roman times had a different objective from the study of philosophy today: their aim was to educate students to lead a good life. The Stoics, in particular, focused on training people in the self-control of the passions so that they would progress toward inner virtue. Our author expresses a similar objective when he directs Titus (and Timothy) to instruct believers how to act in an upright manner.

TRANSLATION MATTERS: "TEMPERATE" AND "SELF-CONTROLLED"

The English reader would not realize that the words "temperate" and "self-controlled" found in Titus 2:2 and 2:5 are translations of the same adjective in Greek: σώφρων. I am not sure why the NRSV has translated these differently, especially since the word "temperate" is not a very resonant word in modern English, whereas "self-controlled" seems to be common in a range of arenas.

2. Abraham J. Malherbe, "Medical Imagery in the Pastoral Epistles," in *Texts and Testaments: Critical Essays on the Bible and Early Church Fathers: A Volume in Honor of Stuart Dickson Currie*, ed. W. Eugene March and Stuart Dickson Currie (San Antonio, TX: Trinity University Press, 1980); repr. in *Paul and the Popular Philosophers* (Minneapolis: Fortress Press, 1989), 126–27.

3. For further discussion on the author's polemic against the opponents, see my comments on 1 Tim 1, pp. 4–7.

The adjective is related to two verbs also found in this passage that add yet another translation option. In 2:4, the verb σωφρονίζειν is translated "to encourage," and in 2:6, σωφρονεῖν is translated "to be self-controlled." In fact, the first verb has a much stronger connotation than "to encourage" and means something more like "call them to their senses" or "restore them to sanity." (In the Translation Matters on "Virtues for Women" in my commentary on 1 Tim 2, I noted the meaning given to the related noun σωφροσύνη is "moderation," one of the Four Cardinal Virtues.[4])

Greek words that begin with σω- (including the words for "savior," "salvation," and "to save") indicate "a deliverance or healing of human persons."[5] When compounded with the root of the word for "mind" (φρον-), we get the idea of "healthy mind" or "sanity." Jerome D. Quinn writes about this word-group in the Pastorals: "The way in which the PE use and understand the *sōphro(n)*- terminology for virtue illustrates how the health bestowed by salvation is linked to the internal moral character that emanates from that healing."[6] In Titus 2:2-8, each of the four groups—older and younger men, older and younger women—is expected to demonstrate this moral virtue that ought to flow from God's salvation.

Throughout Titus 2, the naming of virtues to acquire alongside vices to avoid defines the contents of the "sound teaching." Each term is a standard ideal for honorable behavior in the Roman Empire: one ought to be dignified, sober, not a drunkard, reverent, self-controlled, etc. The longest list of moral standards is directed toward the younger women in 2:4-5:

1. love their husbands
2. love their children
3. be self-controlled
4. be chaste
5. be good managers of the household
6. be kind
7. be submissive to their husbands

Each of the first six items is only one word in Greek, which makes the listing read like an invoice of qualifications to be checked off.

---

4. See above, "Translation Matters: 'Virtues for Women,'" p. 16.
5. Jerome D. Quinn, *The Letter to Titus*, AB 35 (New York: Doubleday, 1990), 312.
6. Ibid., 313.

Even though these are all so-called traditional Roman family values invoked by the author to counter the work of his opponents and to restrict the activities of women, some modern commentators are influenced by his prejudicial view of Cretan culture.[7] Their interpretations rely on a mirror reading of this list of virtues that the younger women ought to display. Luke Timothy Johnson exemplifies this approach: "What is surprising is that these are qualities that need to be taught [to the younger wives]. Is this a sign of the *savageness and incivility* of the *native population*, that responses ordinarily thought to be 'natural' should require teaching?"[8] Johnson expresses surprise that the women of Crete would need to be taught to love their husbands and children when this ought to be their "natural" response as domestic women.

Bruce W. Winter combines the author's negative views of Crete with his own suspicions about the younger women's behavior, conjecturing that "they had been influenced by some of their secular married sisters."[9] In his mirror reading, Winter assumes that the wives "lack interest in the welfare" of their households because they must be told to be "good managers of the household."[10] Similarly, he believes they must be neglecting their husbands and children since they need to be taught to love these family members, stating, "The neglect of her husband as well as her children presumably in favour of a social life that might involve casual extramarital affairs is also commented on."[11] It is astonishing that Winter disparages the younger women as "presumably" seeking out "a social life that might involve casual extramarital affairs." Not one thing in the text suggests this possibility.

The older Christian women on Crete also encounter the critique of a modern scholar. Philip H. Towner picks up on the author's command that older women ought not to be slanderers or slaves to drink. Claiming that these are "shortcomings of a certain kind of older wife,"[12] Towner

7. More discussion of the ancient bigotry toward Cretans can be found in my chapter on Titus 1.

8. Luke Timothy Johnson, *Letters to Paul's Delegates: 1 Timothy, 2 Timothy, Titus* (Valley Forge, PA: Trinity Press International, 1996), 234; my italics.

9. Bruce W. Winter, *Roman Wives, Roman Widows: The Appearance of New Women and the Pauline Communities* (Grand Rapids, MI: Eerdmans, 2003), 168; my italics. Winter's use of the adjective "secular" is completely anachronistic to this time and place.

10. Ibid.

11. Ibid.

12. Towner, *The Letters*, 723.

decides that "his [Paul's] intentional echoing of this stereotype is meant
to ensure that Cretan Christian older women rid themselves of this
'typical' reputation. They were to show themselves as older wives who
had successfully emerged from *the Cretan way of life*."[13] Here we see
clearly that Towner accepts the ancient negative stereotypes about the
culture of Crete and reads those together with the author's patriarchal
perspective on women's behavior.

These three commentators take for granted that there were some actual
bad behaviors characteristic of women and of Cretan women in particular that elicited such teachings from the author of the Pastorals. But
from the perspective of a feminist hermeneutic of suspicion, it is completely invalid to assume that there is a historical basis for our author's
special concern about the women in this hypothetical community. Instead, since the patriarchal assumptions of the author are in plain view,
we need to continue to question his reliability as a witness as well as his
authority as a moral theologian. In my opinion, we should also distrust
commentaries that perpetuate and even add to such negative gender
and ethnic stereotypes.

TRANSLATION MATTERS: "TO TEACH WHAT IS GOOD"

The word καλοδιδασκάλους, translated by the NRSV as "to teach what is good"
(Titus 2:3), is a noun that may also be understood as "good/right/apt teachers."
A compound of "good" and "teachers," the word is unique in ancient Greek.
The author of the Pastorals uses it to claim that virtuous older Christian women
are the best and most appropriate teachers for younger women, especially in
how to fulfill their household functions.

The teachings in Titus 2:2-8 are aimed at the same four groups of
people found in 1 Tim 5:1-2, but the author places them in a different
structure, as this diagram shows:

1 Tim 5:1-2	Titus 2:2-8
Timothy ought to relate to	*Titus ought to* teach
A—older man	A—older men
A¹—younger men	B—older women (*who then teach*)
B—older women	B¹—younger women
B¹—younger women (*in all purity*)	A¹—younger men

13. Ibid., 724; my italics. Towner believes that the apostle Paul wrote the Pastoral
Letters.

In both cases, the younger women break the literary pattern established by the author. In 1 Tim 5, the clause "in all purity" is added as if "Timothy" might need to exercise extra caution with these females.[14] In Titus 2, "Titus" is supposed to teach the older men, the older women, and the younger men, but it is the older women who are assigned to teach the younger women. The author's grammar and his expectations distance Paul's young delegate Titus even further than Timothy from such evidently problematic young women. The older women are positioned as a buffer between Titus and the younger women. For some conservative groups and churches today, this kind of woman-to-woman ministry continues to be the only approved teaching role for female Christians.[15]

In American colonies in the early seventeenth century, this approved model of older Christian women training the younger women served as justification for Anne Hutchinson's practice of teaching in her home. The story of how she was accused and tried for heresy is told at greater length in the following excerpt from Neil Elliott's *Liberating Paul*.

The Politics of Anne Hutchinson

It was not immediately clear to women among the Puritan dissenters who colonized New England whether, and how, the bold experiments in Calvinist theocracy would affect their own liberties. A number of more independent-minded women and men in Boston were drawn to the home of Anne Hutchinson, a remarkably erudite and devout Puritan, the mother of thirteen children, whom the colony's governor, John Winthrop, described as "a woman of haughty and fierce carriage, of a nimble wit and active spirit, and a very voluble tongue, more bold than a man; though in understanding and judgement," he felt compelled to continue, "inferior to many women." The conversations in Hutchinson's home centered around learned discussions of the preaching in local pulpits.

The ministers of the Bay Colony did not appreciate such unsolicited reviews of their sermons. The General Court of the Colony arraigned Anne Hutchinson on charges of "troubling the peace of the

14. See the chapter on 1 Tim 5 for my thoughts on this possibility.

15. Examples include Titus 2, a mentoring program for Christian women (http://titus2mentoringwomen.com); Inspire! Women's Mentoring Program (http://www.inspirewomensmentoringministries.org/public/main.cfm); Titus 2 International Women's Ministry (http://www.titus2345.org); and Creative Ladies Ministry (http://www.juliabettencourt.com/articles/mentoring.html).

commonwealth and the churches," citing her defiance of previous admonitions to desist from promoting such of her opinions as were "prejudicial to the honour of the churches and ministers thereof."

The transcript of the trial includes a tortuous exchange between Anne Hutchinson, who insisted she had violated none of the colony's regulations, nor done anything beyond what was customary for any of the men assembled in the courtroom, and Governor Winthrop, whose eagerness to declare her guilty and pronounce a sentence of banishment was scarcely restrained. Their exchange revolved around two passages from Paul's letters. Winthrop pressed the accused woman to admit to having taught in the presence of men in her house, in clear violation of 1 Tim 2:12 ("I permit no woman to teach or hold authority over a man"); she repeatedly denied that any but women were present in the meetings she led, on the authority of Titus 2:3-5 (older women are to "train the younger women").

The brutal suppression of activist religious women found justification in a flurry of sermons from Puritan pulpits. Anne Hutchinson's condemnation became an immediate precedent. In Puritan sermons preached over the next twenty years, the cherished Pauline admonition to wifely subordination to the husband (Eph 5:22 [repeated in Titus 2:5!]) was now supplemented by warnings against the "notorious" example of Mrs. Hutchinson. Even in England, the rise of agitation by independent women in the churches was suppressed by reference to the sentence in the colonies. "Henceforth," inveighed the Reverend John Brinsley in Yarmouth, England, in 1645, "no more Women Preachers!"[16]

Neil Elliott

One ancient pedagogical ideal is prominent in Titus 2:1-8: that teachers need to be worthy of imitation by their students. The older women (2:3-5) and Titus himself (2:6-8) are supposed to function in that capacity along gender-exclusive lines. For the author, the conventional labeling of moral virtues and domestic roles as either masculine or feminine necessitates such a gendered educational process. As in 2 Tim 2, where Paul serves as an example for Timothy and the other male officials, Titus needs to demonstrate exemplary behavior for young men. Again we

16. Neil Elliott, *Liberating Paul: The Justice of God and the Politics of the Apostle* (Minneapolis: Fortress Press, 2005), 4–6.

⁹Tell slaves to be submissive to their masters and to give satisfaction in every respect; they are not to talk back, ¹⁰not to pilfer, but to show complete and perfect fidelity, so that in everything they may be an ornament to the doctrine of God our Savior.

TRANSLATION MATTERS: "FIDELITY"

The word πίστις, translated by the NRSV as "fidelity" (Titus 2:10), may also be translated as "faithfulness," "faith," "trust," or even "belief." Clearly, here the Pastor is commanding slaves to be faithful to their masters. But it is disturbing, or at least ambiguous, that the slaves' faith is defined by their activities as bound workers and not by their trust in God, and that this kind of faithful service supposedly shines like an "ornament to the doctrine of God" (2:10).

---

come across a tension expressed in the question: Can a male leader serve as a role model for female believers? In Titus 2, the answer is no, which is why the older women must be lifted up as the "good teachers" of younger women. By the very definition of masculinity as the antithesis of femininity, Titus cannot exemplify proper conduct for any woman. Instead, he ought to function as "a model of good works" for the younger men.

Even though this short exhortation falls into the same pattern of advice-giving found in the previous eight verses, I am separating out Titus 2:9-10 because these two verses were among the verses most used to justify slavery in the American South, and thus they deserve much more focused attention.[17] Here I have incorporated three interpretive essays in order to dig deeper into the history and interpretation of the teachings on slavery.

Interpretive Essay: Slaves and Masters Living Together

As was true for 1 Tim 6:1-2, the author of Titus directs his attention only to "slaves" and not to their "masters" (Titus 2:9). Yet we know that persons in both categories were present in the initial audience for the letter, and not only that, but there were some males and females in both

17. See also the Interpretive Essays above on 1 Tim 6:1-2.

groups as well. It is worthwhile, then, to consider the power dynamics of the patriarchal household, describing some of the ways in which Roman ideals of masculinity and femininity intersected with the social construct and economic realities of slavery.

Looking back to the Roman Empire on the legal, cultural, and ordinary daily domestic associations between master and slave, mistress and slave, husband and wife, parents and children, and slaves and children, modern Western readers get only a glimpse of the interpersonal complexities that permeate that world. The articulated foundational principles that underlie the household dynamics are hierarchical and indeed patriarchal in nature. The cultural ideal is that a husband-father-master stands at the pinnacle of a pyramid, and he possesses the authority to instruct, supervise, discipline, command, and make decisions regarding every person in subordination to himself. His own self-mastery would serve as an example of moral excellence: "Just as the elite man mastered those on whom he depended, at least in fantasy, so he created a proper male body by mastering the servile and feminine within himself."[18] This is how he could demonstrate his true masculine power.

However, even though the image of a pyramid seems stable because it has a wide base of support, we can look at the domestic structure in a different, even opposite, way. If the human building blocks of wife, children, and slaves prove to be less solid than the ideal, the male personage at the very top might teeter and even fall, so that for all his legal and traditional power over others, the male head-of-household is also subject to being controlled by those same people. His honor depends on the proper behavior of those "underneath" him. Should slaves, wives, or children defy him, ignore him, steal from him, talk back, or bring shame upon themselves in any way, then his own social status is at risk. Looking at the domestic pyramid from this perspective, there must have been at least some uneasiness (personal and/or cultural) on the part of masters toward their slaves. Would his slaves be loyal to the household and its people, business, and reputation or not? An often-repeated proverb warned, "You have as many enemies as you have slaves,"[19] and

18. Sandra R. Joshel and Sheila Murnaghan, "Introduction," in *Women and Slaves in Greco-Roman Culture: Differential Equations,* ed. Sandra R. Joshel and Sheila Murnaghan (London: Routledge, 1998), 13.

19. Quoted by Seneca, *Ep. Mor.* 47.5. For further ideas on the slave as "domestic enemy," see J. Albert Harrill, *Slaves in the New Testament: Literary, Social, and Moral Dimensions* (Minneapolis: Fortress Press, 2006), 145–63.

slaveholders debated how to ensure loyalty while not associating too closely with the slaves.

The perceived masculinity of the master is supported or destroyed by his strategies for slave management. Yet, positioned at the peak of the domestic pinnacle, the male householder has to work to achieve a social steadiness. As Murnaghan and Joshel state, "Reliance on women and slaves, whether as individuals or as types, meant a constant and intimate involvement with the very figures from whom the master or husband was striving to distinguish himself."[20] To be perceived as a "real man" he has to generate a powerful yet temperate discipline over himself and his slaves, even as he lives and works in close proximity to these human instruments who legally belong to him. It was a delicate balance to achieve, much less maintain.

The author of the Pastorals attempts to reinforce all of these cultural expectations for the household and its individual members. He diagrams the patriarchal structure and its dynamics with words, situating each person in his or her supposed proper place: male slaveholders at the top; their wives in a subsidiary position; and both groups above (especially younger) children and all those who are enslaved (1 Tim 3:1b-5). These high-status men ought to be "real men," as shown by their self-mastery, as well as the submissive behavior of their dependents. The author displays anxiety about the gender-appropriate functioning of some of these male heads-of-households. In his mind, there exists a very real risk that their families might be disrupted by some of the opponents (1 Tim 4:1-3; 2 Tim 3:1-9; Titus 1:10-11). The solution is for the male head-of-household to assert control over his subordinates.

In addition, in the Pastorals the domestic hierarchy becomes the template for the house-church itself, so that only masters (male heads-of-households) may aspire to authoritative roles in the church. While the author explicitly rejects free female heads-of households as teachers of men (1 Tim 2:11-12), he does not even ponder the possibility that slaves (male or female) might serve in this capacity. It is beyond his imagining that a person of such low status, of suspect masculinity and questionable virtue, and unable to legally marry or claim legitimate children and thus form his own household could ever teach a component of the "household of God" (1 Tim 3:15). The enslaved male cannot assume ecclesial authority because he possesses no domestic authority. He has not

---

20. Joshel and Murnghan, "Introduction," 13.

had the training or the experience thought to be necessary for leadership nor the legal rights and honorable status that would corroborate his command.

In the next section, Emerson B. Powery provides a critical reading of both 1 Tim 6:1-2 and Titus 2:9-10 from an African American perspective. Writing from his own teaching experience as a New Testament professor, he also lifts up writings by enslaved persons who fled the United States for Canada during the antebellum period. One noteworthy contribution made by this essay is Powery's emphasis on the presence of Christian slaveholders in the community of the Pastorals. He proposes, and I agree, that the author of the three letters was likely a slaveholder himself.

The Pastor's Commands to Enslaved Christians: 1 Timothy 6:1-2 and Titus 2:9-10

An Interpretive Context

Every year in my introduction to the Bible course, students carefully read Paul's letter to Philemon. Imagining nineteenth-century US society, I divide the class into two groups—abolitionists and pro-slavery advocates—and we utilize "Philemon" as the primary point of debate in supporting these respective causes. Each time, students are shocked to discover how effective this short letter can be for the pro-slavery position. They are equally shocked to learn that enslavement in ancient Roman society was just as bad as the version in the "New World." Recently, one student even thanked me for teaching him that slavery was in the Bible. Of course, I didn't "teach" him this idea. We simply discussed passages that he had overlooked throughout his teenage years, or he might have heard sermons that allegorized these passages as if they were speaking to contemporary work contexts of bosses and employees. For the knowledgeable reader of the Bible, it is difficult to overlook the numerous passages that address enslavement throughout both testaments. Furthermore, condemnation of slavery is rare in biblical texts, even if hints of abusive practices exist (see Deut 23:15-16; 24:7; 1 Cor 7:21; 1 Tim 1:10). Sadly, the history of race relations in the United States makes it difficult to attend to these biblical passages in contemporary settings.

Historically, many African Americans have read certain sections of the Pauline collection critically. This critical resistance has more to do with how interpreters have used these Pauline passages against African Americans during the more than two hundred years of enslavement in the United States than by any actual reading of those passages themselves. In the antebellum period of the United States, we encounter writings from ex-slaves that illustrate such resistance to a "plain reading" of the New Testament texts that arose from the many examples of white ministers preaching "slaves obey your masters." Frequently, the theological rationale from these "scriptural" sermons was simply this: in order to obey God, one *must* obey the "earthly master." They would argue that this is what the Word of God declared.

In her autobiographical novel, Harriet Jacobs, who escaped bondage in 1842, provides an example of one of these sermons from the "master's minister," a Rev. Pike, who preached this message in the home of a free African American.

> Pious Mr. Pike brushed up his hair till it stood upright, and, in deep, solemn tones, began: "Hearken, ye servants! Give strict heed unto my words. You are rebellious sinners. Your hearts are filled with all manner of evil. 'Tis the devil who tempts you. God is angry with you, and will surely punish you, if you don't forsake your wicked ways. You that live in town are eye-servants behind your master's back. Instead of serving your masters faithfully, which is pleasing in the sight of your *heavenly Master*, you are idle, and shirk your work. God sees you. You tell lies. God hears you. Instead of being engaged in worshipping him, you are hidden away somewhere, feasting on your master's substance; tossing coffee-grounds with some wicked fortuneteller, or cutting cards with another old hag. Your masters may not find you out, but God sees you, and will punish you. O, the depravity of your hearts! When your master's work is done, are you quietly together, thinking of the goodness of God to such sinful creatures? No; you are quarrelling, and tying up little bags of roots to bury under the door-steps to poison each other with. God sees you. You men steal away to every grog shop to sell your master's corn, that you may buy rum to drink. God sees you. You sneak into the back streets, or among the bushes, to pitch coppers. Although your masters may not find you out, God sees you; and he will punish you. You must forsake your sinful ways, and be faithful servants. Obey your old master and your young master—your old mistress and your young mistress. *If you disobey your earthly master, you offend your heavenly Master.* You must obey God's commandments. When you go from here, don't stop at the corners of

the streets to talk, but go directly home, and let your master and mistress see that you have come."[21]

Rev. Pike's concern with idleness was an attempt to control the time and activity of the enslaved even when they were on their "free" time, particularly when they were not in the presence of earthly masters. In this brief summary, Jacobs reports that Pike repeated the phrase "God sees" five times and includes one "God hears" for good measure. Pike's "God" was the all-seeing, ever-present "heavenly Master," who functioned as the master's overseer, virtually managing the affairs of the enslaved in the absence of the earthly master. To "disobey" the one was to "offend" the other. Pike weaves together a theological conception that moves beyond the cited, biblical texts for his sermon (which seem to be Eph 6:5-7 and Col 3:22-25). It was an ineffective venture for those in attendance: "We went home," writes Jacobs, "highly amused at brother Pike's gospel teaching."[22]

During this same period, African Americans who had access to literacy and a Bible recognized that teachings in white sermons failed to mention or curtail earthly masters' abuses. In 1848, Rev. William Troy left Essex County, Virginia, and followed the routes of the Underground Railroad north to Canada. He describes his experience of attending a customary, interracial religious gathering of blacks and whites back in Virginia: "I used to go to church regularly, but never heard them preach from, 'Masters, render unto your servants that which is just and equal.'"[23] Troy and others recognized that Col 4:1 provided the potential for fairness, even though it upheld the institution itself. African Americans began to develop such critical readings of Pauline passages in order to survive. What Rev. Troy did hear was a sermon in which 1 Tim 6:1-2 played a prominent role.

Now you brethren that suffer affliction, should endure it as good soldiers, enduring all hardness. Paul says to his son Timothy, "Let as many servants as are under the yoke count their own masters worthy

21. Harriet Jacobs, *Incidents in the Life of a Slave Girl: Written by Herself*, ed. L. Maria Child (Boston, 1861), 106–7. Retrieved at http://docsouth.unc.edu/fpn/jacobs/jacobs.html.

22. Ibid., 107.

23. Benjamin Drew, "Rev. William Troy," *A North-Side View of Slavery: The Refugee; Or, the Narratives of Fugitive Slaves in Canada; Related by Themselves, with an Account of the History and Condition of the Colored Population of Upper Canada* (Boston: J. P. Jewett and Company, 1856), 355. Retrieved at http://docsouth.unc.edu/neh/drew/drew.html.

of all honor, that the name of God and his doctrine be not blasphemed." And they that have believing masters, let them not despise them. These are holy injunctions, and must be adhered to. Be contented under all circumstances with singleness of heart to God, not giving railing for railing, but with fear do the will of your master. Count not your slight affliction dear, for God your Father hath so decreed from all eternity that you should suffer, and if you despise the imposition of God, you cannot enjoy his spiritual benefits.[24]

Regrettably, unlike in Eph 6:9 and Col 4:1, there are no comparable instructions to masters urging them to treat their slaves justly within the Pastoral Epistles, and this nineteenth-century white minister did not include any. Furthermore, this minister emphasizes the eternal nature of this enslavement and the inability of enslaved believers to experience any "spiritual benefits" unless they accept their earthly subjugated bodily condition. Such sermons omitted any biblical safety net the nineteenth-century disenfranchised might have received against the physical violence, sexual exploitation, and psychological warfare from their earthly masters. Harriet Jacobs lived out this experience firsthand. One of her assessments of Rev. Pike's sermon was to compare the spiritual lives of the slaveholding leaders to her enslaved brothers and sisters: "Many of them (enslaved African American believers) are sincere, and nearer to the gate of heaven than sanctimonious Mr. Pike, and other long-faced Christians, who see wounded Samaritans, and pass by on the other side."[25] As the freedom narratives attest, many of Harriet Jacobs's contemporaries developed effective strategies to defuse the debilitating religious experiences promoted by the slaveholding minister. They knew that the Pauline letters needed to be read in alternative ways. Paul's "servants, obey your masters" would not be the final biblical word. They knew that love—since God is love—would have the final say.

The Presence of Christian Slaveholders in the New Testament

In the ancient Roman world, approximately one out of every five persons was enslaved.[26]

24. Ibid., 356.
25. Jacobs, *Incidents*, 107.
26. Keith Bradley, "Slavery in the Roman Republic," in *The Cambridge World History of Slavery*, vol. 1, *The Ancient Mediterranean World*, ed. Keith Bradley and Paul Cartledge (Cambridge: Cambridge University Press, 2011), 250–51.

Strabo (d. 24 CE), an ancient historian and philosopher, recalled a popular proverb when describing the ancient slave markets in Delos, "Merchant, sail in and unload your ship, your cargo (of slaves) is already sold."[27] He reports that Delos would import and export thousands of slaves daily. In this environment, it is no surprise that many early Christians were enslaved believers. As Paul writes to the Christians at Corinth, "For in the one Spirit we were all baptized into one body—Jews or Greeks, slaves or free—and we were all made to drink of one Spirit" (1 Cor 12:13). Other New Testament passages highlight their presence as well (1 Tim 6:1-2; Titus 2:9-10; 1 Cor 1:26; Gal 3:28; Eph 6:5; Col 3:22). It may be more surprising for contemporary readers to learn that slaveholders were prominent members of early Christianity. Philemon, who was Paul's "dear friend, and co-worker" (Phlm 1:1) and a prominent church leader in Colossae was a slaveholder. Mary, John Mark's mother, hosted a church on her property and was wealthy enough to hold slaves, including one named Rhoda a "slave girl" (παιδίσκη, Acts 12:12-13).[28]

Although there is little specific evidence, the author of the post-Pauline Pastoral Epistles may have been a slaveholder as well. If so, this may explain the absence of any reciprocal teachings for slaveholders when he turns to addressing the behavior of enslaved persons in 1 Tim 6 and Titus 2. Some early Christian writings of the first and second centuries contain instructions for both parties (Eph 6:1-9; Col 3:18-4:1; *Did.* 4.10-11; *Barn.* 19.7).[29] However, even in Ephesians and Colossians more commands are given to the enslaved than to the slaveholders, supporting Wayne A. Meeks's assertion that "the ethos of the leaders [of the Pauline churches] is rather more that of the owners than of the slaves."[30] This can equally be said about the communities envisioned in the Pastoral Epistles. For example, the appointment of Christian leaders (i.e., overseers, elders, and deacons) for the young religious movement is restricted to those male household heads, who

27. Strabo, *Geography* 14.5.2.

28. The NRSV translates παιδίσκη as "slave-girl" for the female character with a "spirit of divination" in Acts 16:16 but prefers simply "maid" for the Christian Rhoda in 12:13. Luke describes both women with the same Greek term, as enslaved persons in the Roman Empire.

29. In the New Testament, the letter 1 Peter likewise gives instructions to enslaved believers and not to slaveholders (1 Pet 2:18-25).

30. Wayne A. Meeks, *The First Urban Christians: The Social World of the Apostle Paul* (New Haven, CT: Yale University Press, 1983), 64.

(frequently?) were also slaveholders (1 Tim 3:2-5, 8-13; Titus 1:5-9). The category of "deacon" could also include women (1 Tim 3:11), implying that in the Pastorals' audience some women may also have been slaveholders—like Mary (Acts 12) and Chloe (1 Cor 1:11). Whether or not the Pastor is a slaveholder himself, he forcefully employs all of his theological rhetoric in order to support Christian (and non-Christian) slaveholders in the community. Jennifer A. Glancy ponders: "[E]xamination of the household codes leads me to ask how the presence of slave*holders* in the congregations shaped the emerging structures and ideology of Christianity."[31]

The Advice of One Christian Slaveholder

1 Timothy 6:1-2
In 1 Tim 6, the Pastor encourages enslaved believers who live under the "yoke of slavery"—a "yoke" from a Greek word, ζυγός, which refers to the crossbeam placed on the neck of laboring animals—to honor "their masters" even if their slaveholders are not Christian (1 Tim 6:1). At least the Pastor acknowledges the burden of enslavement as a yoke! In the next verse, the Pastor directs some of his teachings specifically to Christians who are enslaved by other Christians: "Those who have believing masters must not be disrespectful to them on the ground that they are members of the church" (1 Tim 6:2). For him the oppression of enslavement has not been lifted by the appearance of God's salvation. While contemporary Western Christians tend to equate freedom with the practice of their faith, freedom was not considered a basic privilege of ancient Rome, and those who possessed it generally subjugated those who did not have it and exploited the authority they had because of it. Apparently, this was also the case in the Pastor's community.

1 Timothy 1:10
The Pastor is, however, opposed to "slave-trading," which he mentions in 1 Tim 1:10.[32] Would this imply that the Pastor advocates for the emancipation of the enslaved in a master's will? Not enough details are provided. In light of the Pastor's opposition to the slave market, we might assume that enslaved believers in these communities were born into their roles rather than purchased in the agora. Children received their assigned status from their birth mothers, which frequently placed younger enslaved

---

31. Jennifer A. Glancy, *Slavery in Early Christianity* (Philadelphia: Fortress Press, 2006), 132; her italics.
32. For more information on this topic, see above "Translation Matters: 'Ancient Vices,'" p. 6.

females in precarious situations with slaveholders. If a slaveholder could not secure slaves from the marketplace, then how else could he ensure sufficient slave labor for their fields and households except through "slave-breeding" practices?[33]

Titus 1:1

In fact, rhetorically, the Pastor was not troubled by using the term "slave" as a positive metaphor. He described Paul's relationship to God in this way (Titus 1:1)[34]—balanced, though, by Paul's apostleship to Jesus Christ—and, by implication, every believer's relationship to God (as in 2 Tim 2:24). In this regard, the Pastor is not different from his hero, Paul (Rom 1:1; Phil 1:1).

Titus 2:9-10

What actions did the Pastor hope to control? Are there hints belying the Pastor's language that may give us some clues into the attitudes of enslaved believers? Five stock phrases appear in the advice of Titus 2:9-10: "Tell slaves to be submissive (ὑποτάσσεσθαι)[35] to their masters and to give satisfaction in every respect; they are not to talk back, not to pilfer, but to show complete and perfect fidelity." A

closer, critical look at a few of these commands sheds light on possible actions of the enslaved.

(1) "Talking back" (ἀντιλέγοντας) is used one other time in the Pastorals, in Titus 1:9, where it refers to those who "contradict" (NRSV) the teaching of the bishop-teacher who preaches "sound doctrine." The term's association with teaching matches its usage elsewhere in the New Testament, where it is translated by different English words in the NRSV. The Sadducees "challenge" (ἀντιλέγειν) Jesus' teaching on the general resurrection (Luke 20:27). Some Jews from Antioch "question" (ἀντιλέγειν) Paul's revisionist history of Israel (Acts 13:45). Finally, some Jerusalem leaders (with Jesus in mind) claim that anyone who makes himself king "challenges" Caesar (John 19:12). From these passages we see that the context of this term usually surrounds specific teaching. In Titus 2:9 then, the Pastor may imply a meaning of "speaking against" one's master, behind their back, not just "talking back" directly to them, as if they were

---

33. Keith Bradley, "The Regular, Daily Traffic in Slaves," *CJ* 87 (1992): 125–38.

34. See also in this volume "Translation Matters: 'Servant of God,'" p. 134.

35. This infinitive is one of the Greek words related to orderliness. For more information, see above, "Translation Matters: 'Disobedient,'" p. 5.

"sassing" them, in our parlance. Instead, the warning not to "talk back" might have something to do with what the masters were teaching within the household churches, as indicated by Titus 1:9. In this proposed situation, perhaps the enslaved believers saw the irony of the Pastor's opposition to the slave-trade (1 Tim 1:10) as "sound teaching," while he still advocated the continuation of enslavement. This would not necessarily have been viewed as an irony at all, by the first-century master class, since there were many landowning elite who also regularly opposed the moral character of slave-dealers.

A few enslaved believers may have occasionally had responsibility for teaching the believers as well. The metaphorical use of male leaders as "God's slaves" (2 Tim 2:24; Titus 1:1) as those who teach opens up interesting possibilities for this prospect. Although this scenario remains unlikely, there are no explicit statements opposing the teaching roles of enslaved believers. On the other hand, the enslaved did not manage their own households, which seems to have been a requirement for teachers in the communities of the Pastorals (1 Tim 3:2-4, 12; Titus 1:7-9). The Pastor's goal

is to maintain order with respect to what is taught, so demanding the enslaved not to "talk back" suggests he is aware of their challenges to the teaching activity of some slaveholding believers.

(2) The second negative command also needs further investigation. The NRSV's translation "to pilfer" (νοσφιζομένους) is preferable to the translation "to steal" in some English translations (e.g., NIV, CEB). The latter translation creates images of enslaved believers committing petty crimes. Within the New Testament, the term is used only in Acts, where Luke describes Ananias's deceptive act with this verb: he sold his own property but *"kept back some of the proceeds"* (Acts 5:2, 3). In Titus, the term implies a connotation of "holding back" from an allotment of funds given to trusted enslaved persons who were granted responsibility to carry out the master's business. If even trusted slaves were willing to "pilfer" from what was entrusted to them, it reveals to us something about the kinds of conditions the enslaved worked under, indeed a "yoke" even in the Pastor's mind.

(3) To provide "complete and perfect fidelity" implies that the enslaved would be trustworthy and reliable in

their activities. In the Pastor's writings, the adjective "good" or "kind" (ἀγαθός) is usually associated with public activities (ἔργα) (compare 1 Tim 2:10; 5:10; 2 Tim 2:21; 3:17; Titus 1:16; 3:1).[36] But what counts as "complete and perfect fidelity" for the enslaved Christian is unclear.[37]

The emphasis in this household code of conduct suggests that the Pastor perceived a lack of orderliness, which was detrimental to the church's public witness, so that all this advice to enslaved believers may imply that previous warnings have not been heeded. Perhaps the enslaved had connected their newfound freedom in Christ to their enslaved status and tried to negotiate the disparity. The Pastor desired to control not only the actions of the enslaved but also their speech. Perhaps the enslaved chose to speak back to their masters, not insolently but when their master's verbal abuse was unbearable. Perhaps the enslaved "stole" but thought of it as additional nourishment when insufficient meals were offered. Perhaps the enslaved could not be completely faithful "in every respect" because, as Jennifer Glancy has convincingly shown, sexual favors were oftentimes expected, especially of female slaves.[38] Were Christian slaveholders bound by the Pastor's challenge to remain sexually pure with respect to their human property, as he commands in 1 Tim 4:12?

The Pastor fails to provide any insight into the expectations, feelings, and desires of the enslaved believers in his community. The acts that the Pastor condemns—challenging the master's teachings, appropriating funds for survival, and even unfaithfulness—may have been the daily acts of resistance the enslaved utilized since they had no legal recourse for the abuse they received.[39] Instead, what the Pastor prefers—as any slaveholder would—is to prescribe the social

---

36. On "good works" as generally used in the Pastorals, see in this volume "Translation Matters: 'Good Works,'" p. 58.

37. For additional comments on the "faith" of slaves, see "Translation Matters: 'Fidelity,'" p. 153.

38. Glancy, *Slavery*, 50–53; Keith Bradley, *Slaves and Masters in the Roman Empire: A Study in Social Control* (New York: Oxford University Press, 1987), 63–70.

39. The challenge of imagining the psychology of the enslaved is admirably promoted in the work of Keith Bradley, *Slavery and Rebellion in the Roman World, 140 B.C.–70 B.C.* (Bloomington: Indiana University Press, 1989); "Roman Slavery: Retrospect and Prospect," *Canadian Journal of History* 43 (2008): 477–500; "Roman Slavery and the New Testament: Engaging the Work of Keith R. Bradley (Special Forum)," *BibInt* 21 (2013): 495–546.

actions of the enslaved and place them in the service of their Christian and non-Christian slaveholders, who manage the households in which the believing communities pray, sing, read Scripture, take communion, and worship. The only contribution the enslaved believer may offer to the community of faith is that her/his service to an unbelieving master may become an evangelical tool for the church (1 Tim 6:1; Titus 2:10).

The Pastor's "Gospel" for Enslaved Christians

The author of the Pastoral Epistles views the world as a member of a slaveholding society and provides a theological rationale to maintain the obedience of the enslaved. He lays out his religious propositions in the following ways:

- the enslaved ought to behave well so that the name of God and the teaching may not be blasphemed (1 Tim 6:1)
- slaveholders are "members of the [same] church"; they benefit by the service as beloved-believers (1 Tim 6:2)
- "whoever teaches otherwise and does not agree with the sound words of our Lord Jesus . . . is conceited" (1 Tim 6:3-4);
- the enslaved who behave faithfully will "be an ornament to the doctrine of God our Savior" (Titus 2:10)
- "the grace of God has appeared, bringing salvation to all," enslaved and free (Titus 2:11)

All of this discourse is given an eschatological thrust because "we" believers—both enslaved and free—"wait for . . . the manifestation of . . . Jesus Christ" (Titus 2:13). This advocate for the slaveholder encourages the enslaved to look to the future for a sense of "hope" and to ignore any earthly benefits. Since God's grace affects the spiritual "salvation of all" (Titus 2:11), it has no immediate ramifications on enslaved *bodies*. In good Hellenistic fashion, the Pastor distinguishes the body—and one's station in life—from the soul. Besides, material benefits of this kind are reserved for "believing masters" only. All of the "Christian" household codes within the New Testament promote the interest of the slaveholders, including their economic well-being, "since those who benefit by their service are believers and beloved" (1 Tim 6:2).

As for their service to the larger church body, enslaved believers—as the property of unbelievers—should strive to win over their unbelieving masters to the new Christian movement by their unrelenting service. To be totally reliable as slaves might alter the hearts of unbelievers (1 Tim 6:1). Their compulsory service has a missionary function. Yet the believer who is both earthly and spiritually enslaved—the one who should "show complete and perfect fidelity" to the master—loses the ability to participate fully in the church body because her/his relationship to the household church is modified and determined by his/her obedience to the believing master. As Rev. Pike preached in the nineteenth century, "If you disobey your earthly master, you offend your heavenly Master."[40]

Why did the Pastor focus on the behavior of believing slaves? Did he think, as Gordon D. Fee wonders, that "the false teachings being propagated in this part of the world were putting considerable tension on the master/slave relationship in the church"?[41] Was such a "false" teaching of social equality generated by Christians who had heard announcements like Gal 3:28 and Col 3:11 at baptism services in the Pauline communities and reflected on their deeper implications? Or, if someone taught that the resurrection has already happened (2 Tim 2:17-18),

wouldn't this belief have implications for present, earthly status categories? If so, the Pastor reacts negatively to such ideas. Clarice Martin states it this way: "the author of the Pastorals issued stern warnings against what might be termed 'egalitarian excess.'"[42]

The theological and moral viewpoint of the Pastor is strikingly different from other similar advice to enslaved persons in the New Testament because he has not included any instruction to slaveholding believers.[43] The Pastor chooses not to advise them on how to treat their property (which was how the enslaved were conceived), following precedents laid out in Roman law and philosophical treatises. By this omission, it is possible that the Pastor assumes that "believing masters" already carried out their service toward the enslaved with care and compassion. They needed no words of warning. The author of Colossians, however, feels differently: "Masters, treat your slaves justly

40. Jacobs, *Incidents*, 107.

41. Gordon D. Fee, *1 and 2 Timothy, Titus*, NIBCNT 13 (Peabody, MA: Hendrickson Publishers, 1988), 137.

42. Clarice Martin, "1–2 Timothy, Titus," in *True to Our Native Land: An African American New Testament Commentary*, ed. Brian K. Blount, Cain Hope Felder, Clarice J. Martin, Emerson B. Powery (Philadelphia: Fortress Press, 2007), 412.

43. Even more striking is the fact that "nowhere in the authentic letters does Paul attempt to establish norms of behavior for slaves" (Glancy, *Slavery*, 141). On the ambiguity surrounding Paul's views on slavery, see Clarice J. Martin, "The Eyes Have It: Slaves in the Communities of Christ Believers," in *The People's History: Christian Origins*, ed. Richard Horsley (Minneapolis: Fortress Press, 2010), 221–39.

and fairly, for you know that you also have a Master in heaven" (Col 4:1). And, Ephesians follows suit with an exhortation to masters: "Stop threatening them, for you know that both of you have the same Master in heaven" (6:9). The author of 1 Peter provides evidence of a diversity of attitudes and reactions among slaveholders: "Slaves, accept the authority of your masters with all deference, not only those who are kind and gentle but also those who are harsh" (1 Pet 2:18). Only enslaved believers, in the Pastor's perspective, needed to be reminded of their moral obligations within the Christian household community. Before we make too much of this comparison, it is important to heed J. Albert Harrill's conclusions in his study. He proves that the household codes of Colossians (which was probably the older of the two) and Ephesians were not Christian challenges to the Greco-Roman slave codes of their day. Rather, they were written to encourage slaveholding masters to remember their place within the larger hierarchy of church leadership.[44] When compared to the injunctions in the Pastoral Epistles, however, the codes of Colossians and Ephesians appear, on the surface, more attuned to the abusive situations of the enslaved.

Conclusion

Unfortunately, many contemporary biblical scholars continue to read the Pastorals' teachings about slavery without any critical engagement, as if they are God's eternal words for the people of God. In his initial comment on Titus 2:9-10, Gordon Fee writes with exclamation, "No one promised that Christian discipleship would be easy!"[45] William D. Mounce can write, "Learning to view a slave's labor not as a duty but as an act of kindness (1 Tim 6:2a) is revolutionary."[46] But this is not "revolutionary." What would be revolutionary, in the ancient world, was the Essene position to abandon the slave system entirely! What was revolutionary in the antebellum period was the abolitionist movement! Instead, in early Christianity, the Pastor's advice was customary and expected within the ancient Roman slavo-cracy of the day. Clarice J. Martin rightly concludes: "Thus, the New Testament writers who utilized the household codes were neither interested in

---

44. J. Albert Harrill, *Slaves in the New Testament: Literary, Social, and Moral Dimensions* (Minneapolis: Fortress Press, 2006), 85–118.

45. Fee, *1 and 2 Timothy, Titus*, 190.

46. William D. Mounce, *Pastoral Epistles*, WBC 46 (Nashville, TN: Thomas Nelson, 2000), 330.

reforming the social order nor interested in social revolution."[47]

What the Pastor added to these hierarchical relationships was Christian theological reflection in order to manage the behavior of enslaved believers as part of the management of, what he called, God's household (1 Tim 1:4; 3:15). When our hermeneutical and theological biases hinder a proper, critical reading of Christian Scripture, we should not be surprised to continue to see divisions and disagreements among contemporary ecclesial groups. Sometimes, we simply must confess that what we read in a biblical passage cannot (must not!) be the final word on the matter. Surely, God is not as limited in imagining a world of justice and peace for all, as are some of these ancient (and contemporary) Christian thinkers.

Emerson B. Powery

Interpretive Essay: The History of the Pastorals' Teaching

Such instructions regarding slaves as are found in 1 Timothy and Titus have reverberated throughout the history of Western civilization in various attempts to organize societies around hierarchical principles as well as by those who seek to profit financially from the sale and exploitation of human beings. The influence of these texts can be observed in the justifications given for the establishment and prolongation of slavery in the "New World,"[48] and their interpretations continue to contribute to race-based ideologies that fuel prejudices against persons of color in the twenty-first century.

Throughout two millennia there is ample evidence for how masters, the elite, and the self-identified "superior races" understood the New Testament verses on slavery. But what did enslaved people themselves think about these teachings? What were they taught about the Bible's stance on slavery? Before the nineteenth century there are few written witnesses to the actual experience of slavery. But as the abolitionist movement developed in the United States, some ex-slaves gave voice to their stories, among the more famous: Frederick Douglass, Sojourner Truth,

---

47. Clarice J. Martin, "The *Haustefeln* (Household Codes) in African American Biblical Interpretation: 'Free Slaves' and 'Subordinate Women,'" in *Stony the Road We Trod: African American Biblical Interpretation*, ed. Cain Hope Felder (Minneapolis: Fortress Press, 1991), 210.

48. See Harrill's noteworthy analysis, "The Use of the New Testament in the American Slave Controversy" in *Slaves in the New Testament*, 165–92.

and Booker T. Washington.[49] There are also the over two thousand oral testimonies collected from ex-slaves by the Federal Writers' Project (FWP) in the 1930s, four excerpts of which are included below. The former slaves relate some of their encounters with the Bible while they were still young, prior to emancipation.

> Hannah Crassen, North Carolina: "The white folks did not allow us to have nothing to do wid books. You better not be found tryin' to learn to read. Our marster wuz harder down on dat den anything else. You better not be ketched wid a book. Dey read the Bible and told us to obey our marster for de Bible said obey your marster."[50]

> Lucretia Alexander, Arkansas: "the preacher came and preached to them [the slaves] in their quarters. He'd just say, 'Serve your masters. Don't steal your master's turkey. Don't steal your master's chickens. Don't steal your master's hog. Don't steal your master's meat. Do whatsomever your master tells you to do.' Same old thing all the time."[51]

> John Bates, Texas: "My uncle Ben he could read de Bible and he allus tell us some day us be free and Massa Harry laugh, haw, haw, haw, and he say 'Hell, no, yous never be free, yous ain't got sense 'nough to make de livin' if yous was free.' Den he takes de Bible 'way from uncle Ben and say it put de bad ideas in he head, but Uncle gets 'nother Bible and hides it and massa never finds out."[52]

> Anderson Edwards, Texas: "When I starts preaching I couldn't read or write and had to preach what Master told me, and he say tell them n-----s iffen they obeys the master they goes to Heaven; but I knowed there's something better for them, but daren't tell them 'cept on the sly. That I done lots. I tells 'em iffen they keeps praying, the Lord will set 'em free."[53]

49. Frederick Douglass, *Narrative of the Life of Frederick Douglass: An American Slave, Written by Himself* (Boston: Anti-slavery Office, 1845); Sojourner Truth, *Narrative of Sojourner Truth: A Northern Slave*, ed. Olive Gilbert (Boston: the author, 1850); and Booker T. Washington, *Up From Slavery: An Autobiography* (New York: Doubleday, 1901).

50. "Born in Slavery: Slave Narratives from the Federal Writers' Project, 1936–1938," Vol. 11, North Carolina, Part 1, Adams-Hunter; https://www.loc.gov/resource/mesn.111/?sp=197.

51. Cited in Norman R. Yetman, *Voices From Slavery: 100 Authentic Slave Narratives* (Mineola, NY: Dover, 1999), 12–13.

52. "Born in Slavery: Slave Narratives from the Federal Writers' Project, 1936–1938," Texas Narratives, Vol. 16, Texas, Part 1, Adams-Duhon; https://www.loc.gov/resource/mesn.161/?sp=57.

53. Cited in B. A. Botkin, *Lay My Burden Down: A Folk History of Slavery* (Chicago: University of Chicago Press, 1945), 26–27. I have altered the quotation when

Hannah Crassen's story reflects a common statement from ex-slaves: that they were prevented from learning to read anything for themselves, including the Bible, and that the main message taught from the Bible was "obey your masters" or, as the KJV put it, "to be obedient to their masters." Lucretia Alexander remembers a recurring and tiresome sermonizing that surely extrapolates from the words of 1 Tim 6:2, which in the KJV says "do them service," and Titus 2:10 "not to pilfer" or, in the KJV, "not purloining." On the other hand, John Bates's anecdote reveals an open struggle between the master and his slave for control over possessing, reading, and interpreting the Scriptures. Two rival discourses about the future—"some day us be free" versus "yous never be free"—are asserted. Recognizing that the Bible is filled with "bad ideas," master Harry confiscates the book, but the victory goes to John's Uncle Ben who secretly obtains, and evidently treasures, another Bible. In a similar fashion, Anderson Edwards knows of a message of freedom that is the opposite of the master's vision. Even Hannah Crassen's master, in refusing to allow slaves to learn to read, senses the dangers posed by a literate slave population. These four reports exemplify the larger disagreement between biblical views of slavery: between the powerful storyline of the God who acts to liberate the Hebrew slaves as opposed to the more socially conventional and ultimately enslaving directives like those in the Pastorals that presume the existence of and foster the persistence of slavery as an institution.

From the perspective of many twenty-first-century Western readers, these sources, biblical and personal, not only seem ancient but also are easily set aside. Their slavery ideology reflects the past contexts in which they were composed and has nothing to do with modern ideals that grant full human rights to all. Yet with regard to these earlier enslavements, we would do well to remember the warning from William Faulkner: "The past is never dead. It's not even past."[54] The long geographic and economic expansion of the United States depended on slave labor as well as on the elimination and subjugation of indigenous peoples. American society still suffers the effects of racial prejudices and race-based slavery, as seen in the neighborhoods and schools that are

---

Anderson Edwards uses the "n-word" to describe himself and his compatriots. I choose not to use this word, because as a white person born in the United States, I do not want to reinstitute any of the oppressive practices of the slave-owners.

54. William Faulkner, *Requiem for a Nun* (New York: Random House, 1951), 92.

still essentially racially segregated,[55] and burdens of greater incarceration and higher unemployment rates,[56] lower life expectancy, and daily psychological stresses borne by persons of color. White persons in the United States also face the legacy of slavery in that the realities of American slavery exaggerate their sense of superiority as a "race" and blind them to the fact that their privileges often come about simply due to an accident of birth rather than to their merit-based achievement.[57] The lived experiences of this slavery are not past at all, for any of us.

Reading the Pastorals' teachings ought to provoke us not only to reflect on the ongoing social and personal effects of the American experience of slavery but also to name and oppose twenty-first-century forms of enslavement. While more modern slaveries do not usually rise to the level of a "slave society" as in the Roman Empire or the American colonies, enslaved persons live in most every country around the world. Grouped under the term "human trafficking," we find boys conscripted into rebel armies, teenage girls forced into prostitution, and tribal peoples exploited as agricultural laborers. Gloria Steinem writes: "No country is safe from this river of human chattel that flows through factories and sweatshops, kitchens and crop-picking fields, red light districts and brothel beds."[58] Persons of faith can participate with any number of organizations that combat such slavery wherever and whenever it appears.[59]

55. Some of the history of our segregated cities is described in Isabel Wilkerson, *The Warmth of Other Suns: The Epic Story of America's Great Migration* (New York: Random House, 2010).

56. For example, see Michelle Alexander, *The New Jim Crow: Mass Incarceration in the Age of Colorblindness* (New York: New Press, 2010).

57. Long-time Boston College teacher and activist Horace Seldon details many more negative effects of racism on whites in the United States in this concise document: "Racism: Negative Effects on Whites," *Convictions about Racism in the United States of America*, http://horaceseldon.com/racism-negative-effects-on-whites/. I also recommend Debby Irving, *Waking Up White and Finding Myself in the Story of Race* (Cambridge, MA: Elephant Room, 2014).

58. Gloria Steinem, "Foreword," in *Enslaved: True Stories of Modern Day Slavery*, ed. Jesse Sage and Liora Kasten (New York: Palgrave Macmillan, 2006), xi; copyrighted by the American Anti-Slavery Group.

59. Evidence on human trafficking is difficult to confirm. One comprehensive website is that sponsored by the United Nations UNODOC, "Human Trafficking," *United Nations Office on Drugs and Crime*, 2016, http://www.unodc.org/unodc/en/human-trafficking/what-is-human-trafficking.html?ref=menuside.

Titus 2:11-15

¹¹For the grace of God has appeared, bringing salvation to all, ¹²training us to renounce impiety and worldly passions, and in the present age to live lives that are self-controlled, upright, and godly, ¹³while we wait for the blessed hope and the manifestation of the glory of our great God and Savior, Jesus Christ. ¹⁴He it is who gave himself for us that he might redeem us from all iniquity and purify for himself a people of his own who are zealous for good deeds. ¹⁵Declare these things; exhort and reprove with all authority. Let no one look down on you.

The early Christian teachings about slavery continue to be problematic to this day, in no small part because they raise serious theological and ethical issues for people of faith. Along with other biblical texts, the Pastorals' teachings on slaves cast doubt on the true nature of God and at the same time have obscured and obstructed the mission of God's people to identify with the oppressed and to bring release to the captives.[60] All the more reason, then, for teachers and preachers to engage these short but historically influential verses through questioning their premises, disputing their continued authority, and weighing them against more liberating biblical witnesses.

TRANSLATION MATTERS: "ZEALOUS FOR GOOD DEEDS"

The word "zealous" (Titus 2:14) is an adjective in English, but in Greek ζηλωτής is a noun with the literal meaning of "zealot." Here it refers to the "people of his own" who are "eager" or "enthusiastic." According to Benjamin J. Lappenga, the word carries two supplementary senses. First, in a Greco-Roman educational context, it can be translated as "imitator" or "emulator" and refers to how a student ought to follow his or her teacher.[61] Surely the translation "imitator(s) of good deeds" should be considered for 2:14 since the Pastorals so often use this method of teaching and learning.

Second, Lappenga notes, "We simply cannot dismiss the significance of the word ζηλωτής for first-century Jews."[62] The term was, of course, adopted by the Zealot party in response to Roman military occupation. In addition, the Jewish

60. Elsa Tamez has written eloquently about this very dilemma. See her comments in this volume on 1 Tim 6, pp. 82–83.
61. Benjamin J. Lappenga, "'Zealots for Good Works': The Polemical Repercussions of the Word ζηλωτής in Titus 2:14," *CBQ* 75 (2013): 712.
62. Ibid., 715.

ideal was that one was "zealous for the law," so that the Pastorals' term "zealous for good deeds" would be understood as another taunt at the Jewish opponents mentioned in 1:10 and 1:14. With the author's polemical stance in mind, Lappenga offers this expanded translation of Titus 2:14: "who gave himself for us in order that he might redeem us from all lawlessness and purify for himself a special people who are, in stark contrast with those among you who are envious for shameful gain, not 'zealots of the law' in the ways that you opponents have twisted it, but 'zealots for good works' in the sense that I have expounded in this letter."[63]

The chapter comes to a close with these few lofty theologically dense statements that are peppered with the author's distinct vocabulary, e.g., "appear," "impiety," "self-control," "upright," "Savior," and "good deeds" (Titus 2:11-15). Even though the passage sounds very much like Paul linking grace, salvation, and Jesus Christ, the sentence structure in Titus 2:11-15 is quite different from the letters known to be written by the apostle. The very positive presentation of what this author calls "good deeds" is likewise uncharacteristic of Paul's moral exhortation.[64]

The broad vision that salvation has been brought to "all" (Titus 2:11) and that "we" (2:13) are waiting in hope for God's glory is certainly inspiring. Yet the larger context within Titus and even the entire Pastorals letter collection gives a different meaning to these verses. The author has previously taught that "lives that are self-controlled, upright, and godly" (2:12) will be lived differently by males and females, as well as by slaves of both sexes. The universality of "he might redeem" and "purify" (2:14) us all results in a more narrow outcome: the people must act out "good deeds" (2:14) that are gender specific. In addition, the author repeats and strengthens his command from 2:1 that the male leader Titus has the authority and responsibility to pass on all these instructions to the social groups within the community.

In the New Revised Common Lectionary, Titus 2:11-14 serves as the Christmas Eve Epistle Lesson for Years A, B, and C. By extracting these four verses out of the chapter, the committee is able to sidestep the scriptural teachings that seek to uphold conventional ideals of femininity and masculinity, the practice of slaveholding, and the authority of men as church leaders. The discourse of Titus 2 unquestionably calls us to a more critical analysis than can be accomplished through a short reading in a holiday service.

63. Ibid., 717.
64. I have discussed this further above, "Translation Matters: 'Good works,'" p. 58.

Titus 3

Orderliness Is Next to Godliness

The third chapter of Titus maintains the depiction of "Paul" writing to just one person—"Titus"—in order to give him directions for teaching a larger group of believers. Many of the desired ethical standards are also found in 1 and 2 Timothy, but here the author links these to a theological statement that has a liturgical tone by referring to some form of cleansing that results in new life. Turning from this positive and stirring exhortation, the author once again denigrates his opponents and their teachings.

The author begins with a directive to Titus—"remind them be subject to rulers and authorities" (3:1)—that is similar to 1 Tim 2:1-2, where the author instructs Timothy to make sure that believers pray for "kings and all who are in high positions." This particular command to Titus emphasizes the hierarchical nature of the Roman Imperial world and the need for individuals to recognize and remain in their proper position within that social location by being subordinated and obedient (Titus 3:1).[1] This concept is even more explicit in Rom 13:1-2, where Paul declares:

> Let every person be subject to the governing authorities; for there is no authority except from God, and those authorities that exist have been instituted by God. Therefore whoever resists authority resists what God has appointed, and those who resist will incur judgment.

1. On the phrase, "be subject to," see above, "Translation Matters: 'Disobedient,'" p. 5.

174

Titus 3:1-8a

¹Remind them to be subject to rulers and authorities, to be obedient, to be ready for every good work, ²to speak evil of no one, to avoid quarreling, to be gentle, and to show every courtesy to everyone. ³For we ourselves were once foolish, disobedient, led astray, slaves to various passions and pleasures, passing our days in malice and envy, despicable, hating one another. ⁴But when the goodness and loving kindness of God our Savior appeared, ⁵he saved us, not because of any works of righteousness that we had done, but according to his mercy, through the water of rebirth and renewal by the Holy Spirit. ⁶This Spirit he poured out on us richly through Jesus Christ our Savior, ⁷so that, having been justified by his grace, we might become heirs according to the hope of eternal life. ⁸ᵃThe saying is sure.

TRANSLATION MATTERS: "EVERYONE"

The word "everyone" in Titus 3:2 (also in 1 Tim 2:1) translates the Greek words πάντας ἀνθρώπους. In earlier English versions (prior to about 1980), this phrase was translated "all men," similar to the original language, which also uses the masculine noun for a group composed of both men and women. More recent English translations opt for the more inclusive "everyone" or "all people," and this more universal meaning—of all men, women, free, and enslaved—is reasonable in the context of these verses.

However, when the author employs the singular noun ἄνθρωπος to refer to Timothy as "man of God" (1 Tim 6:11; 2 Tim 3:17), it is clear that he is referring to a male person.[2] The singular is also used in Titus 3:10, where "anyone who causes divisions" would be more literally translated "a *man* who causes divisions." In that case, the masculine gender noun shows that the author envisions his most serious opponents as male and not female.

Our author does not go so far as to state that rulers are divinely appointed or that insubordination toward them smacks of insubordination toward God. However, by inserting the dense theological explanation of 3:3-7, he does affirm that by following this Pauline teaching one demonstrates that God has saved "us" from a former wicked "disobedient" way of life and has now cleansed "us" for a new "obedient" life. Both Titus and 1 Timothy express this kyriarchal opinion that behaving submissively toward rulers is an important manifestation of living a good life.

2. See also "Translation Matters: 'Everyone Who Belongs to God,'" p. 125.

In Titus 3:2, the author also advocates for civility, gentleness, and courtesy on the part of the believers toward "everyone." Since this instruction comes after the one to be subject to authorities and before the description of what "we ourselves were once," the author is clearly writing about people outside the community. Although there is no evidence that the Christian communities were experiencing substantial conflict with those outside its boundaries, the author wants to forestall such a situation. Throughout the letters, he has explicitly talked about how behavior by younger women (Titus 2:5), slaves (Titus 2:10), overseers/bishops (1 Tim 3:7), and younger widows (1 Tim 5:14) might be perceived by outsiders. His persistent advice that everyone should demonstrate good moral conduct is meant to remind believers that they represent God, Christ, and the community to those outside.

A Wholesome Order

The author's pervasive concern for order is reflected in the letter's final exhortation to submissive behavior (Gk. *hypotassesthai*). This admonition concerns the relationship of the entire community to "rulers and authorities" (Gk. *archais [kai] exousiais*), presumably the civil authorities of the Roman Empire (Rom 13:1). This is not a dramatic shift from the previous discussion of behavior within the household (Titus 2:1-15), for the Greco-Roman world understood the household and the state to be intrinsically related. Order in one fostered order in the other, and disorder in one led to anarchy in the other (Cicero, *Republic* 1.43).

The concern for civic behavior continues with the exhortation to obedience, for the infinitive has the specific meaning of obedience to those in authority (Gk. *peitharchein*). In the third phrase ("to be ready for every good work"), however, the author is clearly referring to Christian life in its fullness and not simply to political obedience. He is, in fact, drawing an implicit contrast to the opponents, who are "unfit for any good work" (1:16). The various arenas of behavior are thus linked by the concept of authority, especially in light of the instruction to Titus in 2:15 to reprove "with all authority." Obedience to political authorities, to church authorities, and to family authorities are all interconnected and such thoroughgoing obedience was regarded as essential to the maintenance of a wholesome order.[3]

Jouette M. Bassler

3. Jouette M. Bassler, *1 Timothy, 2 Timothy, Titus,* ANTC (Nashville, TN: Abingdon, 1996), 205.

⁸ᵇI desire that you insist on these things, so that those who have come to believe in God may be careful to devote themselves to good works; these things are excellent and profitable to everyone. ⁹But avoid stupid controversies, genealogies, dissensions, and quarrels about the law, for they are unprofitable and worthless. ¹⁰After a first and second admonition, have nothing more to do with anyone who causes divisions, ¹¹since you know that such a person is perverted and sinful, being self-condemned.

Christians through the centuries have found meaning in the assurance of salvation and hope of eternal life found in Titus 3:3-7, which is read as the epistle lesson for Christmas Day in Years A, B, and C of the New Revised Common Lectionary. Some of the terms in this short passage echo Paul's theology. For example, as in the Titus 3 passage, 1 Cor 6:9-11 starts with a list of vicious types that the believers "used to be," and then goes on to explain how God "washed," "sanctified," and "justified" them. Jesus Christ and the Spirit are also named in 1 Cor 6:9-11.

> Do you not know that wrongdoers will not inherit the kingdom of God? Do not be deceived! Fornicators, idolaters, adulterers, male prostitutes, sodomites,[4] thieves, the greedy, drunkards, revilers, robbers—none of these will inherit the kingdom of God. And this is what some of you used to be. But you were washed, you were sanctified, you were justified in the name of the Lord Jesus Christ and in the Spirit of our God.

In addition, Titus 3:5-7 sounds especially close to Paul's understanding of salvation, except that the key element of faith is absent. Also, different words and ideas emerge in this passage. Some of them are typical of the author: "passing our days" (3:3; 1 Tim 2:2), "Savior" (Titus 3:4, 7), and "appeared" (3:4). Some have not been encountered in any of the Pauline letters, including the Pastorals: "despicable" (3:3) "goodness" (3:4), "loving kindness" (3:4), "water" (3:5), and "rebirth" (3:5). The author's typical assertion—"the saying is sure" (3:8)—completes and confirms this dignified affirmation.[5]

4. On the word "sodomites," see in this volume "Translation Matters: 'Ancient Vices,'" p. 6.
5. See above, "Translation Matters: 'The Saying Is Sure,'" p. 29.

TRANSLATION MATTERS: "I DESIRE"

In Titus 3:8, the NRSV translates the verb βούλομαι as "I desire." This Greek word carries a range of meaning depending on the context: "I wish/want/desire/should like/would have/am willing." This word appears also in 1 Tim 2:8 and 5:14, and in each case, the author uses this first-person singular verb to emphasize the weight of Pauline authority for an important instruction.

- 1 Tim 2:8: "*I desire*, then, that in every place the men should pray."
- 1 Tim 5:14: "So *I would have* the younger widows marry, bear children, and manage their households."
- Titus 3:8b: "*I desire* that you insist on these things."

The word "desire" in English does not quite convey the forcefulness of the Greek word as the author employs it. Clearly, he is not simply expressing a wishful thought, but rather what he thinks of as an apostolic directive.

One last time, the author directs Titus to insist on the necessity for good works.[6] By setting these works in opposition to the kinds of speech-acts that he thinks of as "unprofitable and worthless" (Titus 3:9), the author returns to establishing a strong separation between believers and the opponents, who in his perception are not believers. As in his attacks on the false teachers in 1 Tim 1:8-11 and 2 Tim 2:23-26, he draws the line between the two sides in both content (the false opinions in 3:9) and in action ("perverted and sinful" in 3:11). Titus is told to avoid their teachings, but even more harshly, to avoid the people themselves.

TRANSLATION MATTERS: "ANYONE WHO CAUSES DIVISIONS"

The Greek adjective αἱρετικός ("factious" or "causing divisions") appears only here in the New Testament. Although it originally meant "one who can choose rightly," it came to be applied in a negative way as "heretical" in Christian writings of the second century CE. Ironically, even though it is the people who "cause divisions" who ought to be avoided, the author himself creates divisions within the community when he counsels "have nothing more to do with" (3:10) such people. As Jouette Bassler notes, "From the author's point of view, of course, this avoidance was a protective strategy to eliminate internal divisions and restore order; he would not have recognized it as divisive."[7]

---

6. See "Translation Matters: 'Good Works,'" p. 58.
7. Bassler, *1 Timothy, 2 Timothy, Titus*, 211.

Titus 3:12-15

¹²When I send Artemas to you, or Tychicus, do your best to come to me at Nicopolis, for I have decided to spend the winter there. ¹³Make every effort to send Zenas the lawyer and Apollos on their way, and see that they lack nothing. ¹⁴And let people learn to devote themselves to good works in order to meet urgent needs, so that they may not be unproductive.

¹⁵All who are with me send greetings to you. Greet those who love us in the faith.

Grace be with all of you.

Many readers of the Pastorals have been induced to relate to their opponents in similar ways, creating harsh incivility in discussions and severe personal disconnection, even shunning. I once served in a church where an interim pastor cited Titus 3:10 as justification for demanding that someone step down from a committee. This lay volunteer was evidently asking the same challenging questions "after a first and second admonition" (3:10)! Such an insensitive application of this verse is not uncommon among some Christian groups. In fact, Jay Twomey's research into the history of interpretation of this passage shows that

> few readers through the centuries have ever questioned the Pastor's motivations behind, or the correctness of, the term "heretic." There have been striking differences of opinion, though, with regard to the treatment of these potentially divisive sectarians. A majority of interpreters seem disconcertingly enthusiastic, at first blush, about taking a hard line on heresy; but many actually mitigate the text's harshest implications, while others try to eliminate them altogether.[8]

Instead, we should be suspicious of the author's labels imposed on those who disagree with his teachings, especially since he does not describe or engage their ideas in any constructive way. This is not a healthy or open model for Christian communities today.

Like many New Testament letters, this one closes with a few personal remarks and greetings. The author knows that Paul organized a team of co-workers who travelled around the Mediterranean basin, sometimes carrying letters from Paul to the churches. Such personal delegations and written communications were crucial elements of conveying Paul's

---

8. Jay Twomey, *The Pastoral Epistles Through the Centuries* (Malden, MA: Wiley Blackwell, 2008), 219.

presence to the early Christian churches.[9] The appointed people and letters also served to create a network of relationships between individuals and communities by strengthening the sense of belonging to a larger movement. Aside from Titus 3:12-13, the names Artemas and Zenas are not otherwise mentioned in the New Testament, while Tychicus appears four times (Acts 20:4; Eph 6:21; Col 4:7; 2 Tim 4:12), and Apollos has a prominent role in both Acts (18:24–19:1) and 1 Cor (1:12; 3:1-9; 21-23). The two verses in our letter construct an elite group of six male leaders, including "Paul" and "Titus." Even such small details reinforce the author's opinion that only men should preside over church teachings and activities.

When the author says in the very last verse "All who are with me send greetings to you," the "you" is a singular pronoun, indicating Titus alone. Similarly, the request "Greet those who love us in the faith" is in the singular form. However, he looks beyond a single recipient in the final benediction: "Grace be with all of you." He expects that this letter, like all of the letters we have from the hand of Paul, will be read aloud as an educational resource for a larger audience of believers. In the social location he envisions, that audience will include a variety of persons: Cretans and Judeans, male and female, older and younger, enslaved and free. The whole point of his letter is that each one ought to take up his or her proper station in the household and the house-church, just as they do in the Roman Imperial order.

---

9. On how Paul used personal representatives in his work, see Margaret M. Mitchell, "New Testament Envoys in the Context of Greco-Roman Diplomatic and Epistolary Conventions: The Example of Timothy and Titus," *JBL* 111 (1992): 641–62.

Conclusion

The Pastoral Letters are troubling texts. Their author has concealed his identity under a pseudonym borrowed from the famous apostle to the Gentiles. The circumstances behind his compositions are opaque; we do not know what was actually happening in his ministry or his social location. He attacks his opponents with sharp polemics, elevates the social status of elite men, and reinforces subordinated positions for women, children, and the enslaved. His teachings are not only offensive to many present-day audiences, but their appropriation has a long and complicated history within Western culture and large portions of the Christian church.

Along with many of the contributors to this volume, I have discussed at great length the author's restrictive teachings for women. His traditional view of female propriety stands as one of the most important distinctions between the Pastorals and the letters that can reliably be attributed to Paul himself. The author of the Pastorals seems to take up the task of "clarifying" Pauline teachings on women. Contrary to 1 Cor 7:8, 25-28, 32-25, 40, he proposes that what Paul *really* wanted was for women to get married and have children (1 Tim 2:15; 5:10, 14; 2 Tim 1:5; 3:6; Titus 2:3-5). And, even though many women—among them, Priscilla, Euodia, and Syntyche—were active in the Pauline mission in earlier times, our author claims that the apostle *really* meant to prohibit women from teaching roles in the church (1 Tim 2:11-12), except with children (2 Tim 1:5) and younger women (Titus 2:3-5). The author's hyper-valuation of

181

men, of their roles, of "true" masculinity, and of male hierarchy conveys his foundational depreciation of any person who does not embody his cultural conventions about gender. Is it any wonder that he seeks to legislate against women's ostensibly female nature and feminine ways, against slaves' supposed servile nature and devious proclivities, and against his opponents' lack of masculine self-control and attractiveness to weak women? His kyriarchical classifications have led directly to a historical disrespect for the majority of lower-status people and to injustices in church and political systems. Such a thoroughgoing patriarchal worldview is particularly objectionable to me as a Christian woman, as it is to many others.

However deplorable we find the author's beliefs and however much we rightly grieve the influence they have had as authoritative texts, it is undoubtedly true that most early readers of the Pastorals—both male and female—would have shared, affirmed, and promptly disseminated their teachings. These churches and believers existed in a culture built on centuries of accepting such a social hierarchy in philosophy, economics, politics, family life, and religious practices. In their social location, primarily within the urban areas of the Roman Empire, during a time of relative peace and prosperity, I imagine that they viewed the supposed differences between the nature and roles of men and women as ordained by God. Their gender ideals functioned as important stabilizers for their families, communities, cities, and provinces. How appropriate it must have been for the churches to acquire such Pauline letters that supported that very ideology. This explains in part why the churches quickly accepted and used the Pastorals as instructional texts, beginning in the early second century CE.

For centuries after and up to the present day, many Christian readers have understood such teachings as divinely given pronouncements about women's roles in marriage and the family as well as in church organization and leadership. Around the year 200 CE, Tertullian alludes to these verses to limit the priestly roles of women: "It is not permitted to a woman to speak in the church; but neither (is it permitted her) to teach, nor to baptize, nor to offer, nor to claim to herself a lot in any manly function, not to say (in any) sacerdotal office."[1] In the late fourth century

---

1. *Virg.*, 9 (ca. 206 CE). The quotation begins with 1 Cor 14:34a but links to 1 Tim 2:12. Similarly, the *Didascalia apostolorum* states: "For it is not to teach that you women . . . are appointed" (3.6.1-2; ca. 225 CE). These citations along with the thoughts of other church fathers on women and the priesthood may be found here: Catholic

CE, Epiphanius of Salamis denounced the Quintillianists as heretical due to the activities of their women: "They have women bishops, presbyters and the rest; they say that none of this makes any difference because 'In Christ Jesus there is neither male nor female.' . . . [But] they have overlooked the apostle's command,"[2] which can be found in 1 Tim 2:12-14. At around the same time period, John Chrysostom preached a homily on this same passage:

> What place has this command here? The fittest. He was speaking of quietness, of propriety, of modesty, so having said that he wished them not to speak in the church, to cut off all occasion of conversation, he says, let them not teach, but occupy the station of learners. For thus they will show submission by their silence. For the sex is naturally somewhat talkative: and for this reason he restrains them on all sides. "For Adam," says he, "was first formed, then Eve. And Adam was not deceived, but the woman being deceived was in the transgression." If it be asked, what has this to do with women of the present day? It shows that the male sex enjoyed the higher honor. Man was first formed; and elsewhere he shows their superiority.[3]

Here Chrysostom asserts another stereotypical opinion that has persisted through the ages—that women are "naturally somewhat talkative"—which leads "logically" to the presumed superiority given to men by the patriarchal biblical interpretation in 1 Timothy.

It is beyond the bounds of this book to engage with the numerous Christian leaders and churches that claim to ascribe divine authority to the teachings about women found in the Pastoral Letters.[4] There remain many organizations, preachers, and scholars who interpret these words in ways that circumscribe the effective ministries of Christian women and promote the three traditional roles for women: submissive wives,

Answers, "Women and the Priesthood," *Catholic Answers: To Explain and Defend the Faith,* http://www.catholic.com/tracts/women-and-the-priesthood.

2. *Panarion* 49.2.5; 3.3. The Quintillianists appear to have been an offshoot of Montanism. See Frank Williams, trans., *The Panarion of Epiphanius of Salamis*, Nag Hammadi and Manichaean Studies 63 (Leiden: Brill, 1987), 22.

3. John Chrysostom, *Homily* 9 on 1 Timothy.

4. Of course, the Roman Catholic Church, Eastern Orthodox Churches, and Southern Baptist Convention (USA) denominations (among others) do not ordain women. Many evangelical churches likewise will not allow women in congregational leadership. For a parachurch organization that promotes the husband's headship and the wife's submission in marriage, see *Gospel, Gender, Flourishing: Council of Biblical Manhood and Womanhood*, CBMW, http://cbmw.org/.

loving mothers, and exceptional homemakers. The views expressed in this commentary are not likely to influence any of these opinions or change any policies. Rather, my intent has been to offer meaningful historical contextualizations and analyses of the Pastorals' instruction so that preachers, teachers, and engaged students of the Bible might gain deeper understandings of the world of the author and then join the struggle to handle these letters with integrity for our own times. Faithful feminist readers today are not at all required to accept the underlying presuppositions of these troubling texts. Instead, once we understand the ancient situation, we are free to resist such teachings in order to fashion a world where each person has freedom from oppression, access to justice, and opportunities for growth as a child of God.

Works Cited

Alexander, Michelle. *The New Jim Crow: Mass Incarceration in the Age of Colorblind-ness*. New York: New Press, 2010.

Arzt-Grabner, Peter. "Neither a Truant nor a Fugitive: Some Remarks on the Sale of Slaves in Roman Egypt and Other Provinces." *Proceedings of the Twenty-Fifth International Congress of Papyrology*, Ann Arbor 2007; American Studies in Papyrology, Ann Arbor 2010.

Robert J. Banks, *Paul's Idea of Community: The Early House Churches in Their Historical Setting*. Grand Rapids: Eerdmans, 1980.

Bassler, Jouette M. *1 Timothy, 2 Timothy, Titus*. ANTC. Nashville: Abingdon, 1996.

Botkin, Benjamin Albert. *Lay My Burden Down: A Folk History of Slavery*. Chicago: University of Chicago Press, 1945; 1958.

Bradley, Keith. "Roman Slavery and the New Testament: Engaging the Work of Keith R. Bradley (Special Forum)." *BibInt* 21 (2013): 495–546.

———. "Roman Slavery: Retrospect and Prospect." *Canadian Journal of History* 43 (2008): 477–500.

———. "Slavery in the Roman Republic." In *The Cambridge World History of Slavery: Volume 1, The Ancient Mediterranean World*, edited by Keith Bradley and Paul Cartledge, 241–64. Cambridge: Cambridge University Press, 2011.

———. "The Regular, Daily Traffic in Slaves." *CJ* 87 (1992): 125–38.

———. *Slavery and Rebellion in the Roman World, 140 B.C.–70 B.C.* Bloomington: Indiana University Press, 1989.

———. *Slaves and Masters in the Roman Empire: A Study in Social Control*. New York: Oxford University Press, 1987.

Brown, Peter. *The Body and Society: Men, Women, and Sexual Renunciation in Early Christianity*. New York: Columbia University Press, 1988.

Clarke, Patricia A. and M. Lynn Rose, "Psychiatric Disability in the Galenic Medical Matrix." In *Disabilities in Roman Antiquity: a capite ad calcem*, edited by Christian Laes, C.F. Goodey, and M. Lynn Rose, 45–72. Leiden: Brill, 2013.

Coates, Ta-Nehisi. *Between the World and Me*. New York: Spiegel & Grau (Random House), 2015.

Collins, Raymond F. "Where Have All My Siblings Gone? A Reflection on the Use of Kinship Language in the Pastoral Epistles." In *Celebrating Paul: Festschrift in Honor of Jerome Murphy-O'Connor, O.P., and Joseph A. Fitzmyer, S.J.*, edited by Peter Spitaler. 321–36. CBQMS 48. Washington, DC: Catholic Biblical Association, 2011.

———. *Accompanied by a Believing Wife: Ministry and Celibacy in the Earliest Church Communities*. Collegeville, MN: Liturgical Press, 2013.

Conway, Colleen M. *Behold the Man: Jesus and Greco-Roman Masculinity*. New York: Oxford University Press, 2008.

Cribiore, Raffaella. *Gymnastics of the Mind: Greek Education in Hellenistic and Roman Egypt*. Princeton: Princeton University Press, 2001.

Dal Lago, Enrico and Constantina Katsari, eds. *Slave Systems: Ancient and Modern*. Cambridge: Cambridge University Press, 2008.

Dewey, Joanna. "1 Timothy," "2 Timothy," and "Titus" In *The Women's Bible Commentary* edited by Carol A. Newsom and Sharon H. Ringe. 1st edition. Louisville: Westminster/John Knox, 1992.

Elliott, Neil. *Liberating Paul: The Justice of God and the Politics of the Apostle*. Minneapolis: Fortress Press, 2005.

Fee, Gordon D. *1 and 2 Timothy, Titus*. NIBCNT 13. Peabody, MA: Hendrickson Publishers, 1988.

Glancy, Jennifer A. "Protocols of Masculinity in the Pastoral Epistles." In *New Testament Masculinities*, edited by Stephen D. Moore and Janice Capel Anderson, 235–64. SemeiaSt 45. Atlanta: SBL, 2003.

———. *Slavery in Early Christianity*. Minneapolis: Fortress, 2006.

Harrill, J. Albert. *Slaves in the New Testament: Literary, Social, and Moral Dimensions*. Minneapolis: Fortress Press, 2006.

Herzer, Jens. "Rearranging the Household of God: A New Perspective on the Pastoral Epistles." In *Empsychoi Logoi: Religious Innovations in Antiquity*, *Studies in Honour of Pieter Willem van der Horst*, Ancient Judaism and Early Christianity 73, edited by Alberdina Houtman, Albert De Jong, and Magda Misset-van De Weg, 547–66. Leiden: Brill, 2008.

Irving, Debby. *Waking Up White and Finding Myself in the Story of Race*. Cambridge, Mass: Elephant Room, 2014.

Johnson, Luke Timothy. *First and Second Letters to Timothy*. AB 35A; New York: Doubleday, 2001.

———. *Letters to Paul's Delegates: 1 Timothy, 2 Timothy, Titus*. Valley Forge, PA: Trinity, 1996.

Joshel, Sandra R. *Slavery in the Roman World*. Cambridge: Cambridge University Press, 2010.

Joshel, Sandra R., and Sheila Murnaghan, eds. *Women and Slaves in Greco-Roman Culture: Differential Equations*. London: Routledge, 1998.

Kartzow, Marianne Bjelland. "Female Gossipers and their Reputation in the Pastoral Epistles." *Neot* 39 (2005): 271–78.

———. *Gossip and Gender: Othering of Speech in the Pastoral Epistles*. BZNW 164. Berlin: Walter de Gruyter, 2009.

Lappenga, Benjamin J. "Zealots for Good Works": The Polemical Repercussions of the Word ζηλωτής in Titus 2:14." *CBQ* 75 (2013): 704–18.

Lull, David J. "Jesus, Paul, and Homosexuals." *CurTM* 34 (June 2007): 199–207.

MacDonald, Dennis R. *The Legend and the Apostle: The Battle for Paul in Story and Canon*. Philadelphia: Westminster, 1983.

MacDonald, Margaret Y. *Early Christian Women and Pagan Opinion: The Power of the Hysterical Woman*. New York; Cambridge: Cambridge University Press, 1996.

Madigan, Kevin and Carolyn Osiek: *Ordained Women in the Early Church: A Documentary History*. Baltimore: Johns Hopkins University Press, 2005.

Malherbe, Abraham J. "Medical Imagery in the Pastoral Epistles." In *Texts and Testaments: Critical Essays on the Bible and Early Church Fathers: A Volume in Honor of Stuart Dickson Currie*, edited by W. Eugene March and Stuart Dickson Currie, 19–35. San Antonio: Trinity University Press, 1980. Reprinted. in *Paul and the Popular Philosophers*, 121–36. Minneapolis: Fortress Press, 1989.

Marshall, I. Howard. *The Pastoral Epistles*. ICC. Edinburgh: T & T Clark, 1999.

Martin, Clarice J. "1–2 Timothy, Titus." In *True to Our Native Land: An African-American New Testament Commentary*, edited by Brian K. Blount, Cain Hope Felder, Clarice J. Martin, and Emerson Powery, 409–36. Minneapolis: Fortress Press, 2007.

———. "The Eyes Have It: Slaves in the Communities of Christ Believers." In *The People's History: Christian Origins*, edited by Richard Horsley, 221–39. Minneapolis: Fortress Press, 2010.

———. "The *Haustefeln* (Household Codes) in African American Biblical Interpretation: 'Free Slaves' and 'Subordinate Women'." In *Stony the Road We Trod: African American Biblical Interpretation*, edited by Cain Hope Felder, 206–31. Minneapolis: Fortress Press, 1991.

Martin, Dale B. "*Arsenokoitês* and *Malakos*: Meanings and Consequences." In *Biblical Ethics & Homosexuality: Listening to Scripture*, edited by Robert L. Brawley, 117–36. Louisville: Westminster John Knox, 1996.

———. "Slave Families and Slaves in Families." In *Early Christian Families in Context: An Interdisciplinary Dialogue*, edited by David L. Balch and Carolyn Osiek, 207–30. Grand Rapids: Eerdmans, 2003.

Meeks, Wayne A. *The First Urban Christians: The Social World of the Apostle Paul.* New Haven, CT: Yale University Press, 1983.

Merz, Annette. *Die fiktive Selbstauslegung des Paulus: Intertextuelle Studien zur Intention und Rezeption der Pastoralbriefe.* NTOA/SUNT 52. Göttingen: Vandenhoeck & Ruprecht; Fribourg: Academic Press, 2004.

Mitchell, Margaret M. "Corrective Composition, Corrective Exegesis: The Teaching on Prayer in 1 Tim 2:1-15." In *1 Timothy Reconsidered,* edited by Karl P. Donfried, 41–62. Louvain: Peeters, 2008.

———. "New Testament Envoys in the Context of Greco-Roman Diplomatic and Epistolary Conventions: The Example of Timothy and Titus." *JBL* 111 (1992): 641–62.

Mounce, William D. *Pastoral Epistles.* WBC 46. Nashville: Nelson, 2000.

Osiek, Carolyn and David L. Balch. *Families in the New Testament World: Household and House Churches.* Louisville: Westminster/John Knox, 1997.

———and Margaret Y. MacDonald, with Janet H. Tulloch. *A Woman's Place: House Churches in Earliest Christianity.* Minneapolis: Fortress Press, 2006.

Quinn, Jerome D. *The Letter to Titus.* AB 35. New York: Doubleday, 1990.

Rawick, George P., ed. *The American Slave: A Composite Autobiography.* 19 vols. Contributions in Afro-American and African studies No. 11. Westport, CT: Greenwood, 1972.

Robinson, Marilynne. *Gilead.* New York: Farrar, Straus and Giroux, 2004.

Rosenmeyer, Patricia A. *Ancient Epistolary Fictions: The Letter in Greek Literature.* Cambridge: Cambridge University Press, 2001.

Sakenfeld, Katharine Doob. "Hermeneutic of Suspicion." In *Dictionary of Feminist Theologies,* edited by Letty M. Russell and J. Shannon Carson. Louisville: Westminster John Knox, 1996.

Saller, Richard P. *Patriarchy, Property and Death in the Roman Family.* Cambridge: Cambridge University Press, 1994.

Schüssler Fiorenza, Elisabeth. *Empowering Memory and Movement: Thinking and Working Across Borders.* Minneapolis: Augsburg Fortress Press, 2014.

———. *In Memory of Her: A Feminist Theological Reconstruction of Christian Origins.* New York: Crossroad, 1983; 2nd ed. 1993.

Solevåg, Anna Rebecca. *Birthing Salvation: Gender and Class in Early Christian Childbearing Discourse.* BibInt 121. Leiden: Brill, 2013.

Stegemann, Wolfgang. "Anti-Semitic and Racist Prejudices in Titus 1:10-16." Translated from the German by David E. Orton. In *Ethnicity and the Bible,* edited by Mark G. Brett, 271–94. New York: Brill, 1996.

Tamez, Elsa. *Struggles for Power in Early Christianity: A Study of the First Letter to Timothy.* Maryknoll, NY: Orbis Books, 2007.

Towner, Philip H. *The Letters to Timothy and Titus.* NICNT. Grand Rapids: Eerdmans, 2006.

Twomey, Jay. *The Pastoral Epistles Through the Centuries.* Blackwell Bible Commentaries. Malden, MA: Wiley-Blackwell, 2009.

Wagener, Ulrike. *Die Ordnung des "Hauses Gottes": Der Ort von Frauen in der Ekklesiologie und Ethik der Pastoralbriefe*. WUNT 2, vol. 65. Tübingen: Mohr Siebeck, 1994.

Wilkerson, Isabel. *The Warmth of Other Suns: The Epic Story of America's Great Migration*. New York: Random House, 2010.

Winter, Bruce W. *Roman Wives, Roman Widows: The Appearance of New Women and the Pauline Communities*. Grand Rapids: Eerdmans, 2003.

Winterson, Jeanette. *Oranges Are Not the Only Fruit*. New York: Grove, 1985.

Yetman, Norman R., ed. *Voices From Slavery: 100 Authentic Slave Narratives*. 1st edition, New York: Holt, Rinehart, and Winston, 1972; 2nd edition, Mineola, NY: Dover, 2000.

Yousafzai, Malala. *I Am Malala: The Story of the Girl Who Stood Up for Education and Was Shot by the Taliban*, co-written with Christina Lamb. Boston: Little, Brown, 2013.

Zamfir, Korinna. *Men and Women in the Household of God: A Contextual Approach to Roles and Ministries in the Pastoral Epistles*, NTOA 103. Göttingen: Vandenhoeck & Ruprecht, 2013.

Index of Scripture References and Other Ancient Writings

Index of Subjects

General Editor

Barbara E. Reid, OP, is a Dominican Sister of Grand Rapids, Michigan. She holds a PhD in biblical studies from The Catholic University of America and is vice president and academic dean and professor of New Testament studies at Catholic Theological Union, Chicago. Her most recent publications are *Wisdom's Feast: An Invitation to Feminist Interpretation of the Scriptures* (2016) and *Abiding Word: Sunday Reflections on Year A, B, C* (3 vols.; 2011, 2012, 2013). She served as president of the Catholic Biblical Association in 2014–2015.

Volume Editor

Sarah J. Tanzer serves as professor of New Testament and Early Judaism at McCormick Theological Seminary in Chicago, Illinois. She has written several essays on feminist interpretation of ancient texts, including "Wisdom of Solomon" in *Women's Bible Commentary* (3rd ed.; 2012) and "Ephesians" in *Searching the Scriptures: A Feminist Commentary* (1994). Her other research interests have included the Dead Sea Scrolls, the Gospel of John, the historically Jewish Jesus, and, most recently, how difference develops in biblical interpretation between Judaism and early Christianity.

Author

Annette Bourland Huizenga serves as assistant dean and associate professor of New Testament at the University of Dubuque Theological Seminary (Dubuque, Iowa). Her research interests include the Pauline letters and communities, women in the early church, households in the Roman Empire, and ancient moral-philosophical education. These subjects all come into play in her first book *Moral Education for Women in the Pastoral and Pythagorean Letters*. She has written several articles about the expectations for women's behavior, clothing, and virtues in the ancient world. In 2015, the University of Dubuque awarded Dr. Huizenga with the William L. Lomax Award for excellence in Teaching and Advising.